KING'S COUNSEL

THE MACMILLAN COMPANY
NEW YORK · BOSTON · CHICAGO · DALLAS
ATLANTA · SAN FRANCISCO

MACMILLAN & CO., LIMITED
LONDON · BOMBAY · CALCUTTA
MELBOURNE

THE MACMILLAN COMPANY
OF CANADA, LIMITED
TORONTO

SIR HENRY CURTIS-BENNETT, K.C.
Photograph by Maull and Fox

KING'S COUNSEL

The Life of
Sir Henry Curtis-Bennett

(Published in England as "Curtis")

by

ROLAND WILD

and

DEREK CURTIS-BENNETT

With Foreword by St. John Hutchinson, K.C.

1938

THE MACMILLAN COMPANY
NEW YORK

Copyright, 1938,
By ROLAND WILD.

All rights reserved—no part of this book may be reproduced in any form without permission in writing from the publisher, except by a reviewer who wishes to quote brief passages in connection with a review written for inclusion in magazine or newspaper.

Set up and printed. Published January, 1938.
First printing.

PRINTED IN THE UNITED STATES OF AMERICA
BY J. J. LITTLE AND IVES COMPANY, NEW YORK

Foreword

By St. John Hutchinson, K.C.

I HAVE been asked to write a short foreword to this most interesting book. I have gladly accepted, as I feel, having been in daily contact for nearly twenty years with Curtis, that I had more opportunity of knowing him well than perhaps anyone else. To be in chambers with a man, especially as his tenant, enables one to see him as he really is; it makes him one's friend for life, one's dear acquaintance, or merely one's landlord. It made Curtis my friend for life. I therefore feel that it is important for those who did not have my advantages to try and see the personal side of the man about whom this book has been written.

I cannot help feeling that the real clue to Curtis was his simplicity. By "simplicity" I do not mean guilelessness, I mean the real simplicity of a person without complexes or great subtlety. Curtis was a very emotional man, easily moved, as most simple men are. He was able to laugh uproariously at himself and to see himself as ridiculous—the most endearing of qualities, which only the simple possess. With his intimate friends Curtis was the most amusing of companions. A case ends suddenly, he may have done a successful "Curtis" (you will find in the book what this is) and will be happy at the success. We go off together to the Savoy Grill, and the fun begins. Curtis loved food, he would hardly admit it, and often have I laughed at his description of a "little meal" (he loved describing meals), two invariable concomitants of which were a *sole Walewska* and a *châteaubriant*. We would go in; he would be happy when Manetta rushed forward to welcome him, pleased when the waiters knew him. He would order a "little meal" and a whisky and soda; he was not a big drinker. He would send for the page-boy and order two stalls at a musical show—it always had to be a musical show. Many of us would never go to a matinée unless it was Shakespeare done in some peculiar way, Tchekov, or some very heavy modern. I never connected matinées with pleasure after I was sixteen, except when I went with Curtis. He liked stalls in the front row—both of us being large it was a great help if there were three—and there, with long cigars in our mouths, we were to be found.

To many legal friends this appeared a terrible debauch. I think it was his sense of humour and our companionship that made it such fun. Curtis never minded being teased. I remember once we were going down to the country in his open Rolls-Royce. It was a coldish day, and we had tucked ourselves well in, with coats and rugs, and had our cigars in our mouths, when, just as he started, a small newspaper boy got in front of the car. Curtis roared at him—the boy stopped still and shouted to a still smaller lad, "Bill, come over quick and look at these two fat old beggars in a Rolls-Royce." No one could have enjoyed this more than Curtis.

When term ended he was at his happiest. He would get into his car, drive down to Folkestone, and his delight became almost an ecstasy if, on arrival in France, because he was Curtis-Bennett, he got the privilege of getting his car off before all other cars. Then he would sit back and start along the straight French roads. Many a time have I been on those trips with him; he was a splendid companion. He loved France. No scholar of the language, he appreciated that urbane and delicious civilization that France alone possesses among the nations of the world. He loved the long straight roads; he was a fast driver but the best and safest I have ever driven with. He loved the villages; he loved running along by the side of the large serene "impressionist" rivers of France. Then, near lunch-time, fresh interest would be aroused, and no one knew better how to enjoy the pleasure of sitting in a charming *Place*, while a carefully chosen lunch was being prepared. He was so interested in the people, in the old men playing dominoes, the old ladies with their chickens in baskets; and when the *maître d'hôtel* remembered him with affection (it was surprising how many simple people remembered him with affection) his cup of delight was full. He did not particularly like Paris or the large fashionable towns (except perhaps Monte Carlo and Biarritz for a short time); it was the real France, the France of the peasantry, of the cornfields, of the vineyards, that really appealed to his affection. He never forgot a face, and he never forgot a road; if he had driven in a district once he wanted no map. And when it was all over he would return rested and happy to England, and the only regret he would feel was that he was not just setting out.

Curtis loved recognition; he liked waiters to know him, and cabmen, railwaymen and men on boats. He also liked famous men to acknowledge him, and no judge would have enjoyed the trumpets on Assize more than he. This was not vanity—he was without vanity—but a simple liking for the outward trappings of popularity and success. His success meant much to him, but by far the deepest feeling in his life, as I very well know, was his love for his son.

He was essentially English; he was very fond of dogs and of watching cricket. He used to have teams down to Boreham, but what I remember best is going to Lord's with him when a Test Match was in progress; I took the sandwiches and he the wine—a distribution entirely to my liking.

I feel that those who read these words will wonder where the brilliant advocate appears. Curtis was not a typically successful K.C., but anyone who watched him in the Courts, sat behind him as a junior, or looked at the result of his cases, could not doubt that in fact he was a pre-eminently successful one; and any policeman, doctor or other person who had been cross-examined by him would bear willing testimony to the ordeal it had proved.

This book will show the great advocate. I have only tried to give you a glimpse of the man. Marshall Hall and Curtis were great personalities in very different ways, but with me and many others there still exists a feeling of loss when we enter the Courts at the Old Bailey that seem empty without his voice, or sit in those seats at the London Sessions from which we had hoped often to watch him, or go to the different Licensing Courts, which seem more drab and less exciting now that we no longer hear the voice that drew so many licences from almost hypnotized benches.

Personally, I hope at times to pick up this book and catch a faint echo of that voice, or get a vague glance at that burly form that meant so much, so very much, to me during twenty-five years at the Bar.

Contents

CHAPTER		PAGE
I	THE FINEST PROFESSION	1
II	EARLY DAYS	11
III	A THOUSAND A YEAR	19
IV	"DOING A CURTIS"	29
V	WARTIME	38
VI	SECRET SERVICE	51
VII	"TAKING SILK"	65
VIII	IN THE FIRST FLIGHT	85
IX	THE GREATEST YEARS—1	98
X	THE GREATEST YEARS—2	121
XI	THE GREATEST YEARS—3	140
XII	TRUE STORIES	148
XIII	A BARRISTER IN THE HOUSE	155
XIV	GREAT MURDER TRIALS	172
XV	WHEN CURTIS TALKED	195
XVI	"HYDE PARK CASES"	209
XVII	STRANGE CASES	221
XVIII	"LAUGH AND GROW FAT"	233
XIX	GREAT ACQUITTALS	249
XX	"A NEW LIFE"	265
INDEX		277

Illustrations

SIR HENRY CURTIS-BENNETT, K.C.	*Frontispiece*
	FACING PAGE
HARRY IN 1902	14
SIR HENRY WITH SIR EDWARD MARSHALL HALL	52
JEAN PIERRE VAQUIER, THE VAIN MURDERER	110
HERBERT ROUSE ARMSTRONG	110
"A DOMINATING PERSONALITY IN COURT"	144
"IMPROBABLE!" MR. NORMAN BIRKETT, K.C., IS CROSS-EXAMINED BY SIR HENRY CURTIS-BENNETT, K.C. CARTOON BY GEORGE WHITELAW	168
"THE INDIAN ELEPHANT, OR CURTIS-BENNETT." CARTOON BY GEORGE WHITELAW	216
CHAIRMAN OF THE COUNTY OF LONDON SESSIONS	256

KING'S COUNSEL

Chapter One

THE FINEST PROFESSION

To MANY thousands of men and women who knew Sir Henry Curtis-Bennett only by name and repute, the impression of him that remained in the mind most strongly was that of a stout though agile figure, genial and impressive, from whose lips there came phrases that ranged the two extremes—tragedy and comedy.

Defender of murderers; after-dinner wit; emphatic pleader for the lives of over fifty men and women who stood in the dock under the shadow of the gallows; suave and boyish jester who turned to himself and his figure for his inevitable "little story." In public, the carefree and extravagant *bon viveur* and theatrical first-nighter; in private, an always emotional man who could not rid his mind of the tragedies that he had seen pass before him.

Even the increasing weight that was a jest on his lips as he died, he knew to be a tragedy. He was caught in a vicious circle: his heart prevented him from taking exercise, lack of exercise added to his girth and that, in turn, affected his heart. He hid that knowledge, and, encouraged by every public speaker who referred to him, Curtis-Bennett capitalized his misfortune and made it into a joke for court and congress.

As if in character for this man of many opposites, he chose to become adept, in his youth, in the sport that would appear to be least appropriate for a man of his build. Cycle racing was the sport at which he excelled, later to be replaced by the enthusiasm of a pioneer for motoring. But in 1900, when he had passed from Radley to Trinity College, Cambridge, he was a tall, slim figure, the aquiline nose and the high forehead giving him good looks of an unusual kind. Early school-days had been marked by occasional brilliance, but when (like all great men) he ran away from his preparatory school with his younger brother, and arrived forlorn and penniless in London, he was too upset by childish adversity to be sent back. Radley brought him few prizes during the two years he was there, and when he was up at Cambridge, he had his mind only on the near future when he would wear wig and gown. His father was then magistrate at Marylebone (later to be chief magistrate at Bow Street), and it was fairly obvious which way his steps would turn. His parents were not wealthy, and he had the further knowledge that whatever material success he was to have, would be of his own making.

His father was the youngest son of the vicar of Kelvedon in Essex, and came of a family which for nearly two hundred years held various benefices in that county. At the Bar he had had a considerable practice though not in the criminal courts, became a magistrate, and presided in turn at West London, Marylebone, Westminster and Bow Street, and at the end of his life was the best known magistrate on the Bench, having raised the position of chief magistrate to a very high standard. Unlike his son he was a slim man, and with his white curly hair and good looks bore striking resemblance to the late Lord Asquith. But before his death in his sixty-seventh year, he became the object of threats from militant suffragettes, who went so far as to attempt to throw him over Beachy Head and sent him a bomb disguised as a cigar box. For the last months of his life indeed, he was always followed by two detectives.

The cycle racing made young Curtis-Bennett a minor hero, for it was a sport then more popular at the Universities, and earned a half-blue. After winning the University fifty-mile championship from scratch, the mile, and the five-mile race, and beating a track record at Sheen and a tandem record at the Crystal Palace, he gained his Blue in July, 1900, and was acclaimed in the national Press as a "new crack who might revive the glories of University racing."

In 1901 he was in the Association Football Trials, but failed to get into the Cambridge team. And in 1902 he was captain of Cambridge University Cycling Club, rode in all the big meetings at Norwich, the Crystal Palace, Manchester, and Sheen, and won the four-mile race in the inter-varsity sports. The footlights provided another interest, but both amateur dramatics and the race track were soon to be forgotten. His diaries show a frequent attendance at the Cambridge Assizes, and when he spent his vacations at Lexham Gardens with his parents, he records a diligent attendance at the Old Bailey, at the chambers of Mr. Arthur Hutton, for whom he was to "devil," and at his father's Court. Less serious were the holidays at Kelvedon Vicarage, in Essex, where his grandfather was vicar for thirty years.

During those early days, Curtis-Bennett's diaries were models of discretion. Perhaps the mind of the born lawyer was revealed in his desire merely to record the facts of his journeys and the precise time-table of meals, excursions, and withdrawals to bed. Certainly they were not written for posterity; but he had made a habit that he kept through life, and he always averred that he was saving himself trouble. Not in a single entry, however, did he reveal what was in his mind and how the events of his world affected the hopes and fears of an ambitious young man who had decided to become a lawyer. He was completely emotionless with a pen in his hand, and while his brain was crowded with thoughts of his own future, he committed to these pages only the matter-of-fact details of his comings and goings.

Curtis-Bennett found himself ushered into the legal profession by willing and ever helping hands. The family records, however, showed no ancestor for many generations in the "finest profession in the world," and indeed there had been few breaks in the line of Bennetts who were country clergymen. His father took the name "Curtis" as a hyphenated prefix to the surname because there were two "Henry Bennetts" practising at the Bar, and confusion resulted. The Essex churchyards are full of tombstones with the name of Bennett, and Curtis in later years made a hobby of visiting them. Further back, this branch of the Bennett family sprang from the Bennetts of Pyt House, Wilts., where they have lived since at least early in the twelfth century.

Twice during his life did he think he was ruined. And though his career, set down in terms of figures, was one that would encourage any young man with imagination and industry to choose the law, he was often worried, and hid real anxiety behind a carefree spendthrift gesture that deceived all his friends.

London was a lonely place, even for one who had relatives and friends. Having taken his degree in 1900, Curtis-Bennett experienced some lack of resolution, did not relish the additional months of work that he would have to settle down to before he achieved his ambition. His diary reveals a certain haphazardness, as if he were trying to kill time. The Earl's Court Exhibition was on, and every night his steps would be in that direction, either by himself or with his brother. His father conducted him to the Courts, to dinners given to Her Majesty's Judges, and to dinner in Middle Temple Hall. He still trained on the race track at Sheen or Mortlake, but time hung heavily on his hands, and he found ample leisure to walk down to chambers. But he could only taste the scent of battle from afar; and at times it was too tantalizing, and he escaped to propel a solitary punt on the Thames. There is very little incident to fill up the page in the diary, and his pen strays languidly downward with the bare account of lonely journeys on foot across London. While in the Temple he saw hurrying clerks and worried barristers—and envied them: in court he watched the wonderful machinery of which he would soon be a part; meanwhile, he went to the Exhibition with Noel, his younger brother.

There were times when he wondered whether it was wise for him to follow the career that had been chosen for him. Often he thought of trying his chance at commerce, thinking that, when he had found a niche for himself, he might stay in it, comfortable and secure, rather than risk the terrific adventure of the Bar. He knew all the pitfalls ahead; he knew that for years he might be in the position of waiting for briefs, sitting the days out in chambers. In commerce, he could at least be active and scout for work; as a barrister, the slightest sign of invitation to a solicitor, even a casual suggestion of lunch with a friend who was on the other side of the legal fence, might have the direst consequences.

Curtis-Bennett never confessed that he did at one time actually take steps to find himself a safe job in the City. There are good reasons, however, to suppose that he offered himself as a salaried employee of a firm controlled by an acquaintance. That the suggestion was not shocking to him was shown at a later period, when he nearly accepted the offer of a secretarial job. But that was when he had everything to lose; just now, before he began a serious period of coaching, he chafed at delay, and took it out of himself by fifty-mile cycle rides out of London.

Another interest was the amateur theatre, which had engrossed his attention at Cambridge but with which he now flirted almost for the last time. "He is becoming quite a famous amateur actor," said the London Press when he appeared in the title rôle of "Jedbury Junior" at the Albert Hall. It was a charity performance, duly attended by Royalty, and although one paper remarked cruelly that charity covered a multitude of sins, the majority of the newspapers that have space for these matters gave an airing to their usual clichés, such as "Mr. Curtis-Bennett figured with much credit in the title rôle, supplying a manly and thoroughly acceptable rendering of the part. . . ."

The manly hero's head was not turned, however. He wrote in the diary: "Gave performance of Jedbury Junior. Drove home and had supper."

And now the results of the examination were through, and the die was cast. Curtis-Bennett at the age of twenty-three was to be called to the Bar of the Middle Temple on November 17, 1902, and would "devil" for Mr. Arthur Hutton.

Before embarking on the strain of sitting in chambers and waiting for briefs, however, he thought it wise to take a cure. He had been suffering from throat-trouble, and Aix-les-Bains was the only treatment. On the day after the coronation of Edward VII, which he recorded with complete impassivity in his diary, merely giving the times of his journeys, he travelled to the South, attended the baths diligently and returned on September 3rd. Now his diaries record his growing interest in a Miss Elsie Eleanor Dangar, daughter of a family very well known in Sydney. He had met her at a dinner party in the spring, had visited her when she was staying with her parents at Marlow, and now travelled, after one night in London, to Braemar, where the Dangars had a house for the autumn. Curtis-Bennett was good-looking, could talk (though he could not write diaries), and had a reputation as an athlete that must have travelled even to Australia. The fact that they went for walks together before breakfast must indicate to the least imaginative biographer that the young legal student had now another ambition. The diaries record the saying of goodbye to "Elsie"; no other page in the leather-covered books refers to anything more human than the catching of a train or the itinerary of an evening spent "sitting at home."

On his return to London halfway through September, he had ten days to wait before going to Euston to meet "Elsie." Thereafter, the diary records a daily meeting, a state call on

Mrs. Dangar, and an invitation to dinner. When Miss Dangar was occupied with other matters, the theatre had to suffice, and Curtis-Bennett went almost every night. His examinations on "Contract" and "Equity" claim but a word or two in the diary, whereas there are many days in which he has to record going to two theatrical performances, and his narrative for one day reads: "Morning Clerkenwell: Lunched with Hutton. Met Elsie and went to see the 'Bishop's Move.' Back by Underground. Rehearsal of 'In Honour Bound.' Took Elsie and Phyllis to concert at the Town Hall."

Even the momentous day that he was called to the Bar at the Middle Temple does not call from his pen anything more than the following: "Monday November 17th, 1902. Walked over to Lancaster Gate with Noel, Tube to Chancery Lane. Spent morning about Temple. Had oysters with Noel at Drivers and lunch at Troc. Met Elsie at Queen's Gate, walked to St. James's Park, home by Underground. Mother and Elsie came to see me 'called.' Dinner in Hall, went to the Oxford with Father."

The oysters with Noel seem from the diary to be the high light of the most momentous day in his life.

What is remarkable is that on the next day, Curtis-Bennett had his first brief. It was with Arthur Hutton for the prisoner, the brief being from Freke Palmer, the great solicitor who was appearing frequently at Marylebone before Mr. Curtis-Bennett senior, and who was to become one of his closest friends, and who briefed him more than any one man. The diarist seems to take it in his stride, and gives it only the curt phrase, "Had first brief"—without even the distinction of an underlining.

That emphasis he left for January 21, 1903, when he writes: "Interviewed Mrs. Dangar. Our engagement allowed to be announced. Elsie and I came back in bus." And by that time he had had four briefs, amassing the sum of five guineas—a feat that is remarkable in itself, but which has no place in his diary.

Three out of the four cases had the honour of being reported, and the cuttings are faithfully preserved. It is not recorded that Mr. H. Curtis-Bennett had anything to add to the plea in mitigation put forward by his leader in his first case; but the story was worth thirty lines in the *Morning Advertiser,* and, what was even more remarkable, his second case was for the defence in a murder case.

During the same month he appeared before his father, who assumed an attitude towards his son of cynical contempt that deceived nobody. This case also received the notice of the *Times,* and now, for the first time, the voice of Curtis-Bennett was heard in Court. What was more, it was reported, and he could produce the cuttings as evidence.

The greater number of cuttings, however, were concerned with his approaching marriage. Between the beginning of the year and April 4th, legal matters did not intrude themselves unduly, though his appearances in court, spaced by some seven days, might be considered frequent by many who spend the first years of their apprenticeship in chambers. In later years he told a story against himself about one of these first briefs: He was asked by a busy barrister to present himself at a certain court, stand on his feet at a certain moment, and remark, "I consent, m'Lord." Unfortunately, the barrister was in too great a hurry to explain what he was to consent to, but with the mention of the name of the client, rushed away. Curtis-Bennett, glad to earn a guinea, but terribly nervous of making a fool of himself, duly attended, and at the appropriate moment, stood up.

"I consent, m'Lord," he said, with a confidence that he did not feel.

The Judge looked at him.

"You *what?*" he inquired.

Something had gone wrong. Even the veriest amateur could not have forgotten the formula, but here it was obvious that the preliminary proceedings had been tragically distorted. Fortunately, as he stood helplessly before the Judge, there was a whisper behind him, and a voice instructed him to apply for the obvious adjournment. The Judge, knowing perfectly well what had happened, chose to be merciful. And Curtis-Bennett earned his guinea, though ever afterwards one of his most frequent nightmares was set in just such a situation—himself standing transfixed on the floor, while Judge and court gazed at him waiting for him to speak the words that he did not know.

On April 4th he was married, and, written at Folkestone that night, the diary page presents the unusually untidy appearance of words underlined. "Wedding Day," he heads it. "Packed clothes and drove round with Noel to fetch Elsie's luggage. Married at 2.30. Elsie and I left at 4.35, met Noel at Victoria, travelled to Folkestone by 5 o'c train. Drove to Royal Pavilion Hotel and stayed there."

The next day fires him only with the enthusiasm of a keen student of railway time-tables. "We went by 12 o'clock boat to Boulogne, both very ill. Had lunch there and travelled on to Paris. Reached there at 6.5. Drove across Paris to the Palais d'Orsay Hotel. Dined there and stayed the night."

They went to Biarritz for fifteen days, had another three days in Paris on the return, and made some resolutions. One of them led to the collection of a series of diaries, eloquent of the tidiness of this man, unique in the light they throw on a strange side of his character. On the day after his return to London, he went out and bought a small, cheap account book. On the left-hand page, he wrote: "April 26th. Cash in Hand £84. o. o." On the opposite page he wrote: "April 26th. Underground £0. 1. 6. Tobacco £0. 3. 0."

Thereafter, for thirty-four years and six months, he wrote down, in a succession of eleven account books, every penny that he paid out, the last words being "Nov. 3," in preparation for his personal stewardship the following day. The other diaries, recording baldly and sometimes with unconscious humour the various activities of the day, were discontinued three years after he had undertaken this new accountancy. And it was no loss; he was a bad diarist, for the entries read as if he were intent only upon providing an alibi for himself at any given moment of the year. He had never tried to put any feeling into his little books; he never recorded a state of mind, an impression, or an emotion. The only comment on life he allowed himself during the seven years in which he kept a record of his movements, is an exclamation mark on his twenty-first birthday. "I enjoyed myself!" Here was a man with an ever rising, effervescent sense of humour; whose best joke, moreover, was himself: he found the whole world amusing and inviting to a creature with a sense of fun. Yet, faced with a blank sheet of paper, he was only able to put down the facts in their most material form. There is no record of his ever having scribbled more than a line or two that represented himself in a lighter mood. A pen was for writing facts; and thus it came about that he had left an astonishingly eloquent record of the money that passed into and out of his pocket. In all, these diaries account for some £150,000—in shillings and pence more often than in pounds. He was a man who wanted to know where he stood in the world; except for when he went abroad on a holiday, he saw before him the comparative figures of what he had spent and what he had earned, every night of his life.

This, then, was the beginning, and the first few days' expenses read as follows: "Underground 1/6. Tobacco 3/-. Wine etc., and Underground 7/9. Lunch and Fares 2/9." On the other side of the page, there were few entries. Fortunately he had married a lady of considerable private fortune, and his father, from whom, however, he could expect no substantial legacy, helped him often. But the six months of that year did not cause him to write more than three entries as his earnings, and in his first year he had earned sixty-one guineas, one brief of five guineas being the greatest compliment so far paid to his forensic powers.

Chapter Two

EARLY DAYS

TALKING of these early days, when he ran about for guineas and spent many hours in his chambers wondering whether he had chosen aright, Curtis-Bennett gave some sound advice to the thousands of other young barristers in a similar state of mind. "It is largely a matter of luck," he said, "but it is wrong to depend on two or three years to decide whether you are to be a success or a failure. You must give the Bar a chance, and if more young barristers who give it up as hopeless, would wait longer than they do—of course many of them cannot, and they should not be barristers—then they would find that there is a living to be made at the Bar without having either phenomenal luck or remarkable brain. You don't need first class brains, but you do need perseverance, and you do have to have one ideal at heart. The luck comes in when you consider the all-important question of health; one day's illness at an early stage of your career, and you may lose the appearance that leads to other work. Solicitors like to see a young man in court—often in court, even if they are earning a guinea. And if not in court, they like to know they are in their Chambers. It's on the very day that you go to Ascot that the solicitor telephones for an immediate conference. If you're not there, he'll telephone another barrister, and ten to one the other fellow is a most likeable young man, a most intelligent and lucky young man who pulls a case out of the fire. Well, that solicitor won't telephone you any more; he'll give his work to the young man who was in his Chambers when you were backing horses after a month's steady attendance in Chambers without the telephone ringing more than twice."

There was personal experience behind the racy way in which he put his advice. He sat for many days in Arthur Hutton's Chambers, paying £6. 10. 0. a quarter for the privilege, and reflecting that it was a waste of time. He seriously suggested during 1903 that he had mistaken his profession and should give it up. What was the alternative this time? The Army! Yet, in the year after his marriage, 1904, briefs came in at the rate of two or three a month, and he was making the appearances in Court which were more valuable than the guineas. He was junior to Mr. Marshall Hall, K.C., in a three-day case against a receiver of stolen pills, which brought him nine guineas in fees and refreshers of two guineas each; the five-guinea brief came on behalf of a man accused of indecency, in which case Curtis-Bennett was junior to Mr. Charles F. Gill, K.C. Gill followed a method that commended itself greatly to him. He was renowned for his attention to details, and had the reputation of being able to pick holes in any prosecution for indecency, a branch of crime in which he was considered the foremost defender of his day. That reputation was later to be handed down to Curtis-Bennett.

It was Gill who taught Curtis the points to develop in certain classes of case. Many a time did Curtis go to a consultation with Gill in such a case and listen with no little interest and, indeed, profit, to Gill instructing the solicitor what to do, what plans to have made, what photographs to have taken, what experiments to attempt—and realise at the hearing to what good use Gill put the results.

Early in 1904, Curtis-Bennett had another cause to wonder whether in fact he had done right in choosing the career of a barrister. On February 29th, Leap Year Day, a son was born, and once again he was assailed with doubts, particularly since he had just been offered a "steady" job. In spite of the protests of doctor and nurse, who advised that his wife should not be asked to discuss serious matters at a critical time, he burst impulsively into the room and declared that it was now obvious that he should accept a secretarial post at £600 a year. He had made fourteen guineas during the two months and the expenses must have been ten pounds. Given the slightest encouragement, he would have packed away his wig and gown for ever. His wife told him not to be foolish.

The young Curtis-Bennett, whom they christened Frederick Henry, but called Derek, received considerable mention in the Press, with other Leap Year Day babies, and the cuttings were carefully filed between paragraphs headed "Walthamstow Brawl" and "Painful Family Case." There was no more mention of the "safe steady job" and at the end of the year, briefs had brought in over £120. Freke Palmer had sent most of them, and in many cases Gill was leading Curtis-Bennett. Nearly all were defences of men and women charged with petty fraud, assault, or sexual offences. The cases made spicy reading in the *News of the World,* embellished, as was the custom in those days, with pen-and-ink drawings of the culprits—all curiously alike, all with the appearance of emotionless puppets propped up and invested with strange, dark impulses for the benefit of the Press. But the young barrister of Pump Court whose name appeared as junior to Gill or Hutton took little part in the proceedings. Still, he was in court, and that was what mattered.

Curtis-Bennett joined the Southeastern Circuit and the Herts and Essex Sessions as soon as possible, for the name would carry him some way, and it was an obvious choice. Brentwood and Chelmsford began to appear in the day-book and, in the next year, 1905, the account book looked healthy enough for him to achieve one of his greatest ambitions. He bought a car.

This daring step was not taken without many inward fears and doubts. Curtis-Bennett, as he watched his son crawling on the rug, felt that all the slings and arrows of harsh criticism were being aimed at him for this gross indulgence in luxury.

A motor car was the possession of a rich pioneer and a crank; it could never be considered as a thing of practical use, but only as the indulgence of a whim. It was a futurist toy, demanding fantastic upkeep, and in return it would transport its daring owner at the speed of twenty miles an hour for half an hour at a time, after which its punctures had to be mended. A salve to his conscience was that this was only a three-wheeler, and cost only £25. Its former history is not recorded, but the bills for repairs, that became equal to its initial value in nine months, suggest that the machine had already seen life. It was purchased on February 23rd, but since it had no hood, and the driver had to stop for rain, it was considered inadvisable to attempt anything in the nature of a tour till the weather was more suitable. But Curtis-Bennett was all prepared before that date. Several repair bills had been paid, he had bought a dust coat for himself and goggles for his wife, and during the week before Easter, he set out by himself on a tour of some five hundred miles, in the course of which he had nine punctures and "great trouble with the Belt." The account book is peppered with payments for repairs, which seemed to be necessary every fifty miles, and it was almost automatic to write "Repairs to mudguard" after every day's journey. Mentions of rain "stopping progress" read like a cricket season summary, but he was undaunted, and when the three-wheeler was sold in November, the weather being then prohibitive for motoring, it was only to make plans for the purchase of another vehicle. He had got the motoring fever, later to become the passion of his life. The tricar fetched £16. 10. 0. and had cost £17 in repairs in seven hundred miles.

In May of 1905 he was concerned in a drama that he had often watched as a spectator—a murder trial at the Old Bailey. The case had more than usual interest, for it was the first time that the evidence of fingerprints had been used to an important degree for the prosecution. For ten years Scotland Yard had been experimenting, but Curtis-Bennett's leader was able

HARRY IN 1902
Photograph by Charles Stiles, Kensington

to make something of a plea out of his submission that "the finger print system was unreliable, and savoured more of the French Courts than of English justice."

The accused were two men named Stratton, who had murdered an old couple before robbing them of a few pounds. There were some witnesses who claimed that they could identify them, and a woman who lived with them both gave evidence that she had found, under the mattress of the room they all inhabited, the tops of some black stockings. In the room where the old couple had been murdered, there were left three similar stocking tops, and it was the opinion of the prosecution that these two men habitually used them as masks. They were called the "Mask Murderers," and it was proved that they were two utter undesirables whose lives and deaths would not have excited any attention had it not been for the peculiar nature of the evidence introduced by the Crown.

Curtis-Bennett appeared as junior to Mr. H. G. Routh, for one of the brothers. It was in the last days of the old "Old Bailey," and it was perhaps because of this fact that the public seats were filled by fashionably dressed women and some well-known men-about-town. Scotland Yard had then some 80,000 fingerprints on their files. And on the cash box of the dead man, there was a print that corresponded exactly, according to the police, with Alfred Stratton's right thumbprint. When Mr. Muir, prosecuting, announced that for the first time in history the police were going to try to convict on that evidence, there was a thrill round the court.

In confirmation, a warder gave evidence that Albert had betrayed his brother while in the cells, but this was only a minor sensation compared with the legal potentialities of the fingerprint system. Mr. Muir had to explain that the system was based on the theory that no two human prints were alike. Obviously, the defence would not accept such a revolutionary theory, and became immediately suspicious of policemen who dabbled in such beliefs. Mr. Routh made the expert take fingerprints of a juryman, and suggested that the impression varied with the pressure exerted. When he brought an expert for the defence, however, Mr. Routh was not so happy. The witness had been a former Home Office expert, and did not agree with Scotland Yard's methods in using the fingerprint system. This witness said that he was prepared to swear that a mistake had been made in the prints, but the whole effect of his evidence was ruined when the prosecution produced his letters offering to give evidence on either side, without knowing what the evidence was to be! Curtis-Bennett now had the unpleasant task of trying to save something from the wreck of this evidence. He failed dismally, for the Judge interrupted with the remark: "Mr. Curtis-Bennett, is there not a limit to whitewashing this witness? It has done your client a lot of harm."

Curtis-Bennett in later years might have thought of a response, but in 1905 the only thing to do was to sit down. . . .

The Judge did not take to the fingerprint system wholeheartedly, and seemed to want murderers in the future to use ink when they left their impressions on cash boxes. "When proper impressions are taken, the system is extremely reliable; but it is a different thing to apply it to a casual mark made through the perspiration of a thumb. . . . The evidence is not so satisfactory as if, for instance, the murderer had taken some ink and made a definite impression. . . . But to a certain extent, the evidence is corroborative. The jury will not like to act on this evidence alone. . . ."

The spirit of the Old Bailey, that was soon to be demolished, seems to have affected counsel in that sordid case. Or else perhaps it was the style of oratory of the day; but here is an extract from the speech for Albert Stratton: "Gentlemen, on some future day, perhaps when this building is gone; if you will picture to yourselves this court you will see the crowded galleries and the serried rows of people sitting behind. You will see the dim gas lamps, you will see the dock and you will be reminded of your own presence in this court where you saw this young man, Albert, arraigned for his life, craning towards you with bloodshot eye and dry lips, the hot breath coming from his mouth. . . ."

The brothers were hanged, and the Press paid great attention to the "new peril to law-breakers." "Finger-prints are to the fore," said the *Referee*. "Forewarned is fore-armed, or rather, in this case, fore-handed, and the criminal classes will very soon make the new system a back number by wearing gloves when committing burglaries."

Looking back on these days with the knowledge of Curtis-Bennett's later triumphs in a particular branch of the law, we have little doubt that the most important case in which he was concerned was an appeal from a motoring conviction. The brief was for five guineas; if he could have looked forward thirty years he would have seen himself writing huge sums of money in his account book for his work in similar cases; it was the first controversial motoring case.

He was briefed with Earl Russell, K.C., to present the appeal of a well-known motorist, Mr. Frederick Coleman, against a conviction for dangerous driving. Mr. Coleman had admitted driving at over twenty miles an hour, but denied that there was any danger. The Colchester magistrates contended that since the speed limit was designed for the safety of the roads, to drive in excess of twenty miles an hour was automatically to constitute a danger. Yet the same Bench, a few days previously, had not alleged dangerous driving against a man who admitted travelling at thirty-nine miles an hour. Now, before the Recorder of Colchester, Earl Russell earned the congratulations of the infant motoring industry by securing the reversal of that conviction and the allowing of the appeal. Not, however, without some trouble, for counsel for the respondents urged strongly that the true interpretation of the law was that speed was the determining factor.

"It is not necessary actually to prove that anyone was in

danger to sustain a charge of driving to the public danger," he said, and added that the onus was on the defence to prove that there was no danger. "Has your car any shield or protection from the wind or dust?" he asked the appellant.

"The dust is usually behind me," was the reply, and there was much laughter at that.

"I agree—and the smell too," said Mr. Jones, who was prosecuting, and the reporter of the Colchester *Telegraph* adds that there was "renewed merriment" at this witty reference to the unpopular motor-car.

During the next thirty years, Curtis-Bennett was to make a fortune from the motor-car; the owner-driver was to contribute a huge annual sum to the legal profession for protection from non-motoring magistrates; and Curtis-Bennett was to be chosen as the foremost living student of the law relating to motoring negligence, as counsel in an historic and perhaps unique motoring case. Small wonder, therefore, that when a passenger in his car exclaimed violently at the folly of other drivers, Curtis-Bennett would smile and say: "Of course. But that's where our money comes from!"

The ordinary run of sessions and police court work brought him no more than a few guineas, and a contact with that strange world that drifts through the dock and departs, leaving behind only a faint memory of squalid crime, terrible cruelty, poverty, and despair. There were few figures of colour and many completely drab creatures whose records told of years of prison and regular appearances before magistrates.

By the end of 1905 the left-hand side of the account books looked better. He had made over £300 in that year. His ambition now was to make a thousand a year.

Chapter Three

A THOUSAND A YEAR

THE YEAR 1906 brought in over £700. He was still chasing guineas energetically, though he had seldom earned more than fifteen guineas on one brief, and often enough several days' work brought in only a few guineas. It was not through lack of conscientiousness, for even when he left his Chambers to play a game of billiards in a Fleet Street saloon, Arthur Hutton's clerks were told that for the smallest detail he must be sent for, and Curtis said that he never moved faster than from that billiards saloon to his Chambers when a solicitor had called. He felt a rich man when ten guineas were paid him in gold—richer than he felt later when he received cheques for a hundred. And even at Ascot, where there was a police court on the course, he sometimes appeared in defence of an alleged pickpocket or welsher between races, took his fee, and slapped it on a horse. "Somehow you feel cleverer when you win money at racing than when you work for it," he said. His father still helped him with occasional gifts, but his wife's parents believed that it would kill his ambition if his wife received more than he earned.

His craze for motoring was his greatest extravagance. The motor of those days was never reliable enough to be used for business, and Curtis regarded it purely as a luxury. Indeed, this pioneer motorist could always be seen as a cyclist when it came to transporting himself to and from the station when they took a country cottage for the summer at Laleham. Curtis bicycled to the train—too often for a day's waiting in Chambers. Yet a new six horsepower De Dion Bouton had cost him

£100, and the garage bill was usually as high as the "household books," every detail of which is to be found in his spidery writing; a bottle of champagne to celebrate the baby's birthday cost him 3*s.* 2*d.*; an apron for the nurse 2*s.*; a bath for the baby 4*s.* 9*d.*; and the curtains were cleaned and Curtis noted it down.

But the money expended on keeping the De Dion Bouton in running order was exceeded when he bought Marshall Hall's car in 1907. He got £75 for the De Dion, and paid Marshall Hall over £200. Now there was a chauffeur, new motoring coats and gloves, a subscription to the Automobile Association (he was one of the first 5000 members) and a fortune on tires. Once or twice, relying on the chauffeur, he visited police courts in the car, prompting his clerk to remark dubiously: "I don't think this car idea is any good. How can it encourage solicitors to give us decent fees when we turn up in a large car with a chauffeur and do a two-guinea case at a police court?"

The new car was a Vulcan, and seldom in the history of motoring can there have been such a vehicle for wearing out tires at over seven pounds a time, and general repairs. But it survived several one-day "tours," and Curtis was immensely proud. The year seemed as if it was going to produce the £1,000 in fees for the first time, and they took a house at Sunninghill, and Curtis joined Bramshot Golf Club and took his first holiday abroad. The account book, as faithful a record of a man's life, ambitions, and fears as has ever been scribbled in terms of shillings and pence, tells the story of the small bottle of brandy bought the day before the crossing; again just before Christmas it tells of Curtis buying a new white waistcoat and a case of wine.

Of some three hundred briefs, only a handful were marked more than "10 and 1," but there was one good case for him when he defended, with Mr. George Elliott, K.C., one Horace George Rayner, sometimes known as Turner. An extraordinary story was told by Mr. Muir for the prosecution.

Rayner's mother, it seemed, went to live under the protection of William Whiteley, millionaire merchant, in the year 1879. The prisoner was then three years old, and six years later a son was born to Mr. Whiteley and the prisoner's mother, and was christened Cecil. George Rayner did not know that he had a stepbrother until 1898, when he asked his mother who he was.

One day in 1907 George Rayner went to have an interview with the millionaire in his business offices in London. Two shots rang out, and William Whiteley fell dead. The police arrested Rayner, and a struggle was made to save him from death as a result of a wound in his right eye. When he had recovered he was charged with the murder, and in his first statement he said his name was Whiteley, and that he had killed his father. He told the same story in the witness-box, claiming that he had rightly asked Mr. Whiteley for financial assistance believing him to be his father. He was condemned to death, but his youth and the suggestion that he was mentally unbalanced resulted in his reprieve and a sentence of penal servitude.

Marshall Hall's Vulcan could not satisfy Curtis-Bennett for long. He had his heart on a new Fiat, and bought it by instalments during the autumn of 1907. In 1908 they moved to Englefield Green, and Curtis took another bold step in going into Chambers of his own in Plowden Buildings. The cost was considerable, and he found that the immediate result was to lose briefs which Mr. Hutton might have passed on to him. He made £800 in that year, but he was in two cases which took the public eye, the "Poplar Scandals" and a case in which Carrie Nation, the well-known agitator against smoking, was fined for breaking a smoking advertisement in a tube train. Curtis also appeared for the Crown in the first two appeals to be heard by the newly formed Court of Criminal Appeal. But for the most part, he earned his £800 at a couple of guineas a time, many of them from the railway companies, with whom he had made an early reputation. In that year, too, he made a friendship that was to last through the years, through a great many cases that were front-page news, a friendship never marred by a quarrel—J. D. Cassels, formerly a newspaper reporter, was that year called to the Bar. One of his earliest stories of Curtis-Bennett concerns a brief they held jointly, marked two guineas. On the day before the case was due to be heard, they were shocked to learn that their client had committed suicide.

"I wonder what made him do that?" said Cassels.

"Possibly worry over the amount we were being paid?" suggested Curtis.

In his new Chambers, Curtis had Sam Humphreys, a great character of the legal profession, as his clerk. The clerk cannot make a barrister, but he can go a long way towards raising his fees and generally enhancing his reputation. Humphreys was an artist at his work and was well-known for his wit and his presence of mind. He was later elected Judge at the annual Dunmow Flitch Trial and generally did much to help to bring the barristers in his Chambers into the public eye.

In 1908 Curtis had earned nearly £2,000, and his name was already becoming well known. "The D. S. Windell Bank Fraud" was one of the most interesting cases. With Mr. George Elliott, he was briefed to defend a young Dutchman named Robert who had been concerned with a charming young swindler in what the judge called the greatest bank swindle since the Bank of England case in 1871. The other accused was a twenty-nine-year-old clerk in a bank, named Francis King. He had made inquiries at various branches of his bank, forged eight signatures and the password of the bank for the day, in his manager's writing, and sent Robert round the eight branches in a taxicab one morning, cashing cheques under the curious name of "D. S. Windell" to the extent of £2,300. By examining 80,000 bank forms, the bankers traced the forgeries to King, and arrested Robert in Spain, where he had been getting rid of the notes. Both prisoners were facetious and pleasant to the police at the time of their arrest. The defence did not put them in the witness box. And young Robert, who described himself in a letter read in court as "a rather precocious youngster, not understood by my surroundings," went to prison for eighteen months.

The motoring craze already began to have concrete benefits for Curtis as early as 1909. Curtis-Bennett was by far the most expert barrister in a motoring case; as yet, judges and magistrates did not want to hear technical details, and the police evidence of motor-cars "tearing past like the wind" was usually sufficient to convict a driver, who was considered as a rich and slightly eccentric danger to the public safety. Curtis-Bennett knew that the police knew nothing about motor-cars; and their evidence could be torn to shreds if only a court could understand something of practical motoring. A case in 1909 and another four years later show the difficulties of these pioneer motorists when the police decided that they should be prosecuted for their twenty-mile-an-hour foolhardiness.

Curtis-Bennett appeared for a chauffeur who was charged with disobeying the signals of two police officers. The magistrate at Marlborough Street attempted to prevent him producing two witnesses and told him that he was wasting the time of the court. The evidence for the defence was that the police had given wrong and unrecognizable signals (a fault which Curtis-Bennett alleged against the police until the end of his life) but the magistrate calmly said that the police were there to give signals, and therefore must have given them! The fine was one pound. Curtis-Bennett asked that it should be increased to one guinea, in order to give him the opportunity of appealing. But in those days magistrates frequently inflicted this sum for dangerous driving, in order to make certain that an endorsement appeared on the licences of the well-hated motorists.

The next year, Curtis-Bennett was himself charged with

speeding. He defended himself and obtained an acquittal. He had driven through a police trap in a country village, and at the time accused the police of comparing their stop watches in order to give identical evidence. He told the court that, when he was stopped, he thought he must have been in a ten-mile-an-hour area, for he was certainly not exceeding twenty miles an hour. He had driven fifty thousand miles in six years, and was most anxious to avoid an endorsement on his licence. This was the first of three summonses, on two of which he was fined, which he received in the course of his motoring career. He framed them and had them hung in his garage at Boreham, where they still are.

But a case more illustrative of the persecution of motorists by the police occurred in 1913, when the "Grey Car Case" was heard. These were the days when the colour of a car, the fact that it was a touring model and of considerable power, convinced witnesses and justices that they were dealing with "road-hogs" in racing cars. Rural witnesses talked of seeing cars rush through villages and turn corners on two wheels, with the sparks flying from the back wheels. Any witness could make a guess at the speed of a car—and those asked by Curtis-Bennett to estimate the passing of ten seconds without looking at a watch, were usually 50 per cent incorrect. The "Grey Car" was driven by John Sallows, a chauffeur, and had killed a woman near Hammersmith Bridge. Sallows had driven on after the accident, and it was not until a month afterwards that the police offer of £100 reward had resulted in his being found and charged with manslaughter. The car had been taken out without permission, and it was proved that the driver and the occupants knew about the accident. The fact that it was a "torpedo-shaped" car, and that there were women passengers, did not help the accused. But Curtis-Bennett suggested that the jury should take no notice of the details which sounded so ominous, and concentrate on the point as to whether Sallows was criminally negligent. He produced plans to show that a buttress must have impeded his view, and obtained his acquittal, though the verdict attracted some notice in the House of Commons. Sallows was fined, and his licence was taken away for two years, on charges of failing to stop after an accident.

Curtis-Bennett himself was always a fast driver, but he had excellent road sense, and he treated the handling of a car as an art and a whole-time occupation. He came to regard it as his only relaxation and, nearly every year, from 1909 onwards, he took a car to France. But, though he realized that in a few years the police would have to take a firm stand against dangerous drivers, he criticized bitterly the fact that they were never educated in the niceties of motoring. If a village constable waved his hand agitatedly up and down as a signal for him to slow down, Curtis-Bennett would stop, call the man to him angrily, and ask him what he thought he was doing.

"If I am driving too fast for you," he said, "summons me. If I am not, leave me alone. But don't wave your arm up and down in that meaningless way. It is not a signal."

When he had police constables in the witness box in a speeding case, he could usually destroy the whole effect of their evidence by a few questions on the actual arithmetic of their tests. He complained that they never seemed to work out the meaning of what they were saying; they did not understand the meaning of speed as related to time, and they did not realize that one second's difference over a short distance meant a vital difference over a long period. He complained that most of them had never driven cars and did not know the full meaning of skids and skid marks, and indeed one of his greatest triumphs in a motoring case was when he made the experts called for the prosecution admit that skid marks, said to have been made by the defendant's car, must have been made by a car coming in the opposite direction.

Curtis-Bennett made only a brief appearance in a sensational case at the beginning of 1911, the "Houndsditch Murders," when five foreigners appeared on charges of shooting and murdering policemen. He appeared for a woman, Luba Milstein. The case excited great interest. The police expected trouble, and threw a cordon around the court before the hearing; the underworld was being combed once again, and the exhibits included daggers and bandoliers of cartridges, pistols and rifles. The Crown, however, decided that Luba Milstein should not be proceeded against, and she was released.

By far the biggest case he had appeared in so far was heard in October, 1911, when crowds surged outside Bow Street, and the police cordon was frequently broken by a mob of people who wanted to see the sporting hero of the moment, Jack Johnson. James White, Bombardier Billy Wells, and Johnson had been summonsed for contemplating a breach of the peace —the breach being the £8,000 prize fight for the heavyweight championship of the world arranged for the next week. It was obvious that the whole future of boxing in this country was at stake, and against the Solicitor-General, Sir John Simon, K.C., M.P., and Mr. R. D. Muir and Mr. Travers Humphreys for the Treasury, the defendants had retained F. E. Smith, K.C., to lead for all of them, while Curtis-Bennett appeared for Johnson and Wells, Mr. Forrest Fulton and Mr. Eustace Fulton for White. F. E. Smith could not attend the first hearing, and Curtis-Bennett himself had only received his brief as he came into court, and only that morning had been approached about the defence. He immediately asked for an adjournment, but the magistrate would only consent if a promise were given that the contest would not take place the following week. Certainly it seemed unfair that, though the contest had been advertised for months past, and the contracts had been signed some time ago, the promoters were being asked to relinquish all hope of getting their money back at a few days' notice.

After argument, the magistrate said he would hear the opening of the case that day. Sir John Simon, an ethereal and delicate intruder into the company of elegant bruisers, famous referees and fans of the great fighting game, submitted that the record of championship fights showed that, in fourteen out of twenty-two contests, one combatant was unable to continue. It was, therefore, clearly a proposed breach of the peace. They might think that the obvious procedure was to send police to watch the fight; but he would not like to answer for what would happen if that course were taken, and in fact a magistrate had once been roughly handled when he tried to interfere at a prize fight. He told how Johnson had, in three such championship fights, reduced his opponent to a condition in which he could not continue. "That fact abundantly justifies my submission that the fourth in which he proposes to take part should not take place within the jurisdiction of this court."

Johnson always thought that his enemies had planned this campaign against the fight. In actual fact, though the summonses displeased most of the sporting fraternity in the country, there was another big section which disapproved of a black versus white championship. This aspect was of course not referred to in the case, and Sir John Simon only protested that the proposal that two men should fight until one or the other was incapacitated, filled him with the greatest indignation.

The hearing was adjourned until later in the week; but by that time "Jimmy" White had realized that he was fighting a losing battle. The fight had been advertised to take place on the following Monday; he could not postpone it, and if he fought the case, it was likely to last several days and cost him a small fortune; when, therefore, the pugilists assembled again before the Bow Street magistrate, Mr. White announced that he was prepared to give an undertaking that it would not take place. Jack Johnson lost thousands of pounds through the cancellation of contracts to write his version of the fight, but he appeared on the music halls. Wells lost the £2,000 he was promised if he would step into the ring against the giant negro; and the boxing public of England, who dearly love a heavyweight scrap and a man of the physique and picturesqueness of Johnson, wondered once more, as they have always wondered, why they were denied a pleasure for which they were ready to pay.

Once again, 1912 showed another jump in Curtis-Bennett's earnings. He was in the two-thousand-a-year class—one of the most rapid rises to that pinnacle ever made by a barrister practising in the criminal courts. He was beginning to get the licensing briefs, but save for a profitable fortnight in March, when he appeared in a case in which thirty suffragettes were charged with resisting the police, there was no case that was out of the ordinary.

In 1913, Curtis-Bennett's father, who had a few weeks before been appointed chief magistrate at Bow Street and been knighted, collapsed suddenly after making a speech at the Mansion House. The circumstances recurred later with tragic similarity. Curtis from the start had appeared frequently before him. Neither of them welcomed it, for Sir Henry was bound to lean against his son's argument and the son was equally bound to feel the weight against him. Such was the rigid code of his father, who always acted in a way that would crush any suggestion that he was favouring the advancement of his son by helping him obtain briefs. Yet in these later years Sir Henry had come to his own son for advice, and showed his admiration for the rapid advance he had made in little more than ten years.

Sir Henry was survived by his wife; a quarter of a century later that gracious lady was to survive her son and have three great-grandchildren.

Chapter Four

"DOING A CURTIS"

WITH a flat in London, a country house that was appreciably bigger, and a family that had been increased by the birth of a daughter, Ann, in 1910, Curtis now lived on a different scale. He was beginning to be able to be more exclusive in the work he accepted, and with licensing and railway briefs making up a solid foundation of his practice, with a pupil paying satisfactory fees for working with him in Chambers, and two fat briefs coming along in the year that swelled his income by no less than £1,200, he was on the crest of the wave. One of these briefs was for the defence in the "Canteen Case," which lasted through the year. Curtis was paid nearly a thousand guineas for his work. In addition, his wife's income had risen: Perhaps it was fortunate that Curtis could not foresee that in two years' time the shadow of the War would force him to live almost wholly on that income, while he himself watched the temporary collapse of his practice.

The licensing cases required tact and diplomacy, combined with expert local knowledge. Curtis liked the work, apart from its remuneration, for at Brewster Sessions there would be a bench of magistrates before whom he could display his well-known persuasive tactics with good effect. Success in making licensing applications depends to some extent on the personality of the applicant; Curtis knew the magistrates from many experiences in court, and they liked to listen to him. But though it might seem that the representation of fifteen or twenty licensees in a day, some of them meeting with no opposition, was not a difficult task, Curtis never worked harder than in the first few months of the year when the Brewster Sessions were on.

He loved to surprise the Bench with his own knowledge of the layout of districts and plans of new licensed houses. He toured the districts before making new applications, and after the heyday of George Elliott, Archibald Bodkin, and Cecil Whiteley, he became the most sought-after barrister in licensing work. His success in court was due to his never-failing patience and politeness; he was particularly pleasant to clergymen who opposed licences, and he had an invaluable gift for making the magistrates personally interested in the applications he put forward. He was never monotonous; that was the secret of his success in a difficult department of the craft of advocacy; and indeed, licensing sessions provided some of his swiftest and most effective shafts of repartee—losing half their effect when set down on paper, but sufficient to provide a welcome moment of levity when heard in court.

Some of his success depended on his audacity. He could present a bench of licensing Justices with the most completely trivial argument and invest it with an atmosphere of profound wisdom. Only those who had heard his remarks when considering the case knew that, behind that impressive mask and portentous manner, he was wondering whether by any possible freak his gamble could come off. One morning, after using up all his arguments to win three applications for licensed houses in one district, he was faced with the problem of finding a reason for the application of another house. "What can we say now?" he asked. "What *is* there to say?"

When he stood up, he put forward the argument that, because this house was the only one in the district belonging to this particular brewery, it would be unjust if the large public accustomed to that brand of beer had to walk several miles—or even use a public conveyance—in order to obtain what they wanted! The application was successful. And not by a vestige of expression on his face, not by a twinkle in his eye, did he reveal his amusement at the success of an argument that was perhaps more attractive than convincing.

Gradually, he became known at the Bar for this audacity which so often proved successful. He regarded no argument as doomed to failure, particularly when he was putting it to a jury or a bench of magistrates. The manner and the trick became known by an expression that is used today to describe a certain combination of honest bluff, cheek, opportunism, and a genius in choosing a phrase and in timing: an action informed with guile yet so ingenuous as to cause a smile. It was called "doing a Curtis." A vague phrase, it is yet perfectly understood by every barrister and solicitor who saw Curtis in action. Curtis used it himself about his own methods, readily admitting that it had "come off" again. He said it of himself, years later, when he had put on weight, about his cycling days.

"It's difficult to believe, Curtis, that you were ever a champion cyclist," said a friend, surveying his ample girth.

"I'll tell you about that," he said. "I chose the outside position up on the bank, and when the starter's pistol went off I turned my wheel down the bank and rode across the front of the other competitors, and they never caught me after that. I 'did a Curtis' for the first time."

Originally, the phrase was used to describe his manner when submitting "No Case" at the end of a prosecution's evidence with one eye on the jury in the hope that even if the Judge had to hold there was a case in law, the jury might be so affected by what he said that they would stop the case themselves. But later, "doing a Curtis" came to mean any typical gesture or move of ingenuous guile.

At the Old Bailey in an important case, the Judge had resumed his seat after the luncheon adjournment before Curtis had returned. A messenger was sent to the barristers' room to find him. As he came into court, calm and unhurried, he looked at the clock and, instead of the expected humble apology, remarked suavely: "It is unfortunate, my Lord, that the clocks in this building are not synchronized. If they were, your Lordship would not be kept waiting. . . ."

He readily admitted his own pleasure at the success of "a Curtis." Considering a manslaughter case, he shook his head slowly, and when the solicitor concerned expressed surprise, saying he had an excellent case, Curtis explained: "It's a very good case. But there aren't enough red herrings. You want a lot of red herrings in a manslaughter case. . . ."

And again, in another manslaughter case, when he was replying to several congratulations after an acquittal: "Yes, I had six hares to start. I started that one first. I saw one juryman fairly leap at it. I knew that one was a safe winner, and so I ran it hard the whole way, and didn't start any of the others."

This was in line with his oft-repeated advice: "Don't confuse the jury. When you have one good point, run it for all you are worth. Repeat it, and din it into them; never let them forget it. You can forget all the other points."

Sometimes he liked to shock the court, so that when the jury considered their verdict, they would still be reeling under the surprise of his pleading. Imagine, for instance, the feelings of a jury, asked to decide whether a defendant was a knave or a fool, when Curtis stood up and said: "You may think my client is a fool. I tell you so myself—he *is* a fool. But you can't convict on that, or the courts would be full."

He often used to say that his client's case was at its best *before* he went into the witness box, the tragic Thompson case being the classic example of his client's insisting on defying his advice.

But the greatest example of the value of this audacious approach, this courageous, seemingly carefree gesture that was so carefully rehearsed, was during a motor-car accident case which presented a not unusual complication. A married man and a married woman, both happy in their separate domestic circles, decided to spend a week together. They took every precaution to hide their identity and their escapade from busybodies; alibis were carefully manufactured, telephone calls were arranged to allay suspicion, and they even garaged their cars and hired another vehicle in which to travel to the country hotel. Their plans were perfect in the execution; but on the way back to London they ran into a man, and he was killed.

Curtis was briefed by a distracted couple who saw themselves and their families, their married lives and their futures, involved in a terrible scandal as the result of one temporary escapade. More tragic than a verdict of criminal negligence, would be the revelation, that would at once follow, that the driver of the car was accompanied by the woman. Their movements would be traced; their escapade would be public property, and their two homes would be wrecked. "I had the devil's own job," said Curtis.

At the inquest, he was able to assure the relatives of the dead cyclist that their claims would be recognized at a figure that was more than generous. He successfully disposed of any suggestion that there should be a prosecution, and he was tying up his brief, sighing with relief, when a police inspector who had charge of the case asked aloud in court: "Wasn't there a passenger in the car?"

In another moment, success might turn into ruin, if the Coroner or the police suggested that this valuable witness of the accident should give her evidence.

Curtis went on tying up his brief. With an air of supreme unconcern, he said: "I don't think the passenger can carry the matter any further or assist the Court."

He had "done another Curtis."

His modesty made it possible for him to utter many a phrase which would have offended if it had not been accompanied by a certain charm of manner and ingenuousness that was proof against insult. Mr. Claude Mullins told him: "I would rather be told I was wrong by you than by anyone else." He was given a licence by judges and opposing counsel that many envied, and even Mr. Justice Avory, least frivolous of all judges, smiled his tolerance at him. Curtis politely asked permission to quote some precedents in a case that seemed hopeless from the start. The Judge, knowing that he was fighting with forlorn hope, admiring him for his tenacity, gave permission with a most understanding smile.

"Certainly you may quote precedents," he said. "*If* they have anything to do with the case at all. . . ."

This presence and manner was undoubtedly his greatest asset. He was not a profound lawyer, and never pretended to be. "If you want law," he said, "you can look it up. To be too deep is a disadvantage. My law library is Ruff's Guide to the Turf and an A.B.C." Yet his three-day speech in the Armstrong appeal is quoted today as a classic in the art of applying the legal statutes and authorities.

His invaluable ability to make friends, and to keep them, served him well in court. He never forgot a name, and whereas some of the leaders of the Bar were too proud to recognize the existence of humble servants of justice, Curtis counted among his friends many of the clerks in country courts who sat at the feet of magistrates and often played a most important part in advising them. These clerks knew, better than any illustrious stranger, the personal idiosyncrasies and prejudices of the local Bench. They helped Curtis, and when he pleaded a case before an unknown Bench, and put forward a certain line of argument, he watched the magistrates' clerk with the corner of an eye. That official might merely frown slightly; Curtis took the hint; and nobody else in court knew why the well-known and genial barrister suddenly changed his tactics and embarked on an entirely new line of country, more in sympathy with the personal feelings of the Bench.

He was sensitive to every tremor in a courtroom; he knew

that magistrates and juries do not form their opinions on legal precedents alone, and he took care to inform himself of their prejudices and their instincts. He knew the value of their opinion of him as a man, and he contrived to see what was behind the masks of their faces, so that, after a great closing speech for the defence, he would often tick off on his fingers those members of a jury who were with him, and those who were still unconvinced by his oratory. "The two women are all right," he would say. "I have the women with me. But there's a man on the right of the back row who doesn't like me. . . ."

He often gained the sympathy of a jury when he subtly flattered the twelve just men and women. "You and I, men of the world as we are . . ." he would say. Or: "When we are driving our cars on the roads of England, members of the jury . . ." Or: "There are people who are not so tolerant as we are, gentlemen . . ."

Then he watched their pleasure, saw them make mental notes that here at last was a man who understood them, who took them at their real worth.

But there was nothing cynical in his attitude to the jury as an institution. He believed the jury system produced justice. He was always admiring the trouble taken by juries to get at the truth; their patience and conscientiousness; and naturally, he had several stories of juries that were against himself.

One concerns a case in which he felt he was sure of one man in the back row, who followed him with every sign of interest, and nodded his head repeatedly when he made his strongest points. Curtis hoped that this man's apparent enthusiasm would spread to his colleagues. To his consternation, however, the man's head continued to nod in agreement when his adversary spoke for the prosecution. Curtis then understood that he was one of those listeners who nod their heads in token of having heard, and taken in, an argument; but the nodding of his head by no means meant that he agreed with what he heard.

Curtis could emerge unscathed through the most daring passage of armed wit with a judge or his "learned friends." He probably went to greater lengths of audacity when addressing the Bench than any man since a predecessor who was very like him in temperament and build and who was known to say to Appeal Judges who were pressing him with questions, "One at a time, please!"

For the defence, with Mr. Archibald Bodkin for the prosecution, Curtis made a decision not to put his client into the box. Now Mr. Bodkin had been counting on a slight breathing space after the evidence for the prosecution, and had no idea that he would be called upon to speak so early in the proceedings. He needed time to collect his thoughts, and had as yet made no preparations. As he sat down at the end of the reëxamination of the last of his own witnesses, Curtis stood up and said: "I call no evidence, m'Lord."

"What's that?" asked Mr. Bodkin.

"*You heard* . . ." said Curtis in a loud voice.

Judges liked him. There are few men at the Bar who can suggest without interruption from his Lordship that the jury should stop the case. "Of course, if you wish to hear my witnesses," Curtis would say, "I can produce a score, fifty witnesses! But do you want to hear any more of this remarkable case?"

And finally, to illustrate this phrase that will live for many years in the vocabulary of the Temple, this slangy and picturesque expression which conjures up so perfectly the portly, immaculate, self-confident figure who might spring any surprise at any minute, there is the story of Curtis in court during a case that was not going at all well for his client. Even Curtis had difficulty in keeping a confident expression on his face while the most damning admissions were extracted from his own witnesses. A solicitor passed near his seat, and Curtis whispered into his ear. The solicitor replied with a short sentence. Upon which Curtis burst into a paroxysm of silent laughter, a gust of quiet mirth that none in court failed to observe. It was as if he had just heard news that completely dispelled his anxiety and revealed, once and for all, the folly of the opposition case. Judge, jury, his own client, and even his learned friend could not help thinking that Curtis had just heard something that would shake the case to pieces. And his confidence was immediately transferred to the case for the defence.

"What did you say to Curtis that pleased him so much?" the solicitor was asked.

"Nothing," was the reply. "I only told him it was raining outside. . . ."

Once, "doing a Curtis" took an unexpected turn. Curtis did the usual submission to the Judge with one eye on the jury. The Judge was hesitating, and the jury was talking. Then came the customary observation from Curtis: "I do not know whether the jury want to hear any more of this case." The foreman stood up and said, "No." "How do you find the prisoner?" said the Clerk. "Guilty," said the foreman. That situation took another two or three hours to put right, and it is satisfactory to record that the prisoner was finally acquitted.

Chapter Five

WARTIME

THE outbreak of war found Curtis immersed in a great year's work, which had already brought in a matter of £4,000. During the last days of July he had planned a motor tour in France, but had turned back at Boulogne and gone to Littlestone for a week-end's golf. The news of war shook him and puzzled him—as it did many others who later claimed to have foretold the calamity. Rumour was no more wild in the Temple than anywhere else, but it was obvious that the ranks of the legal fraternity would be depleted.

When in 1915 the appeal was made to every man at least to make an offer of his services to the country, Curtis made the pilgrimage to a recruiting office, a rotund, embarrassed, and somewhat pathetic figure. He knew his application was a waste of time.

He surprised an ordinary recruiting office with his presence, and was turned down for any kind of service without so much as an examination. Curtis was only thirty-five, but already the lack of vigorous exercise to which his muscles had been attuned at Cambridge, his strained heart, and his natural inclination to fat, had given him a generous figure that even a recruiting doctor could discern as the sign of ill health.

In 1915 the War had touched him with more than its ordinary gesture. He was briefed in spy cases, and ever afterwards there was to live in his brain a memory of tragic men, brave or cowardly, who stood in the Old Bailey or before a court-martial with their defence in his hands—but with little hope of escaping conviction. The authorities were remarkably punctilious in ensuring that spies caught in this country were given the full privilege of a trial. The War Office instructed solicitors to brief counsel in their defence, and the Judges—when it was a civil trial—were always insistent that the procedure should be precisely according to custom. The smallest departure from custom in the prosecution, and there was a possibility of a hard and fast case being unsuccessful. The Law was not to be shaken by the "exigencies of war" or any similar interferences.

Early in 1915 Curtis-Bennett defended Carl Muller, who was proved to have been a regular visitor to one of the best known of the spy forwarding addresses in London—a bakery in Deptford High Street. Muller had always been demanding money from the German Intelligence Service.

He was picked up by the police in Newcastle after Peter Hahn the baker had been cross-examined at Scotland Yard. He was tall and lanky and in a perpetual state of terror when Curtis advised him as to his defence. He spoke English with hardly a trace of an accent, and for some time he resisted the imputation that he was, in fact, a German. But Curtis learnt that actually he spoke German and French as well as Flemish and Dutch. Muller and the baker were tried together at the Old Bailey in 1915 and found guilty of espionage. Hahn received seven years' penal servitude, escaping the death penalty after proving that he had been under the influence of Muller. Muller was sentenced to death, but Curtis advised an appeal. Here again he was unsuccessful. In June, when Muller was removed to the Tower in a taxicab, it broke down, and a crowd formed to jeer at one whom they immediately recognized as a German spy. On the night before his execution he collapsed completely, but in the early morning when he went to face the firing party, he expressed a wish to shake hands with the soldiers.

On May 11, 1915, the "Security Services" sent out telegrams to the ports of England asking for an immediate report on any young man of unknown description and any nationality, who might give as his business the selling of cigarette lighters; the net was to bring in a drug-taking Jew, and Curtis was to have the first of several briefs that caused him pain and embarrassment and sometimes real sorrow. "It was an unpleasant task," he said, "but I considered it to be my duty, and I fulfilled my duty as far as I was able."

The young Jew traveller in cigarette lighters was Robert Rosenthal, an ex-criminal who had been offered his freedom if he undertook espionage for Germany. It was by the wildest chance that he was apprehended, for the authorities had nothing more to go on than that he was expected in England shortly. A letter had been intercepted in the post which gave these bare details, and only a few hours after the telegrams had been dispatched, news came that such a man was waiting to catch a boat at Newcastle. When he was brought to London he "confessed" that he was a German soldier; actually he had spent very few years in his own country, most of them without employment, until the outbreak of war. He was only twenty-three years old, a completely contemptible, cowardly type, and had no hesitation, in the extremity of terror, in offering his services to England now that he was caught. During the trial by court-martial, however, he bore himself well, encouraged by Curtis, though, since he had admitted both his German nationality and his intention to work as a spy in England, there was little defence available, and his counsel could do no more than put forward in extenuation the plea of his youth and his inexperience, the fact that he had done no harm, and that he had been more or less forced into this occupation. These pleas were of no avail, and Rosenthal was one of the youngest spies to be executed in this country, being hanged at the Tower, owing to the military exercises then taking place within the confines. Before his death, he tried twice to hang himself in his cell, and was dragged to the scaffold crying his innocence and protesting his willingness to do any service for England in return for freedom. Even the defence of such a man was an unpleasant task, and Curtis was not anxious to repeat the experience. But in the autumn, after a busy fortnight in which seven spies were caught, he defended two men of dramatically differing temperaments. Among the riffraff sent to England by Germany as "agents," there was hardly one in a hundred who was considered in the Fatherland as a "gentleman," Lody being a shining exception to the general rule. The majority were poorly paid, ill-equipped mercenaries who had never deserved a moment's admiration for the dangerous game they played.

Perhaps the next most gallant fighter in the "war without arms" was Fernando Buschman, the young, good-looking, Latin-faced violin-player who said he was travelling for a Dutch firm in England, trying to sell cheese and vegetables, and other commodities, but who was found to have descriptions of warships in his notebooks. His papers contained letters that left no doubt of his purpose in England, and the only query in his case seemed to be why this intelligent young man had ever become mixed up in the espionage business, and why he had ever attempted to pose under such obviously false colours. Curtis could do little or nothing with his defence, but when the inevitable sentence of death was spoken, Buschman faced his judges like a brave man and said: "I thank you for the scrupulous justice I have received."

In the Tower, he asked for his violin, that instrument with which he had charmed the landladies in his lodgings wherever he had stayed in England. Throughout the nights he played unceasingly, and Curtis was touched when Buschman sent him, through the guard, a score of music that he had himself composed. On the eve of his execution, he was again playing till a late hour, and when they came to take him out, he kissed the violin passionately in farewell, showing a Latin temperament that he had carefully concealed when on his trial. He was smiling when the shots rang out that killed him—one of the most pathetic and fatalistic spies who ever blundered through England in the War.

Later it was discovered that he had volunteered for this work apparently from his own choice, for he was a rich young man who could easily have remained in Brazil, where he had been educated, without being touched by the War.

His trial had taken place at the Westminster Guildhall in the morning of September 20; that same afternoon, Curtis went to the Old Bailey to defend a very different type of man. This was "Reginald Rowland," or more correctly, Georg T. Breeckow, a professional musician who had posed as a rich American travelling in England for his health. The pose was a good one, for he had spent several years in America, and, somewhat strangely, was supplied with plenty of money. He had served a short time in the German Army before being sent to England equipped with a code for use in messages which he was to transmit through Holland. His good American accent, only vulnerable when guttural German syllables intruded in moments of stress, served him well, and if it had not been for his accomplice Breeckow might well have gone free for many months. The accomplice was Lizzie Wertheim, a British subject by marriage who kept a boarding-house in Bloomsbury. Before attempting any inquiries which might result in obtaining information of value, Mrs. Wertheim and Breeckow splashed their money about the West End, riding in the Park, visiting the most expensive restaurants, and generally making contacts with a class of society well above that of a boarding-house keeper. It was not until the flashy and dazzling woman began touring the Scottish ports, in a large car with her maid, and staying at the best hotels where she hoped to meet naval officers, that the authorities became suspicious. Their fears were confirmed when they intercepted a message from Breeckow to Holland to the effect that Mrs. Wertheim's suddenly increased wealth had gone to her head, and that he had difficulty in restraining her extravagance. The lady was watched, and though some of her mysterious movements were explained by the fact that she was buying cocaine for herself, there were other matters which decided the authorities to arrest the pair.

Mrs. Wertheim was most indignant, Breeckow terrified and nerve-shattered. Once again there was no possibility of Curtis putting up a good defence, for when it was explained to him that the eagle on his American passport had its claws on the wrong way, and was short of a feather or two, Breeckow broke down and wrote a full confession. The trial was at the Old Bailey, before three High Court Judges and a jury, and he was sentenced to death, Mrs. Wertheim receiving ten years' imprisonment, it being successfully argued that she had acted throughout under the influence of the man. Curtis appealed against the death sentence, but without result.

When Breeckow was assisted out of his cell five weeks later to face the firing squad, he was delirious with fear. He babbled incoherently, and dragged out of his pocket a lady's handkerchief, which he asked should be tied round his eyes in place of the official bandage. The handkerchief was too small, and while the soldiers waited, the commandant knotted it to the bandage to provide a makeshift cover. And in point of fact, Breeckow the musician, unlike the courageous Buschman who had found solace in his music before his last appearance, died from heart failure before a bullet touched him. As the order to fire was given, he slumped forward in the wooden office chair that was always used for executions in the Tower. He was dead.

Most of these spies were first questioned by Mr. Basil Thomson, later Sir Basil, the head of the C.I.D. at Scotland Yard. He was an expert at sharp-shooting his questions so as to take suspects off their guard, and though there was never a suspicion of the "third degree" about his examinations, he could change his tactics with a rapidity that bewildered many a man who imagined he had nothing to fear.

Curtis-Bennett came to know Basil Thomson well, and since it was his preliminary word that usually left Curtis without a leg to stand on when he appeared in court to defend a spy, he came to have a very high regard for his ability. Their friendship was to last through the years.

Another spy defended by Curtis-Bennett was the close-shaven, iron-jawed German-American who never revealed his real name, but who was known as Irving Guy Ries. He had been picked up by the German espionage service in New York, and had actually been a film operator, though he tried to pose as a merchant in England, and went to considerable trouble to give substance to that illusion. Here was another case of a man facing a firing squad mainly because he was kept short of money by his employers, for it was a letter addressed to him through Holland, and containing the exact amount usually supplied to spies, that led to his being suspected. Ries had had to make application for further funds; and with a criminal lack of imagination, German Intelligence sent him the sum that was known to be the usual monthly payment. Confirmation was soon forthcoming that his American passport was forged, and another spy stood facing a court-martial on October 4. Curtis did his best, but it was sufficient to prove that a man had been in communication with a known spy address for him to be convicted. The charge against Ries, indeed, was that he had "done an act preparatory to the commission of an act" prohibited by D.O.R.A.; "namely an act preparatory to collecting information that might be useful to the enemy." His refusal to give his correct name was from an honourable motive, for he wished to save his parents from the knowledge of his end. And when he faced the rifles, he provided evidence of his bravery. "You are only doing your duty, as I did mine," he said, and shook hands with every member of the firing party.

Curtis-Bennett did not relish these briefs, and would have evaded them if it had been possible. Always sensitive to atmosphere, he shrank from the grim reality of this phase of the War. He could not bring himself to regard these blundering, doomed creatures as dangers to the State whom it was wise to do away with, and he was not the type to perform his duty and forget. The day of the executions, he suffered acutely. But there was no other course open to him. And it is perhaps illustrative of the attitude of the War Office that these spies were given the free benefit of defence by one of the leading counsel of the day.

Curtis-Bennett next defended, in October, 1915, a man whose first trial resulted in a disagreement of the jury, brought about by Curtis-Bennett's eloquence.

The prisoner was a British subject who was on a music-hall tour in Germany when war broke out. In Ruhleben, he took advantage of the better treatment afforded to those who professed to favour Germany, and in due course it was suggested to him that he might undertake spying for Germany. When he came to England, with a story that he had been released owing to ill health, he was naturally allowed to travel where he wished, and no suspicion fell on him till "Security Services" —that department which found so many chinks in the spies' armour—intercepted the scores of two songs, signed by "Jack Cummings, Palace Theatre, London." No such person existed, and further, chemical treatment of the scores revealed messages written between the bars of music. It was with some difficulty that "Jack Cummings" was proved to be identical with a music-hall artist then appearing in a trick cycling act in Glasgow; but when he appeared before Mr. Thomson on suspicion, the prisoner admitted that he had promised to serve the Germans in order to obtain his release, but had in fact never any intention of keeping his promise once he had arrived in this country. He explained away the presence of secret ink in his luggage, and admitted that he had at one time endeavoured to obtain a position in the Postal Censorship Department. The only fact which incriminated him seriously was his dispatch of a secret message in the score of music, though here again he had something of an excuse, for he said that if the Germans had suspected him of obtaining his release on false pretences, he feared that he would be assassinated.

His story had the makings of a good defence in it, and when he appeared before a judge and jury at the Old Bailey, Curtis-Bennett presented a reasoned and convincing explanation of his actions. As to the message in the score of music, he suggested that there was nothing there that could not be read in an English newspaper, and that obviously the prisoner was merely trying to send something that would keep the Germans quiet, that would earn him money, and that would preserve him from an attack which he genuinely feared.

Curtis was in his element with the jury. He played on the fact that the prisoner was the first British national to be accused of espionage during the War, and after his long and emphatic speech to the jury, the foreman announced that they could not reach agreement upon a verdict.

There was, however, some surprise when it was announced that there would be another trial with a new jury.

The new trial was held eight days later, and the prisoner was committed to penal servitude for life—no doubt the previous jury's disagreement had saved his life.

This view was also taken by the Press. "The public will undoubtedly feel that the sentence is lenient," said the newspapers, "seeing that the prisoner is a British subject. We can only assume that there were circumstances which led the judges to take this view of the crime, and we rely on what we know of them in believing that the punishment is adequate."

Ten days later two detectives walked into a quiet London hotel and confronted a woman named Eva de Bournonville with the charge of being engaged in espionage.

The following day, when Basil Thomson showed how letters signed by herself yielded to certain treatment and showed writing in invisible ink, she said: "How did you find out?" Then she asked to be allowed to speak to Mr. Thomson alone. "You know," she said, "I hate the Germans, and really want to work for you. I was trying to make them believe I was working for them. . . ."

Before Curtis-Bennett received his brief to defend her, she had told a great deal more about herself to the authorities; and her information, added to what was known already, again caused astonishment at the naïveté of the majority of spies sent to England by the German Intelligence Service. Eva de Bournonville was a Swede who was short of money—and perhaps that tells the gist of the story. She had travelled widely about Europe in various occupations, and had a ready command of languages like most of her people. She was well-born and moderately intelligent, and she believed that if she played a simple game of double-bluff in England, she would be safe, and would earn the miserable eight pounds a week offered her for risking her life.

It was easy to get to England with her Swedish passport, and through friends that she had met in Europe she endeavoured to obtain references good enough to get herself into the "Security Services"—"in order to help the English."

Here, however, she failed, and for some months she tried to earn her salary by making childish inquiries from everyone she met about the situation of anti-aircraft defences, the number of "regiments" at Wellington Barracks, and the movement of troops at Tidworth. When she moved to an hotel much frequented by officers on leave, and began asking young subalterns similar questions, they reported her. When arrested, she still had in her possession a cheque, which had innocently been sent through the Danish Legation addressed to a nonexistent Belgian prisoner. Her letters were easily recognizable and read, and it was obvious that she might stumble on a series of facts of real value.

Once more, therefore, Curtis-Bennett was given a brief that

was hopeless from the start. Eva de Bournonville had no defence, and the best her counsel could do was to plead that she had been led to imperil her life in this way by the German Military Attaché at the Legation in Denmark. Mr. Justice Darling passed the death sentence, this sentence being later commuted by the Home Secretary to penal servitude for life.

Curtis railed at the hopelessness of his task in these cases, but there was no possibility of avoiding them. The briefs from solicitors instructed by the War Office fell even more frequently on his desk as "Security Services" dealt efficiently and rapidly with Germany's new drive to learn England's secrets. Much of his time was also taken up with appearances before the Tribunals that sat in judgment on claims to "indispensability." He was always at home before the magistrates who formed these tribunals in town halls and guild halls, and the work seemed never-ending, for it was seldom that any man was given release from military duties for more than a few months at a time. Twice more he appeared at the Old Bailey and in courts-martial in spy cases before he gained, for the first time, an acquittal for a suspect.

This was the only suspect brought to trial who was not convicted, and certainly the evidence against him appeared to be very slight.

His name was Johann Christian Zahle Lassen, a Dane who professed to be travelling in whisky but, unfortunately for himself, appeared to be trying to do business only in those towns where the foreigner was least desired in war time. His story to Basil Thomson was that he wished to buy whisky here and resell it in Copenhagen, though when it was asked how he proposed to pay expenses by taking a few dozen bottles back with him, and why he must travel to Newcastle to make his purchases, he was unable to give an answer. There was no evidence that he had been corresponding with a known spy address—the proof of which was sufficient for the prosecution —and it seemed that the only dangerous ground traversed by

Lassen was that he had been introduced to Count Brockdorff-Rantzau, the German Ambassador in Copenhagen, and had told him something of the disappointing effects of the Zeppelin raids on London. He was pressed to tell whether any suggestion of payment had been made for this or any other information, but this he strenuously denied. There was also a Dr. Katz whom he admitted meeting in Berlin, but the elderly and somewhat bewildered Dane confessed that he never knew Dr. Katz was a member of the German Secret Service.

The court-martial at the Westminster Guildhall at the end of January, 1916, did not know what to make of Johann Lassen, but after two days' hearing, and under the spell of Curtis-Bennett's vigorous denunciation of the prosecution, ordered the prisoner back to Denmark with the warning that he would be wise to renounce all ideas of returning to England during war-time.

Curtis defended at seven more courts-martial and an Old Bailey spy trial during 1916. Most important of the spies whom he was briefed to defend was a young and volatile German who could actually speak not a word of English. His name was Adolfo Guerrero, and he posed as a Spanish journalist sent to London to write articles for a well-known Madrid newspaper. As soon as he arrived, he took steps to secure permission for his Spanish mistress to join him. But Raymonde Amonderain got no further than the English coast. She was arrested in order to see if she could shed light on the activities of her lover. She treated Basil Thomson to such an exhibition of temperamental fireworks when he suggested that she liked the Germans, that he was persuaded she knew nothing of Guerrero's real work in life, and she took little or no part in the collection of evidence against the suspect, her only experience of this country being a prison cell before she was sent back to Spain. Guerrero, when arrested, stuck doggedly to his story of his Spanish newspaper connections, even in the face of the editor's denials. It was made certain that one part of his story was true, however. He was in truth a twig of the Spanish nobility, but it was also certain that he had been seduced from neutrality by German agents then very active in Spain. The court-martial in July took three days owing to the necessity for translating every word into Spanish for the prisoner's benefit, and Curtis-Bennett made a great fight for him, wielding with great effect evidence in the form of a letter Guerrero had written to Spain in which he had said: "I like the English expansive and frank character."

But it was not through his counsel's efforts that Guerrero avoided the extreme penalty. He was sentenced to be shot, and in a heartbroken appeal from the death cell, Guerrero asked to be allowed to see his mistress once more before they were parted forever; he also asked her to obtain permission to be married. Neither request was granted, but his sentence was commuted to one of penal servitude for ten years.

Raymonde Amonderain revealed, before she left, yet another example of the curious lack of imagination on the part of the German Secret Service. Her lover had asked her to call at an address in London for papers. It was the same address that had been used by other spies.

Curtis-Bennett's efforts on behalf of the spies he defended aroused such admiration that a senior member of the staff of the Secret Service who was usually the chief witness for the prosecution, told him that he was too good, and jokingly suggested that he should not be allowed to defend spies. The joke was continued, an order was drawn, in official language "prohibiting" Curtis from defending any more. This Curtis prized, and had hung up in his flat.

Chapter Six

SECRET SERVICE

ONE evening early in 1917, Curtis fell in with his old friend Sir Archibald Bodkin as they walked westward from the Temple.

Sir Archibald as Director of Public Prosecution was in charge of all proceedings against spies and others who were to be tried for serious War offences.

Suddenly Sir Archibald said: "My good friend, I know of a job that would suit you down to the ground."

Without further explanation, he took Curtis-Bennett by the arm and led him to offices at the corner of Charles Street, Haymarket. It was the headquarters of the Secret Service, nerve centre of the British counter-espionage system.

In a few weeks, Curtis-Bennett was in the uniform of a lieutenant of the R.N.V.R. and a member of the headquarters staff of the Secret Service.

It was long past the days when British Intelligence, "starting from scratch" five years before the War, practised crude school-boyish experiments with invisible ink and rice paper, but not yet had the great "spy scare" quieted down; and throughout England, men and women were still hearing suspicious noises at night which they were sure meant preparations for sabotage, were still seeing messages being transmitted to German cruisers a hundred miles away by the flapping of a bedroom blind in the wind, were still attributing the most elaborate private lives to inoffensive German governesses and naturalized Germans who were innocent as the day.

Curtis-Bennett's immediate chief had been concerned, the

day before the outbreak of war, in the netting of every German spy then in England. The public, however, was disposed to think that the country was overrun with spies, that the most confidential government departments were manned by them, and that such a thing as an efficient counter-espionage system was nonexistent. Curtis-Bennett found that that unenviable reputation was a blind; German agents who came to England were given all the rope they needed, provided that eventually they hanged themselves.

He took to this strange game of bluff and double bluff with enthusiasm. They had found a square peg for a square hole. He was the man of the world among the soldiers, sailors, and policemen with whom he was now working, and they used his supreme ability to read character and motive to great effect. It is no exaggeration to say that after a short time, he was in possession of as many secrets of the anti-spy war as any other man in England. He was one of the favoured few who were given a sight of completed documents after they had been decoded or translated. These translations were made by a special department, but, as a precaution, no man was allowed to deal with an entire page; the work was split up among the staff, so that not until the document reached the highest authorities, could it be read in its entirety.

Unlike the policy in other countries during the war, England insisted on legal business as usual even when taking action against those who might be dangerous to the nation. The Law Officers of the Crown had to be satisfied that the military authorities throughout the country had acted with strict legality. Decisions as to the course to be followed were dictated by Curtis-Bennett, who thus found himself on the other side of the espionage game.

It was a busy life and a happy one, though he lost all touch with his home life, and contented himself with one-room flats, first in Bury Street and then in Albemarle Street, where his wife saw him occasionally. Gone were the week-ends at Bore-

SIR HENRY WITH SIR EDWARD MARSHALL HALL
Photograph by Aitken, Ltd.

ham, the house in Essex to which his father would have retired had he lived, and to which Curtis-Bennett had moved in 1916; gone too were the long motor drives on which he could relax, and the golf that he found so good for him. His hours were unconventional, and his meal-times unregulated. He was the soul of discretion about his work, and only to the most intimate members of his family were there revealed some of the dramas in which he took part—and those long after the War, after he had left the Secret Service. He was no mere officeholder in naval uniform, keeping to regular hours at a desk, and it is known that on several occasions he took an active part in the outdoor life of an investigator. The naval uniform was not worn for days at a time, and his wife was more than once surprised to find him in civilian clothes. Once she heard her name spoken behind her in Bond Street. She turned to find him standing in the street, in a lounge suit. He had not been able to resist surprising her.

One of the most dramatic stories told by Curtis-Bennett of those War days concerned the conspiracy in Paris that preceded the Russian Revolution. The British Intelligence Service knew most details of the secret conferences that were being conducted. It was known that the downfall of the régime was cut and dried, and that very shortly the result of those Paris intrigues would seriously threaten the Russian front. There was nothing to be done, but it was both the policy and the function of his department to be informed and prepared for the worst.

It was decided that all communications in this connection passing between Paris and Petrograd should be tapped. In war-time, many things are forgiven, but it was a ticklish problem to have to examine the papers of an ally travelling through England. One of the most important emissaries of the Russian Revolutionary Tribunal in Paris planned to carry dispatches via England, join a convoy in Scotland, and proceed to Petrograd. He was a distinguished general of the Russian

Army, travelling of course in uniform; and when he landed in London, he carried a common sack bound with rope, handcuffed to his wrist for additional safety, and sealed with the Imperial stamp. This bag contained a number of locked official pouches.

Curtis-Bennett used to say that in every respect, even to the employment of women decoys, the story of the Russian general followed the finest examples of William le Queux. The general was an imposing figure, and though on the face of it he should have felt himself safe in the territory of an ally, he was taking no chances. He was secure in his diplomatic privileges, was officially engaged on high State business, and enjoyed every hospitality and facility from the authorities of an allied Power. But a State Intelligence Service is sometimes obliged to strain the laws of etiquette.

Attempts were made to persuade the gallant officer to stay in London for a time; he proved inflexible in his purpose, even in the face of the most seductive female temptations. He caught the night mail to Scotland without having given any hint of being amenable to the many pleasures set before him by the ingenuity of British Intelligence. But the word had gone forth that he must not leave England before those papers had been examined.

Three men travelled in the same train, and in their pockets they had two drugs that could not fail to render the General insensible for several hours. In the country hotel of a little Scottish port, they found an opportunity of doctoring the General's coffee. They satisfied themselves that he had drunk it, and walked confidently into his bedroom that night. As they walked in, a powerful flashlight was directed straight into their eyes, and they had the uncomfortable feeling that they were also faced with a revolver. The General seemed to be drug-proof.

He embarked next day, and a harassed special agent sent word to London that the plot had failed. But it must not fail.

The convoy would be stopped. They must try again—and succeed. This time, they could use a special drug; the urgency of the position must justify the taking of grave risks.

By special signal, the convoy was stopped, and in consequence the General was informed that pending sailing orders he must postpone his departure and remain ashore. He returned to the hotel with bad grace, and that night, he unsuspectingly swallowed the drug. This time there was no flashlight in their eyes when the three agents entered his room. They released the handcuff with a master key and took the bag intact with its contents.

In those days it was impossible to transport the elaborate testing paraphernalia for secret ink and for other mysteries. It was necessary for the documents to be sent back to London for the treatment of experts. A "Clear the line" order had gone out, and a special engine was waiting at the Scottish port with steam up. It left immediately for London with the precious bag, and was met by Curtis-Bennett at the London terminus, in the early hours of the morning.

The experts concerned had been warned for immediate and urgent duty, and within half an hour of the engine's arrival in London, the contents of all the pouches were being subjected to the most technical treatment, and were then carefully repacked.

A difficulty was presented by the broken rope and the broken seals. An expert was meanwhile engaged on making a die that could be used for restamping the seals. The rope was given to assistants with instructions that at all costs, an exactly similar piece must be found. Covent Garden Market was combed, and the requisite piece of rope obtained.

The "Clear the line" signal was sent out again, and within eight hours the engine was on its return journey to Scotland. The General still slept, and when he woke up he found the sack still handcuffed to his wrist, the rope was uncut, and the seals unbroken. He sailed to Petrograd with the feeling, no doubt, that though an attempt had been made on his diplomatic immunity, it had failed. The Russian Revolution was no surprise to the authorities in England; the detailed plans for the collapse of the existing régime; the names of the chief conspirators, and the probable extent of their revolutionary activities were known in London before they were known in Petrograd.

And a very tired, but vastly pleased barrister in naval uniform, went to bed after twenty-four hours on duty.

Security Services daily provided comedy and tragedy, a macabre or farcical succession of O. Henry short stories. Through their hands passed the cases of an astonishing company of men and women, the dregs of the streets and the docks, fugitives from other lands, and suspects who were betrayed by their own involuntary impulses. Curtis-Bennett was the preliminary adviser of their probable innocence or guilt.

It was said of him that he could tell at once whether a man was lying or telling the truth. Most barristers are psychologists, and here was a man who later in life was to have a national reputation for judgment of character, gaining invaluable training for himself and at the same time giving invaluable service to his country. Much of it was tentative work, particularly when Security Services, playing the game of double bluff, supplied "information" to the enemy, for which German money was actually paid over. Very soon after 1916, British agents were working for the German Intelligence Department in England. Some of them had crossed the frontier into Germany, posing as traitors or as German-born citizens, and were sent back to England for the collection of information.

They had instructions to obtain posts in munition factories or in Government Departments, in arsenals or at training depots; and one duty of Security Services was to see that these men reached their objectives. The information they sent back to Germany had a double purpose: it confused headquarters, led the German staff to come to curious decisions;

and it not only resulted in large sums of money being paid into this country (to the material advantage of the counter-espionage departments) but in addition provided valuable information as to exactly what the Germans wished to know, and what plans they had in contemplation.

Curtis-Bennett's work in this connection was delicate. The details given had to be plausible, and the success of the pseudo-German spies in this country had to be marked but not too sensational. On many occasions, Curtis-Bennett would ponder deeply on the advisability of allowing "X" who had received orders to obtain a post in a North country munitions factory, to "succeed" in his application. Was it not time that "X" reported a failure? Was he not becoming too good an agent to be true? Had it been discovered that his last piece of information was entirely false? Curtis-Bennett, aided by the key men of his department, thought with the brains of the other side, put himself in their position, announced a decision on which a man's life might be at stake.

The most brilliant exponent of this most hazardous branch of espionage was a young officer whose real identity was known to no other man except the Chief. He had the peculiar gift of talking French with a German accent, and German with a French accent. He had been a regular officer before the War, but at the outbreak of war he had volunteered to fill the most dangerous rôle of all. He would enter Germany, pose as an Alsatian with a grievance against the English, and suggest that he work in England as a German agent. He knew what risks he faced, and he knew the thoroughness of the German investigation into the bona-fides of a German agent. He told Curtis-Bennett subsequently that as a part of the test in Germany, he had been put through a third degree that must have been terrifying to a man with so perilous a secret. Over a period of twenty-four hours, he was waked up every hour and questioned for ten minutes. Insinuations were made that he was an English spy; he was told that, if he would confess to being a spy, he would be allowed to sleep in peace, and would be repatriated; his mind was played upon, he was flattered, he was bullied and informed that the War was over and there was no more need for pretence. But he kept his senses. It was only part of the routine test undergone by all applicants for important posts in the German Intelligence Service.

Coming to England soon after the Silvertown explosion, he received orders that munition factories all over the country must be blown up. German headquarters wanted to read in the English papers of terrible disasters week after week. Dockyards, ammunition dumps, arsenals, and factories must burst into flame. Security Services got to work.

It was, however, a difficult task. The department could provide the explosions, and Fleet Street photographers could obtain pictures of devastating wreckage in various parts of the country. The reports that went back to Germany from their paid agents could be dictated, but the difficulty was that the German Intelligence Department judged the results mainly from the English newspapers, and it was not feasible to alarm the British public every week by an account of a disastrous explosion that would seriously stem the tide of shells and guns.

German Intelligence was told that the production of armaments was practically crippled. Sabotage was what German Intelligence wished to hear about; very well then, they should be told.

Curtis-Bennett could never conceal his admiration for the chief actor in the drama, the young officer who walked in daily danger of death as a traitor. He planned with him his future movements, and with the information at his disposal of the character and history of every man in German Intelligence, sought to read the thoughts of the opposition like a skilful chess-player. The comparison is strangely applicable, for long after the War there was a dramatic meeting between a former officer of Security Services and the Chief of the German Intelligence Department. The two men met in London, and each discovered that his intimate knowledge of the character, history, and mentality of the other was so complete as to be embarrassing. Each had had in his possession, during the War, a complete record of the other's upbringing, education, tastes, and dislikes; each had been accustomed to thinking "with the mind of the other." And they sat down and played chess, two men who had no secrets from each other.

Curtis-Bennett was equally well known in Germany. He learned that German Intelligence had photographs of him from his early youth. He was studied critically; his career was examined, his every decision analysed. All to one end: so that, in this strange game of bluff, the character readers on one side could hazard a guess as to the reactions of the metaphysicians on the other.

The greatest coup of the young officer was to send to Germany the "secret plans" of a "mystery battleship" that existed only in the minds of the Naval Intelligence Service. The ship was supposed to have miraculous qualities, a speed unheard of even in these days, and armaments that were invincible. It was said to be awaiting a chance to make a raid that would settle, once and for all, the future of the German fleet. Perhaps it was with some envy that its imaginary plans were drawn up, but it was the German Intelligence Staff that asked for the actual plans, and the young officer received a large sum of money for supplying them.

Security Services were most ingenious when it was decided to "keep alive" a spy who had been shot in the Tower. The essential information extracted from the spy was his method of transmitting messages. He had a fairly obvious go-between, but the Department wanted to check every link in the chain. The handwriting department, where any kind of handwriting, on any kind of paper, in any language, could be copied, made short work of producing an exact facsimile of one of his reports. He was dead, but for some time afterwards his salary came regularly to England for his use, reports were left for him, and he was congratulated on the information that he had been sending. The Germans were eventually believing anything they were told, particularly after the "fantastic" story of the "landships" proved to be true. And in return, Security Services were receiving indirect reports of every activity developing in the enemy mind.

A critical time came when the officer mentioned above was recalled to Germany. It was customary for spies to remain in England only for four months at a time, after which they were removed from possible temptation, and returned to undergo another test. Once more the officer took his life in his hands and pitted his cool brain against the "third degree," conscious that, even for a man without a guilty secret, the test was a considerable hardship. He emerged once again successful, and returned to England with express orders that he must somehow penetrate into the British Intelligence.

Here indeed was a situation likely to appeal only to a poker player: an Englishman paid by the Germans to impersonate an Englishman. After an artistic delay, he was "appointed" one of the staff. He sent descriptions of naval guns that would have appeared valuable to anyone without his special knowledge, plans of fortresses that had been scrapped or which were obsolete, and full information about his superiors.

These were nerve-racking days and nights for a man who was always highly strung. Curtis-Bennett had private worries as well, for he could not prevent himself from looking forward to the time when he must try to pick up his lost practice. He had saved little money, and had it not been for his wife, who kept Boreham Lodge going, he would have suffered even more severely. He was himself living on the small salary appropriate to a lieutenant in the Navy. In 1917, he was moved to the civil side of counter-espionage work. He still ranked as a Naval officer on the reserve, and still wore uniform. Sir Basil Thomson was then head of the C.I.D. and was chairman of an informal committee, perhaps the most important and powerful in England, to interview suspects. Sir Basil, though himself an expert in cross-examination, welcomed an adviser of Curtis-Bennett's talents. In October, 1917, Curtis-Bennett became his assistant, a member of an august triumvirate which included, as its third delegate, a military officer who was frequently changed.

The committee, which was unnamed throughout the War, and which indeed was never mentioned even in court, knew all the secrets of espionage. It sat in a long room overlooking the Embankment, and when the prisoner entered, accompanied by two detectives, he had to walk towards the desk of Basil Thomson, flanked by the desks of Curtis-Bennett and the third member.

There was dead silence as he came into the room. But as he reached the desk, Basil Thomson would request him to be seated, in an armchair that faced his inquisitors and ensured that his face would be in the full light.

There was something peculiar about that armchair. Basil Thomson noticed that whenever the suspect was faced with a critical question, when he realized that perhaps his life depended on his answer, he would draw himself forward by the arms, as if to extricate himself from a position of inferiority. He remarked on this to Curtis-Bennett.

"Don't you know?" said Curtis-Bennett. "Go and sit in it yourself."

Basil Thomson faced Curtis-Bennett as suspect to judge. "I felt at once an irresistible desire to raise my face to the level of his."

"It's a low chair," said Curtis-Bennett. "Always, when you want to get the truth out of a man, put him in a chair lower than yourself." And Basil Thomson ingeniously capped this by suggesting that in a court of law, the cross-examiner should be accommodated in a kind of lift, and should be elevated above a witness before his cross-examination began!

In that low chair sat Mata Hari, Casement, and a host of others: spies, or innocent but suspected men and women whose appearance spoke eloquently enough of their curious international background; mercenary agents, working the most dangerous game in the world solely for cash; gallant gentlemen who became agents solely out of a sense of duty; small, inefficient, and contemptible spies who were self-doomed before they got halfway across the room.

Curtis-Bennett had great admiration for Basil Thomson's methods. He was an expert cross-examiner, specializing in that rapid and unexpected change of tactics which confused a guilty man. He could be softly blandishing, polite, and conversational; suddenly he would change to a fiercely incredulous and impatient critic. Curtis-Bennett showed that he could be an imposing figure. He was suave and skilful in his questioning; but if he found that he was not gaining confidence he would stand up, loom over his desk, and present an indignant front.

The combination of Basil Thomson and Curtis-Bennett was perfect. They took turn and turn about with questions that torpedoed the defences of a guilty man. Much of the information was already in their possession before ever a suspect came into that office, but there was a possibility of adding to that knowledge by judicious questioning. It was here that Curtis-Bennett's knowledge and skill at cross-examination proved of such a value.

It was not all routine work. There was drama, sometimes pathos, in that room. And an eyewitness of the scene has given a picture of Curtis-Bennett at a time when the emotional strain of those days had made him a tired man, physically and mentally fatigued as a result of long days and nights of work. "One of the suspects," he relates, "was a young German Naval officer who had been rescued from a vessel destroyed by mines off the Southeast Coast. All his papers had been rescued, and although he was on his way to the United States the papers showed beyond doubt that he had been engaged in espionage in England. He was caught red-handed, and had already been before the interviewing committee twice. Now, the third time, he thought he was answering for his life.

"He was twenty-three years of age, clean-limbed, with fair hair, and frank blue eyes. Curtis-Bennett invited him almost paternally to sit down. Politely, he bowed to his interviewers and prepared to answer questions with composure, though he thought there was no escape from the firing squad. His English was perfect, and when he hesitated over a word, he apologized with a smile. He was cornered, unable to deny his guilt. But he would divulge nothing. Neither Basil Thomson nor Curtis-Bennett tried to bluster. The atmosphere was tense and melancholy.

"He was dismissed, and he knew that he would not see that committee again. He stood up, clicked his heels, and bowed. 'Gentlemen,' he said, 'before leaving your presence, you will perhaps allow me to apologize for failing to answer many of your questions. But while thanking you for the courtesy you have shown me, I am consoled by the knowledge that had our positions been reversed, each one of you would have behaved as I have done.'

"He bowed again, and was gone. The moment the door closed behind him and his guards, Curtis-Bennett—always emotional, and who had been affected by the human side of the tragedy—said: 'My God! I should like to run after that fellow and shake him by the hand.' He had seen a gallant youth in distress, and for the moment sentiment had been the paramount feeling in his heart."

In the case of the young German officer, however, there was an anticlimax that provided the final touch of drama, an O. Henry situation that Curtis-Bennett appreciated to the full, although he had so entirely placed himself within the identity of the other man that it did not serve to lessen his grief. The officer did not know that the worst fate that could befall him was internment as a suspect, for he had been arrested outside the three-mile limit. Curtis-Bennett knew that, but his emotion was expressed on the part of the individual who was certain that he was on the way to a blank wall and a firing squad. It was a perfect example of the way Curtis adopted the personality of another human being; it was some time before he could put out of his mind the torment of that admirable young man who had so signally revealed his character.

Chapter Seven

"TAKING SILK"

AFTER the War, Curtis had to make a difficult decision if he were coming back to a practice with which he had lost all connection for two years. His name had been absent from the newspaper columns, and he feared that the public would have forgotten all about him. He had decided, however, to "take silk." Only two K.C.'s had been appointed during the War, and the list was likely to be the longest in history. "Taking silk" is always a dangerous matter for a Barrister. If he has a good practice at the Junior Bar it by no means follows that with the magic letters K.C. after his name he will enjoy similar success. He was now in competition with the best brains the Bar had to give, and as far as the criminal Bar is concerned there is little room for more than one or two King's Counsel who specialize in Criminal and Licensing work. But, with a large number of others, including Patrick Hastings, one of his oldest friends, he was duly sworn in before the Lord Chancellor and took the Oath, which ironically enough includes the words: "For any matter against the King where the King is party I will take no wages or fee of any man."

On the face of it this would mean that a K.C. must never appear for the defence; for some time indeed it was the practice for a K.C.'s clerk to ring up the authorities when a defence brief came in, to obtain formal permission to take sides against the King and for a small fee to be paid for it.

His decision was soon justified, and even though Marshall Hall was still very much in the forefront, within three years the name of Curtis-Bennett was mentioned in nearly every big criminal case. As in the early days of his career, his old friend Freke Palmer played a large part. Freke Palmer kept a list of the fees he paid to counsel during every year that he was in practice. As long ago as 1888 he was briefing such men as Charles Gill, Bargrave Deane, Arthur Hutton, Marshall Hall, Forrest Fulton, Sir Charles Russell, and C. W. Mathews—this at a time when Curtis was at school at Eastbourne, a ten-year-old boy winning most of the races at the sports. In the year of Curtis-Bennett's call, Freke Palmer was paying considerable sums to Gill, Clarke Hall, Arthur Hutton, Richard Muir, Clavell Salter, Montague Shearman, Lord Coleridge, Charles Mathews, A. H. Bodkin, E. G. Hemmerde, W. M. Upjohn, J. C. Priestley, and Marshall Hall. In the first year of his call, Curtis received just over £17 from Freke Palmer. In 1908 he was third in the great solicitor's list after Rufus Isaacs, K.C., and William Clarke Hall. In 1909 Curtis-Bennett headed the list; in 1910 he was second to Marshall Hall; in 1911 second to Richard Muir; and in 1912 he was first, with Marshall Hall second. In 1913 he was first, followed by Barrington Ward, Stuart Bevan, Ellis Hume-Williams, Marshall Hall, St. John Hutchinson and Holman Gregory. In 1914 he was third after Bodkin and Hume-Williams. In 1915-16 Curtis was first, with Marshall Hall second, St. John Hutchinson third; and in five years following his "taking silk," Curtis headed that representative list four times out of five. Freke Palmer's records show that up to 1925 he paid Curtis £7,077—this in spite of the fact that Curtis was not called until 1902; up to 1925 he had paid Marshall Hall £5,700 and Sir Charles Gill £3,340. And six years later, in the year 1931, he records that he paid Curtis-Bennett £10,400 and Marshall Hall £5,700. There can be no more excellent illustration of the way Curtis reached and overtook every other rival at the Bar.

Time was heavy on his hands before he was demobilized in March, 1919. But when he first attended London Sessions he was met by such a welcome from his colleagues that he knew there would be little delay before he was once again "in the swim."

He took off his Naval uniform for the last time with relief and entered in his account book the sum of £130, his gratuity. Perhaps, he thought, it would be some time before he again entered such a large sum. But he was soon in harness on some well-paid cases.

The earliest case to bring good fees was the representation of the Grahame-White Aviation Company, against an airman's claim for malicious prosecution. He appeared with Sir Edward Marshall Hall, and his brief was marked 200 guineas, the case lasting for over a week. Curtis was called upon to play only a small part, but when in October the National Canine Defense League were looking for a well-known barrister to "defend" a dog which had been ordered the death penalty for savaging, Curtis had all the publicity that he could possibly require and more than he desired.

Naturally, the fact that a K.C. had been employed to appear for the life of a dog attracted a great deal of public attention. Twenty thousand signatures had been obtained on a petition for a reprieve, and there were processions in the streets, appeals on public hoardings.

The dog, "Bobs," a nondescript animal reputed by its defenders to possess an almost human passion for going to the pictures, and an intelligence that seemed considerably more acute than that of some of the thousands who devoted weeks to efforts for its salvation, had been sentenced to be destroyed by the West London magistrate after witnesses had spoken of its ferocity.

The dog became the hero of the week, had its portrait painted by a famous animal artist, and was photographed in every conceivable position.

Curtis had been in two minds about accepting the brief. He was always fond of animals, but he had practically decided against appearing in circumstances of such mass hysteria when his children impressed upon him that he should change his mind. In actual fact, the fate of Bobs received more attention from the Press than had some of the human beings Curtis had defended on charges of murder.

Once again people wrote to the newspapers calling attention to the fact that "in no other country in the world" could there have been such a furore over the fate of an animal. The photographers were busy throughout the week, and even contrived to take pictures of the dog in court, while some of the newspaper stories were painfully whimsical.

Bobs was usually fitted with a muzzle, but when it appeared in court with its owner, a little girl of thirteen, the muzzle was taken off for appearance' sake. Evidence was given that Bobs had on two occasions attempted to bite policemen, and several witnesses had said that it was a most ferocious animal—the worst they had ever known. Six months before, the owner had been ordered to keep it under proper control as a danger to the public, and the climax had come when a policeman on attempting to separate it from a dog fight had been savagely attacked.

Curtis said he could produce fifty witnesses to say that Bobs was a quiet animal, and cross-examined the policeman and other adverse witnesses with great humour. One of them said: "I always carry a supply of stones in my pocket to throw at Bobs to ward off the attack I always anticipate. He has come at me, and I have told him that if he came nearer I would give him a whack on the nose."

"When the dog heard you say that, he went away?" asked Curtis.

"He runs at people and frightens the children. He growled in a bad manner and grabbed me."

Curtis asked: "Where?"

"In Seymour Street."

"What part of you?"

"My trousers—and not in a friendly way."

But Curtis knew that the finest evidence could be given by the appearance of the dog itself. He himself had advised that the muzzle should be taken off, and towards the end of his appeal he had the dog passed to him in court and took it in his own hands. Fondling its head, he continued his appeal, one hand in his pocket and the other caressing the dog. After giving a promise that it would henceforth be kept in proper control, his appeal was granted, and immediately afterwards, processions formed outside the court announcing the "great news" that Bobs had been reprieved. But Curtis walked quietly out of the court without saying a word to anyone—hoping that the snap the dog had made at his hand while on the table had been due to nerves. . . .

In 1919, Curtis was back again into his old form, and with considerable satisfaction was able to put down the sum of £5,000 as his year's earnings. At the close of the year, he appeared in the famous Douglas-Pennant Inquiry with Mr. Tristram Beresford for Colonel S. Janson.

The Honourable Violet Douglas-Pennant had been for a short time Commander of the Women's Royal Air Force. She had been dismissed and had made such allegations against several officers and against the general morality of camps during the War, that the House of Lords had voted in favour of a Select Committee being appointed to report. Miss Douglas-Pennant had alleged that she had been dismissed because she had tried to improve the conditions in those camps, and had made specific allegations of conduct which were so grave that many parents had forbidden their daughters, who had served in the W.R.A.F., ever to make mention of the fact. The House of Lords had appointed the Committee after an astonishing speech in that privileged chamber by Lord Stanhope. Miss Douglas-Pennant had also made her allegations while privileged, otherwise she would have been immediately faced by writs. A Colonel was the central figure in one of her most serious allegations in which she had said that he had been surprised *in flagrante delicto* with a girl in the camp.

Miss Douglas-Pennant was, therefore, in the position of a plaintiff in an action for wrongful dismissal. Curtis-Bennett's client had asked for a court of inquiry and failing that, a court-martial to inquire into any allegations made against him.

Earl Stanhope was one of the witnesses moving for the appointment of the Committee in the House of Lords. He had said in the House of Lords that the reason why the Government refused an inquiry was that they feared that scandals would come to light. He then proceeded to give instances of immorality in the camp. Miss Pennant, he declared, had discovered that the colonel in charge of the camp had allowed girls to return intoxicated in the early hours of the morning. Miss Pennant had been dismissed after giving orders that would improve the situation.

At the inquiry the chairman of the committee now asked Earl Stanhope whether he had been satisfied with these charges and whether they were true or based on "mere gossip at the Club."

Lord Stanhope at first said that he had been satisfied of their truth, but later desired to withdraw some of the statements he had made in the House of Lords and made particular reference to Curtis-Bennett's client, who was the officer concerned in the incident that had been cited.

The most biting attack upon Miss Douglas-Pennant was made by Sir Gordon Hewart (now the Lord Chief Justice) on behalf of the Air Ministry. He said that the reason for her dismissal was that she was unable to make a success of her job. "It is a lamentable fact that this lady came to this position saturated with suspicion, thinking the whole world was against her."

Mr. Patrick Hastings said: "It should have been her duty to supervise the obscene jester, but it seems to amuse the lady even now. The behaviour of this lady is, in fact, incredible from beginning to end."

The committee made public some of their conclusions immediately after the inquiry and declared that the accusation against the officer was entirely untrue. Miss Douglas-Pennant had alleged that officers in the camp did not want a searchlight turned on conditions there. "It was clear to me that I was dismissed because of my efforts to get these matters right," she had said.

The committee said her accusations, unsupported by evidence, deserved censure. Their findings in full were announced in a White Paper, and during the next month the House of Lords debated the findings and heard Lord Stanhope withdraw his imputation against any individuals and apologize to the House for using unjustifiable expressions.

It was revealed that the cost to the State for the inquiry would amount to over £10,000. This was Curtis-Bennett's first appearance in the House of Lords and was a useful case to be in shortly after "taking silk." The next time he appeared in the Lords was many years later in the historic de Clifford case.

At about this period when Curtis was rapidly making his way towards the £10,000 a year mark, the Press frequently tipped him for official posts as they became vacant. He was twice forecast as the new Chief Commissioner of the Metropolitan Police, and other expectations were that his name had been considered as a possible Director of Public Prosecutions after the resignation of Sir Charles Mathews.

But Curtis did not want any of these posts, and indeed, as he totted up a total income of over £11,000 in the year 1920, the wisdom of his decision could not be contested.

At that time the crime calendar began to have a most sinister appearance. It was the beginning of a period when, to quote the words of Mr. Justice Darling, immorality was rife in the cities, and there was an immediate increase in a certain kind of case in which Curtis was to gain very considerable renown.

To cope with the growing evil, the police began to make periodic drives against the more outward signs of immorality. There was a steady stream of alleged abortionists to the court to be dealt with by the Judges when convicted, with uniform severity.

One of the worst of the abortion cases was that of a Doctor Devi Sasun, a coloured man who went to prison for ten years for the manslaughter of a girl on whom he had performed an illegal operation.

Curtis got him acquitted of the charge of murder after cross-examining three doctors and Sir Bernard Spilsbury. The evidence was that the police had taken statements from 116 women who had been treated by Sasun over a period of fifteen years.

Sentencing another abortionist (defended by Curtis), Mr. Justice Darling called attention to the need for a strong law. "Such practices have increased since the War," he said, "and I myself believe that the consciences of a great many people have been deadened to the mischief and the crime and the sin of such practices. . . . The common subject of conversation among young men and girls is pregnancy."

Curtis enjoyed conducting a cross-examination in which he could tear to pieces the evidence of a doubtful witness. After a morning's hard work during which he had been on his feet without a rest, he would appear as fresh as when he began and say: "That's the kind of day I enjoy."

One of his best successes was when he appealed against the conviction of a clergyman alleged to have accosted young women in the Strand. As usual two constables were the only witnesses for the Prosecution, and Curtis asked them if they had not noticed that the defendant had a limp? The police thought they were being led into a trap and were emphatic that the man they saw behaving improperly was not physically afflicted. Curtis then had everything his own way, producing evidence to show that the clergyman had a pronounced limp as the result of an accident. An easier victory came when he appealed against the sentence on a company director for procuring a false passport for a young girl whom he took to Paris. She was only sixteen, but he was able to prove that she herself had wrongly stated her age; and when he asked her to stand up in court she revealed herself as a girl with every appearance of being at least twenty years of age. Curtis put the girl's father in the witness box and said: "Do you know the Defendant approached your wife on the question of marrying her?" The father agreed. "In fact they are now married," suggested Curtis. The answer was that the trip to Paris had been followed by marriage.

The Gambling and the Lottery Law brought more briefs. There was the famous "Golden Ballot" prosecution in which Curtis defended the organizer. The promoters, whose bona fides were beyond question, had mystified the police considerably. In the advertising literature it had been announced that after a hundred years of doubt somebody had discovered a method of holding a lottery without infringing the Act. It was asserted that this was an original and legal scheme which had been copyrighted, but having collected a large sum of money—over a quarter of a million pounds—the promoters had advertised several prizes for a plan for allocating the prizes. As the proceeds were for an admirable charity, the police had at first held their hand; but they had been forced to take action against what they considered to be a breach of the law. Mrs. Hilda Leyel, the organizer, had admitted that, though she had taken legal advice on the subject, the committee had so far been unable to decide on a method of allocating the prizes.

That was when the police had first interviewed her. Before summonses could be applied for, however, she had gone round the country by car distributing the prizes; a pearl necklace to a cook, a motor car to a man who could not possibly afford it. The prosecution stated that Mrs. Leyel had worked very hard and very successfully and had charged nothing for her services. This was a lottery for a real charity purpose. Curtis said that he thought Mrs. Leyel must have been badly advised. All the prizes had been presented by generous donors and had not been deducted from the receipts. His client was not a rich woman and would have to pay any fine out of her own pocket.

The Magistrate agreed with all the compliments that had been paid to the organizer of the "Golden Ballot." "She is a very capable and generous-hearted person, and her object was absolutely genuine," he said. But at the same time he fined her £40 for her hard work, and as a result of having ensured a huge sum of money being paid to a War charity.

Since the War, Curtis had become something of an enthusiast for racing. He had always put a pound or two a week upon a horse, and he went to race meetings near London whenever possible and acquired something of a reputation in the Temple for being a good judge of horses and a good punter. In the Press there was some mention of an eminent judge and a well-known K.C. having been successful with a "double" at enormous odds and in Curtis-Bennett's account books there was frequent mention on the credit side of the results of his betting.

But he gained more knowledge of the racing game when he was briefed in the spring of 1920 in one of the longest and most complicated "Turf Conspiracy Trials" ever to be heard in England. It lasted almost to the end of the year, and Curtis-Bennett's earnings from his defence of one of the accused reached a total of two thousand guineas. It was a strange case. Curtis had only the watching brief with C. S. Zeffertt when a certain Peter Christian Barrie, a horse dealer, and one Walter Hopkins were charged with conspiring to obtain from Messrs. Wetherby and Sons the sum of £167. 19*s*. 6*d*. representing the stake money of the Faceby Plate run at Stockton Races in the preceding October. It was alleged that Barrie in the name of A. Pearson entered a horse called Coat of Mail, and that a three-year-old named Jazz was substituted for it and won the race after starting favourite at 5 to 2 against. Coat of Mail, it was stated, was in Surrey at the time. Mr. C. F. Gill, K.C., the Hon. Reginald Coventry, and Mr. Vernon Gattie conducted the prosecution and Mr. Huntley Jenkins and Mr. Walter Frampton appeared for Barrie and Hopkins.

When arrested Barrie was stated to have said that Hopkins was responsible. He said he had a friend called Pearson who had entered the horse for the Stockton Races. Hopkins when arrested said he had had none of the stake money.

Photographs were produced of the two horses. A witness said that Hopkins had tried to sell Coat of Mail for £1,000, and that he said he wanted to get rid of it. The prospective purchaser heard certain rumours and eventually refused to buy it.

That was the first day's hearings; but during the following week two more men were arrested. One was Cyril Lawley, who was accused of obtaining money by false pretences, and the other was Curtis-Bennett's client—Norman Weisz, a rich diamond merchant, who was charged with conspiring to commit the same offence. The persons alleged to have been defrauded in the case were the stockholders of Cheltenham Races, for Weisz and Lawley were said to have been concerned with a horse which had been brought on the Cheltenham Race Course, hooded and rugged and with bandages on, fifteen minutes before it raced away with the Malvern Selling Hurdle Race. Its name was Silver Badge and the stake money of £189. 15s. was sent to Lawley.

The real truth of the matter, said Mr. Gill, was that there was no such horse as Silver Badge. Lawley was posing as the owner of an imaginary horse, and the horse which arrived at Cheltenham on the morning of the race had until recently been known as Shining More. It had previously been taken to

London by Barrie and subjected to some treatment in consequence of which its colour became darker. The disguise was successful in Cheltenham, and later witnesses described how after its success the horse was restored to its original colour. The stake money was a small consideration, said counsel, and the real object of the fraud was an opportunity of backing the horse at long odds. Weisz won £1,500 as a result of two bets.

The police had been most industrious, and produced as the first witness a stable hand who had taken Shining More to Hampstead and met the mare again three days later. By this time she was darker and had a white star on her forehead. Barrie had explained that this was the result of using some American dope and asked the stable hand to try to clean the stuff off with gasoline. This was unsuccessful. Another method of disguise had been to pull and trim the tail. Weisz had been at Lawley's house at Epsom and, when arrested in his Hatton Garden office, had declared it to be a preposterous charge as he had bought the horse and had paid for its upkeep and training fees. The bail allowed was heavy, Hopkins having to find £1,000, Weisz £600, and Lawley £100.

The next day Mr. Henry Persse, the well-known trainer, described how Hopkins had bought Jazz from him for £800. The jockey who rode Coat of Mail at Stockton described how he had been most impressed with his mount, but later he had seen Jazz and realized that this was in fact the horse that carried him to victory.

A bookmaker's accountant told the court something of Weisz's betting account. He had won £500 on Silver Badge at Cheltenham at 10 to 1, and had mentioned to the witness later that he had heard rumours about the race and would repay the money if they were true. A course bookmaker stated Weisz had won another £500 on Silver Badge from him. This witness had also spoken to Weisz later about the rumours, and the defendant had again promised to repay his winnings if they were true.

Weisz had bought Silver Badge after the race, but Lawley's statement that the horse had been purchased at Bristol from an army dealer was disproved.

At the close of the case for the prosecution, Curtis made an attempt to suggest that there was no case against Weisz to be sent to a jury for trial. "The facts, so far as he is concerned, are not in dispute," he said. "It is merely the construction to be put upon them. Really the only allegations against him are that he knew Shining More was to be substituted for a horse entered as Silver Badge and that he won considerable sums from bookmakers by backing it." Curtis was now joined in court by Mr. Douglas Hogg, K.C., who led him at the trial. All the other defendants agreed that Weisz had known very little about racing, and represented him as a man who was always honest. The evidence of their activities was truly astonishing. The horse Coat of Mail had always been known as a pathetic-looking animal with a very poor record. When the photographs of Coat of Mail and Jazz were compared, the Judge agreed that there was no similarity. "They look like an advertisement of 'before treatment' and 'after treatment,'" he remarked.

The accused men other than Weisz were said to have boasted of the ease with which horses were "rigged" in England, and when they came to describe Weisz, they spoke of him as "a most absolute ass" who took tips from any tipster, a newspaper boy on the street, or a casual friend.

Mr. Hogg told something of his life story. He was an Hungarian Jew with an income of £10,000 a year, and he had been persuaded that he would be in a much more magnificent position if he owned race horses. He sometimes bet £500 a day, though he professed knowing nothing of the vocabulary of the racecourse, and admitted that he had thought a horse to be good because he had seen people feeling its legs and back. He had asked his own bookmaker for tips and, such is the luck of the beginner, had won £600 from him on his own tip of a 12 to 1 outsider. The gang had invited him to a West End hotel to meet a rajah who might buy pearls; there was no rajah when he got there, but he had played cards with an Australian squatter and had been told he had lost £2,000—the squatter later being convicted for card sharping.

He had believed one of the accused when they sold him a horse to run in the Grand Prix at Auteuil, though Mr. Gill, prosecuting, said that he, though not a racing man, knew that Longchamps was the venue of that event.

In spite of a plea for a light sentence, Weisz received fifteen months imprisonment, and with the appeal Mr. Hogg and Curtis could do no better for their client.

It was the end of the greatest racing fraud case of the decade. It was hoped that the conditions referred to by the accused were not generally true on the race courses of England, but it was noticeable that the police redoubled their efforts in an attempt to grab the crooks who were making vast fortunes from their unfortunate victims on the racecourses and in private card games. Gambling was on the increase, and the confidence trickster, profiting by the money that flowed easily in London at the beginning of the boom, was playing a variation of all the old ruses of "Rich Australian Squatter," "Spanish Prisoner," and "Newly Discovered Gold Mine."

The Press feared that the Turf was in a bad way, and though the Jockey Club and other racing authorities had always efficiently administered their stringent rules, the punter in the Sport of Kings was still being victimized by expert and audacious rings of sharks.

That case raised Curtis-Bennett's earnings for the year to £11,000. It had been somewhat unexpected, and his thoughts immediately flew to a new motor car on which he had set his heart. It was his first Rolls Royce, an open tourer with an aluminum bonnet that marked it as something unique in England. He went to buy it with boyish impulsiveness and could now boast that he owned the ultimate perfection in vehicles. He drove straight down to see his son at Radley and to show him the car, which he named "Silver Badge," saying that the new treasure was the result of his industry on behalf of a man who had become unfortunately involved in the Great Painted Horse Case.

Though not so remunerative, two murder trials in which Curtis-Bennett was concerned in 1920 attracted as much public attention as the "Painted Horse" case. One of these murder trials was that of the "Golder's Green Murderer," a sex-obsessed habitual criminal with a dark background. His name was Arthur Andrew Clement Goslett; he was dark and sallow, and in his veins there coursed Negro, French, and English blood. Before the War he had played a dangerous game in West Africa, operating in the diamond markets for the illicit diamond buyers, serving his sentences when he was caught, returning to that profitable branch of crime as soon as he was released. Just before the War, Goslett came to England and married—whether legally or not was never known. He joined the Royal Naval Air Service, showed a good knowledge of engineering, and soon received a commission. For some time he held a position of some responsibility, but the authorities became suspicious both of his movements and of his company. He was shadowed by the Secret Service for suspected espionage, but passed successfully through the test of a cross-examination at Scotland Yard. The result was promotion in the Service. Goslett celebrated the occasion by "marrying" again.

Women were his obsession, and the stout Mrs. Goslett did not satisfy his amatory instincts. Nor did his latest "wife." In 1919 he went through a form of marriage with a certain Daisy Holt, and although he now had a good job in a Government aeroplane factory, found that it was a grave responsibility to maintain three homes. Nor did he always "marry" the girl of his choice; when he saw a woman he coveted, Goslett invariably left the "wife" who accompanied him, and made an attempt to extend his experience as a lover.

In January of 1920, he "married" a fourth time. His official home was with the real Mrs. Goslett, but it was with Daisy Holt that he was most concerned, and Daisy was about to have a baby. Soon, the fourth "wife" was also pregnant. Goslett could handle her without difficulty; but Daisy insisted that the man she believed to be her legal husband should start a home with her. He told her the true facts; Daisy suggested that he leave his wife; but instead, Goslett shirked the exposure and said that Daisy should pose as the widow of his brother and come to live in the little house at Golder's Green.

It was a plan doomed to failure. Though he had gathered two wives under one roof, there were two others in their own homes. And Goslett, who had grown to adopt a careless attitude towards human life while in the gold-fields, decided to simplify his complicated existence by the removal of at least one of his responsibilities; the least-favoured, the first and only legal Mrs. Goslett.

Daisy attempted to force a showdown before her ill-fated predecessor. But Goslett would not admit before her that he had lived a life of deceit, and it was Daisy who told the poor woman. The younger woman expected a scene; strangely enough, Mrs. Goslett seemed unmoved; the days of romance were dead for her; her thoughts were only on the possibility of her husband buying her a new house. . . .

One night Goslett asked his wife to accompany him to inspect a house that he promised to rent. Their way led near the river bank. As they walked along the bank, Goslett produced a tire lever, struck his wife savagely over the head, and flung her dead body into the water. He then returned to the house where Daisy awaited him; he thought he had reduced his domestic worries by 25 per cent.

He made no attempts to cover up the crime. He was arrested within twenty-four hours, and charged first with bigamy and then, when they had found Mrs. Goslett, with murder. He made eight statements to the police, six of them being confessions. And though it was hardly possible that he nursed any hope of being able to escape the penalty for murder, he blamed Daisy Holt in most of them.

"I was induced to do it by Daisy Holt," he said. "I had intended to do it on a previous night this week, but my heart failed me. I killed the best woman. I am going to have the rope, I am going down under. . . . When I returned home I intended to poison myself, but Daisy was frightened and said she would like to live for the sake of the child."

Curtis-Bennett was briefed for the defence. It seemed a hopeless case. But he fought valiantly to prevent the admission of the statements as evidence, suggesting that they had been wrongly obtained from his client. Goslett had written at the end of one statement: "This is King's evidence." He had insisted on adding this strange remark, said the police, but Curtis suggested that he had done so because the police had offered some hope of leniency if he would make a full statement. The case attracted national attention, not because of any particular glamour attaching to the prisoner, but because of the great legal fight made by his advocate. Curtis, with the help of witnesses, also represented Goslett as slightly insane. At his work he had been known as "crackpot," and "The Mad Skipper."

"There is not a scrap of evidence, apart from the confession," said Curtis in his final address. "I cannot imagine stronger evidence of the unstability of his mind. . . . It shows hallucinations of the worst kind. If he thought he was forced by some irresistible impulse to kill his wife, then he was acting under an insane delusion."

But the Judge would not admit that definition. "You are not to consider whether the prisoner is eccentric or abnormal," he said, "but whether he was mad. I have never heard of a murderer who was normal, and it is well for society that that is so. The suggestion that he murdered under a delusion, is no defence."

That was virtually the death sentence. The jury confirmed it after only a short retirement. And Goslett, after making a will in favour of his fourth "wife," the poor misguided girl who was shortly to have his child, died on the scaffold still protesting his bitterness against Daisy Holt.

But if that case had interested the public because of the point of law in the definition of insanity, the other murder trial brought an even more debatable question to the fore; no other than the "unwritten law": "Is murder ever justified?"

The facts were undisputed. The prisoner was one Edwin Semmens, a young man who had married an even younger wife during the War. There was some doubt about the legality of the marriage, however, and when the husband went abroad soon after the War, the wife became friendly with a Major Ditcham, a married man living in the same London hotel, and evidently told him her doubts as to the genuineness of her status. When Semmens returned to London, suffering from malaria and other illnesses, it was to find that Major Ditcham's wife had left London for the country, and the Major and his own wife were engaged in a guilty intrigue. Among the papers in his wife's pockets he found one from the Major which read:

"DARLING LITTLE WOMAN:

"What I have been dreading all the time has happened. I have to go down; I hate and loathe the woman, but I can't very well refuse. I love you, and shall never love any other woman. And you are all that means happiness to me. Nothing, absolutely nothing, will make me give you up. Good-bye, sweetheart, with all my love.

"Yours,
"POM-POM."

The next day the angry husband bought a revolver. He wrote a letter to the Major, and received the reply: "I have been informed that you have discovered my attachment for Mrs. Semmens. As she is not your wife, you have no legal claim on her. Under the circumstances I don't consider that she should return to the hotel. As far as she is concerned, she is not to blame. The fault is my doing. I cannot tell you where she is."

Mrs. Semmens, however, wished to collect her luggage at the hotel. She arrived with a woman inquiry agent, and requested her husband, who met her by appointment, to hand her her personal belongings. The inquiry agent stayed outside a room while they went to collect her things. As soon as the door closed, she heard a shot, and the husband said: "There is one for you."

Curtis-Bennett produced a doctor to describe the mental effects of the illnesses suffered by his client, and his words must have impressed the jury. For from their retiring room they sent a note to the Judge: "We are agreed there is no intent to murder. Will you please advise us as to what verdict to return in the circumstances?"

The Judge was in a quandary—and admitted it. "The finding is a remarkable one," he said. "If there was no intent to do bodily harm, the verdict should be 'Not guilty.' You are the judges of fact. I am here to administer the Law. The prisoner was either sane or insane, and if he shot with intent to 'spoil her beauty,' that is grievous bodily harm."

But the jury would not declare that Mr. Semmens had committed murder because he had shot his wife for her unfaithfulness. After a few minutes they returned with a verdict of "Not guilty." Mr. Semmens seemed bewildered; Curtis-Bennett, smiling and congratulatory. And the Press, with one accord, headed their comments with the old, ever fascinating headline, "The Unwritten Law," and opined: "The Judge's warning seems to have passed unheeded. The verdict suggests that the jury upheld a husband's power of life and death over an unfaithful wife. Such an attitude is dead against the law of these islands. It means, in practice, a death sentence for marital infidelity. . . ."

Possibly Curtis-Bennett also wondered whether the remarkable case of Edwin Semmens would be quoted as a precedent whenever similar circumstances arose. But, as far as is known, the man who shot his wife for unfaithfulness, and was acquitted of murder, never served by his experience to save another outraged husband from the penalty of his impulsiveness.

Chapter Eight

IN THE FIRST FLIGHT

IN DECEMBER, 1920, Curtis had another good brief for 200 guineas for the prosecution with Charles Gill, in the Eastbourne Crumbles murder trial.

The accused were Field and Gray, young artisans who had been arrested for the murder of a young London typist—Irene Munro. Irene had gone to Eastbourne in August for a holiday by herself. Three days after taking lodgings she went out for a walk, and the next day her body was found on the lonely Crumbles, the head crushed in with a heavy stone.

The trial was held at Lewes—a sleepy country town which awoke to activity only when the old-fashioned pomp and ceremony of the Assizes brought a horde of people for a murder trial. Curtis later appeared in several more murder cases at Lewes. He usually stayed at Brighton, and returned refreshed after the seaside air. Although he never enjoyed prosecutions, he took the utmost care over the Crumbles murder case, knowing that against him Sir Edward Marshall Hall, Mr. J. D. Cassels and Mr. John Flowers were assembling their defences in what was certain to be a trial commanding great public interest.

Both the prisoners pleaded "Not guilty," and showed an indifference and calm as they stood in the dock that Curtis found only comparable, in later years, to the confidence of Armstrong.

Jack Alfred Field, who was only nineteen, deliberately yawned in the dock and thrust his hands deep in his pockets as he listened to the preliminaries. William Thomas Gray, the other accused, who was twenty-eight, appeared more concerned; but when they were given seats in the dock they both leant back with their arms crossed and listened to Mr. Gill's cold, precise voice, telling the terrible details of the crime, with apparent lack of interest.

Irene Munro was under eighteen years of age. When she came to Eastbourne for her holiday she was poorly dressed and lonely. She was seen in company with the prisoners going towards the Crumbles in the afternoon. A plain paper bag had been found on the dead girl's body; it would be, said Mr. Gill, an important piece of evidence. The discovery had been made by a thirteen-year-old boy who had seen the foot of the murdered girl sticking up through the shingle. A long green coat trimmed with black fur was shown; then a crumpled dark straw hat which had been crushed over her head with a stone. "The evidence in this case," said Mr. Gill, "was corroborated in so remarkable a manner as to carry conviction in the mind of any person who considered its value."

And indeed the prosecution seemed to have been able to find witnesses who could testify to every movement of the two prisoners. A barmaid knew them by name, and had seen them just before they went to meet Irene. Workmen had seen them go towards the Crumbles, and although they produced an alibi in the form of a girl who had said she had spent the afternoon with them, the evidence was conclusive. Poor Irene had perhaps not been an entirely respectable character: she had agreed readily enough to accompany the two young men to a place which was notorious for its alfresco romances. But when she got there, for some reason or other, she resisted the advances of the young men, and she had paid for it with her life.

One of them had stunned her with a stick he carried, a peculiar weapon with a bulldog's head as the handle. The marks of the bulldog's ears were imprinted in the flesh of her cheek, and when they found that she was unconscious and might cry out when she recovered, one of them had killed her with a stone and then dragged her over the shingle and buried her in a pit. J. D. Cassels called his client Field, but Marshall Hall did not call Gray. Mr. Gill seldom liked to leave more than a minor part of his duties to his juniors. In this case Curtis examined the witness who produced the plan, and did not again rise to his feet.

The death sentence on Field and Gray, two callous and unconcerned murderers, on December 17, was received with complete stoicism, and when they died together in February they went to the scaffold without flinching and without distress, having made no confession.

In January, 1921, Curtis appeared in one of his most profitable and most important motor cases. The defendant was a man well-known in many circles. As he was driving his car on the Great North Road, it had skidded and mounted the bank, killing one child and injuring two others. Curtis-Bennett's brief was marked 200 guineas. The defendant, who was charged with manslaughter, had to contend with considerable local feeling, and the evidence of police and other witnesses, who estimated his speed at sixty-five miles an hour, and asserted that after the accident he had said: "I might have taken it too fast."

There was applause when witnesses made statements inimical to the defendant. Curtis made considerable capital out of the fact that one witness, a district councillor, was well-known locally as a critic of the speed of motor cars passing through the village of Baldock. The most damaging witnesses were members of one family. One of them admitted that he had said that he would like to be on the jury. Several young members of the family gave evidence, and one of them said that the car had "come up the hill in a flash." Curtis smiled to himself and took out his watch. "I will count the seconds on my watch," he said, "and I want you to tell me how long it took the car to travel from the crossroads to the top of the hill." The witness stopped him at the third second. "Thank you," said Curtis. "As the distance was 250 yards, from your description, the car must have been travelling at 180 miles an hour!"

But in spite of his destruction of the evidence against his client, and a strong plea that he was the victim of local feeling, the defendant was sentenced to twelve months' imprisonment for manslaughter. If he had wanted, Curtis could have made much more of the plea that local feeling had assisted in his conviction. He received anonymous communications on black-lined paper, of which the following is an example: ". . . And Christ took little children in His arms and blessed them, and said 'whoso offendeth against one of these, it were better he had a mill stone around his neck and were cast into the sea.'"

He appealed against the conviction, pleading that the accident was entirely due, not to excessive speed, but to the condition of the road, and a slight accident when the driver had touched the accelerator instead of the brake. He also protested with vigour against the conduct of the prosecutor, Sir Richard Muir, who had put to the defendant no fewer than eight questions, all alike, which tended to show that he had bought the car for no other purpose than that it would go at great speed. "These questions were wrongly put," he said, "and had elicited from the defendant the fact that he had had an unfortunate past record of accidents." Mr. Justice Avory: "By repeating the question many times, Sir Richard Muir was casting the fly over a lazy fish until he bit."

It seemed indeed that the Appeal Judges agreed with Curtis-Bennett's submissions. The summing-up, they said, had been unfortunate, and they did not agree with the manner of the prosecution. But the appeal failed, and Curtis was most indignant, because he held that his case had been hopelessly prejudiced by unprecedented conduct aimed at the exposure of the defendant as an habitually dangerous driver.

In July, 1921, Curtis had a noted victory in obtaining the reversal of a conviction against a well-known clergyman who had been arrested for "a Hyde Park offence." It was the first of his great defences of prominent men whose conduct in the Park led them to be accused of offences which resulted in some cases in a sentence of infinitesimal importance compared with the disgrace that attended their arrest. His client was a clergyman then in charge of the English Church at Brussels. He had been a Cambridge Blue, chaplain in the Navy, chaplain to King Edward and King George; he had been married twenty-five years and was a devoted husband, and had come to England to preach at the Chapel Royal.

One evening, after visiting friends at Maida Vale, he had walked in Hyde Park and it had begun to rain. He had spoken to two women who had laughed at his gaiters, and one of them had made a remark to him about the Church and had asked him for money. The clergyman had walked on, the woman accompanying him. But they had gone no more than a few yards when a policeman arrested him. He had tried to assist the woman, saying that she was a friend, and that had led to her release. For "annoying the woman," he had been fined £5 by the Marlborough Street Magistrate, the police saying that he had spoken to several women and forced his conversation upon them. Two women had complained of his conduct to the officers, but had refused their names and addresses.

The appeal was heard at London Sessions, and Mr. Travers Humphreys, for the respondent magistrate, said that it was unfortunate that people should make complaints and refuse to give their assistance. But the police had followed the clergyman, and if there was any explanation of his conduct the authorities would be as glad as anyone else. Curtis, after outlining his client's distinguished career, produced three admirals to speak for his character and put his client into the witness box. He obtained a decision quashing the conviction without great trouble, the Chairman saying that although the police had given their evidence fairly, the inference drawn from their statements had been incorrect.

Curtis-Bennett's next murder trial gave him the opportunity of leading for the Crown. The accused was Thomas Clanwaring, a shock-headed, dark half-breed who was accused of murdering Alice Maud Lawn, the proprietress of a general shop in King Street, Cambridge. He was opposed by Mr. A. C. Fox Davies, and the defence had received over two hundred letters offering financial assistance for Clanwaring. Curtis took two hours over his opening speech, talking conversationally to the jury without a trace of bitterness or persecution in his outline of how Clanwaring, according to the Crown, had committed the murder.

It was a curious case. Clanwaring arrived in Cambridge with a fantastic story of having lost his speech through being blown up in the Silvertown explosion. But he had plunged into cold water at the Letchworth public baths and had miraculously recovered it. The night before the murder he had been so short of money that he sold his cap for a shilling. The morning after the murder he changed coppers into silver and silver into pounds. The dead woman was in the habit of keeping a great many coppers in her shop. Her body had been found lying at the bottom of the stairs, a gag in her mouth, her forehead broken by a chopper, and a piece of string round her neck. Someone had washed his blood-stained hands in a bowl that stood near by, and wiped them with a tea cloth. Money which had been in a cupboard was missing, although there was £600 in notes upstairs. The murder had occurred in the afternoon, and Clanwaring could account for every hour of the day except that fatal hour in which Miss Lawn had died. "If you feel that there is any doubt in your mind that Clanwaring committed this murder," concluded Curtis, "then he is entitled to the benefit of that doubt."

Strangely enough, although Curtis was so expert in dealing

with the time element in a case, it was on the question of time that Clanwaring was acquitted. The defence established that he had been in a public house 1,000 yards from the shop, six minutes before he was supposed to be in the shop. "Walking at the rate of four miles an hour," said the Judge, in addressing the jury, "it would take him thirteen minutes to walk that distance. And was Clanwaring likely to walk at even four miles an hour?" And indeed, Curtis had had some difficulty in eliciting reliable evidence from some of his witnesses. One of them, for instance, stated that he had started the morning by drinking a pint of beer at the "Dog and Pheasant"; after breakfast he had had a pint of beer at the "King William"; he had then drawn his pension and had two pints of beer at the "Rose and Crown"; he thought he then went back to the "King William."

"You were a little doubtful by that time," suggested Curtis.

The Farrow's Bank case at the Old Bailey lasted for thirteen days, establishing a record for the new court. Curtis defended Walter Crotch. The trial had been postponed from the previous Old Bailey Sessions, Curtis needing more time to prepare the defence of his client after new evidence had been called following nine days' hearing in the police court. Thomas Farrow had been manager of the bank, which closed its doors at the end of 1920 with a deficiency of two million pounds. Crotch had been a leading director, and the accountant, Frederick Hart, was the third member of the trio to be charged.

The closing of the bank had meant immense suffering throughout the country, for nine thousand pounds a year had been spent in advertising in religious papers which found their public among frugal and thrifty people. It had paid good dividends over a number of years, and it had been diligently represented that the bank was solvent and prospering. But it was alleged that the balance sheets were false, and the Attorney General, who was at the time that brilliant advocate Sir Gordon Hewart, K.C., M.P., stated in his detailed opening speech that the trading loss in twelve years was over a million pounds. Farrow's Bank had begun the fashion of advertising, and other banks had followed suit. Excellent results were obtained from this method of obtaining new clients. Then, when accountants had made an inspection of the books, they reported to Farrow and Crotch that the assets would not realize five shillings.

Curtis-Bennett's client, according to one of the witnesses, had shown remarkable philosophy when presented with this statement. He had thrown up his hands and said: "It cannot be helped. I knew it would have to come sooner or later. Well, I shall now be able to retire and start writing books."

"Well, Crotch," they said to him, "you seem to have a sense of humour." He had replied: "If I believed in a hereafter, I know exactly what I should do, but as I do not, I shall just have to face it out."

As soon as possible Curtis took up this point of Crotch's alleged remarks. "Mr. Crotch has written a number of serious books on immortality," he said, "and was very much hurt by that statement."

The case for the prosecution was that for no less than twelve years Farrow had been guilty of duping the public. He was, in fact, nothing more than a common thief. Mr. Cecil Whiteley, for Farrow, asked the jury to say that he honestly believed what he was doing was within the law and in the interests of the shareholders. He had had no birth or education, and had risen to a position of eminence through his desire to found a halfway house for people of small means who could not borrow money from joint-stock companies, and who often fell into the hands of moneylenders.

"The whole of Mr. Farrow's life," said Mr. Whiteley, "has been devoted to protecting the poor classes from the moneylenders. At the present moment all the money he possesses in this world is exactly one hundred pounds."

The cross-examination of Farrow by the Attorney-General

revealed the astronomical figures which were involved in the collapse of the bank. Expenses were exceeding income year after year; in 1919 the expenses were over £200,000, and the earnings were less than £80,000. Up to the end of 1919 the total amount of writing up of the investments of the bank was over £1,500,000.

Most of the time was spent in cross-examination by the Attorney-General of the principal defendant, and when at the end of a fortnight Curtis rose to speak for Crotch it was almost a foregone conclusion that the verdict would be one of guilty. The summing up had lasted for nearly four hours, and Mr. Justice Greer had used some very plain words, and had said that when they had found out that there was only one way to keep alive this financial child of Mr. Farrow, they had connived to keep on until they were found out.

Farrow and Crotch were sentenced to penal servitude for four years, and Farrow made a long speech to the Judge in which remorse and self-pity were very evident: "I had no idea there could be found twelve of my fellow countrymen who could unanimously say Farrow is a criminal. Thank God I have six children who still believe in the honour of their father, and although I am going down will bravely hold up their father's name with pride even to an unbelieving world."

Crotch was less personal. "I never intended to inflict any injury on the public," he said. "I had great dreams in my life as a young man of public service, and now my one desire is that you will give me the opportunity of coming back soon to a decent and useful life as a good citizen."

Before the year 1922, the names of Curtis-Bennett and Marshall Hall were often being linked in comparison. Their methods were very different, but Curtis was getting some of the briefs that might have gone to Marshall; and when it came to a question of deciding on a man of the world for the representation of a client, many solicitors chose Curtis. It was said of Marshall Hall, with some truth, that if you were a guilty man, you could do no better than brief that handsome, impressive giant in the hope that when he came into court, he might pull the case out of the fire by the sheer majesty of his presence and his stubborn insistence on obtaining his own way. But, if you were innocent, and had a perfect case, Marshall Hall might choose to conduct the case in a certain manner, fall out with opposing counsel and the Judge, create a minor scene in court, and find himself involved in a side-issue upon which the jury might decide the case.

Curtis rarely quarrelled, and then only when sure of his grounds as for instance, in the Almeric Fitzroy case, when his objections to the attitude of the magistrate (Mr. Mead) were supported by the Press of the whole country; and his particular protest against Mr. Mead's handling of the case was vindicated in signal manner at the appeal. Frequently enough he used to say that he had been "livid with anger—simply livid!" But when doubt was expressed of the truth of this obvious overstatement, he would smile tolerantly, and qualify it by saying that he had been "a little disappointed." He knew that a jury favoured an even-tempered and confident advocate, and he took every opportunity of showing them that of all the counsel asking for their consideration, here was the man who knew the facts of the case, who was most willing to help them with explanations, and who seemed to have every detail of the case at his finger tips. Curtis could adapt himself to any company; he never made the mistake of overestimating the intelligence of a jury, but he could explain a point to them with sympathy and perfect diplomacy.

He interrupted others with perfect timing and skill—purely in order to reveal his intimate knowledge of the facts for the benefit of the jury. For though he would say that the jury system was the best in the world, and believed that, in the main, Justice was served, he knew that when it came to the time for the twelve good men and true to consider a nice point, they could not help being affected by the personalities of the men who had presented the facts to them.

To illustrate the predicament of a client with a poor counsel, he was fond of telling the story of the nervous young barrister, who began:

"M'Lord, in this case my unfortunate client—M'Lord, as I say . . . M'Lord, my unfortunate client—"

"Go on," said the Judge. "Go on. So far the Court is with you. . . ."

When he represented himself as knowing more about the cases than any man in court, he was often doing himself no more than justice. He attached a great importance to a "view of the scene," and particularly when a policeman was in the witness box, he mentioned this. "You're sure of that?" he would say to a witness. "You're quite sure of that? I've been there myself, you know . . ." And often enough a police witness would try to strengthen his own evidence by a slight exaggeration. Then Curtis would pounce. "If only the police would stick to the facts, and tell only what they know to be true," he said, "they would fare better in court. Too often they try to improve upon the facts."

His consideration for the jury and his desire to help them—as distinct from his wish to appear to them in a favourable light—was also shown by the trouble he took in explaining documents. Counsel often do not take the trouble to refer to documents exhibited, as being points which are not very material. But Curtis would take them over to the jury and show them and, after his explanation, would say: "Now are you quite sure you understand what they mean? Is there any point about them that I can make more clear?" The jury appreciated such help, and remembered their adviser when they came to consider the verdict.

There were clients who thought that, if they briefed him, his appearance would draw attention to their case. And in one instance recounted by Curtis, it appears that the proceedings would have ended earlier if it had not been for his popularity with a jury. The Judge intimated that he thought the jury might have heard enough. Eleven of them agreed, but the twelfth wished to hear the defence. Afterwards he was asked why. "Well," he said, "I admired Curtis-Bennett's voice so much when he cross-examined that I was anxious to hear him making a speech to us."

And indeed, among those who came to hear him from the public gallery, there were many who were experts in the art of speaking. He had quite a following from the stage, knowing many famous actors in the Garrick Club. Seymour Hicks was a regular attendant at big trials in which he appeared, and admired his methods greatly. Discussing the relative requirements of an actor and a barrister, Curtis said that he wished he could have all the advantages that are available on the stage. "After all," he said, "an actor has an atmosphere favourable to him. He has an audience that wants to hear him; he has scenery, lights, every mechanical aid to make him more acceptable to that favourable audience. In a Court of Law, a barrister has to create his own atmosphere; he must win over his audience without external aid; sometimes I wonder whether it would not be a good thing if I could have soft music while I make the speech for the defence!"

An actor said to him: "The most difficult feature, to me, would be that your part is not written for you." Curtis replied: "That's the only part of an actor's job I could not manage! I could not learn a part and speak it."

Curtis showed the truth of this when he went to the House of Commons. He was worried because he had written copious notes for his maiden speech and must continually refer to the manuscript. Whereas the half-page of note paper with a few scribbled headings on it, which he seldom looked at, gave him the chance of standing free and unfettered in court, his brain concentrated on the chronological order of his argument, his hands free for those few restrained gestures.

One attribute of his always pleased the solicitors. They said that "he always knew who was paying his fees." There are counsel who will disdain to consult their clients, and have dealings only with the solicitor who instructs them; Curtis would chat in court with the most humble and disreputable defendant who had caused him to be briefed, and he came to court always with a sincere confidence and a determination to do his best within the limits of his powers for his client. He could not bring himself to adopt a cynical attitude; the power of his oratory was a mirror of his own belief in his client; and even after his faith in a client was rudely shaken, on an occasion when he had reposed faith in his innocence to an unusual degree, Curtis continued to "take home with him" his professional reliance on the innocence of the men and women he so skilfully defended.

The case in which he had been so badly deceived was that of a man charged with murder. Curtis felt very strongly that he was a victim of circumstances, and could not get out of his mind that a great wrong would be done if he was not cleared of all guilt. He was able to obtain an acquittal on the charge of murder, but his client received ten years for manslaughter. The appeal failed, and Curtis resolved to do his utmost to right the wrong. He determined to seek an interview with the Home Secretary to see if something could be done for the man, and had actually been arranging a meeting when he returned to chambers and found the solicitor on the telephone. Before Curtis could say a word, the solicitor said: "I've just been to see our man in jail. He's very pleased indeed, and wishes me to congratulate you on getting him off with only ten years. He considers himself very lucky. . . ."

Curtis said to himself: "Never again do I make up my mind personally on a case! After this I'll take a case and do my best on the evidence. . . ." Needless to say, he broke that resolution on the next occasion when his client pleaded "Not guilty," and indignantly contested the evidence.

Chapter Nine

THE GREATEST YEARS—1

Curtis-Bennett's greatest year, a year of work that was all in the public eye, was 1922, when he loomed ever larger in the headlines and noted in his account books an ever-increasing standard of fees to give solid support to this flattering mirror of his career. Up to date he had appeared in forty-eight murder trials, for defence or prosecution. But few of them had been notable, and he had not yet handled by himself one of the startling cases that had put Marshall Hall's name at the top and kept it there for many years. In these days, it is the fashion to say that there are no more "great" murder trials; certainly there has never been a year of such dramatic court-hearings as 1922; and in the records of crime for the last twenty years, three of the cases in which Curtis appeared that year will remain in the public memory. Merely to mention the names conjures up all their drama and tense excitement. They were the Armstrong murder trial, the trial of Ronald True, and the trial of Mrs. Thompson and Bywaters.

Curtis-Bennett's knighthood came in the New Year Honours. He welcomed it since it would repay him for the lost time caused by his work in the Secret Service. The official reason given was "for work in the Criminal Investigation Department," but as a fact, he would have welcomed the honour more two years before, when he had been more nervous of the effect of his absence from chambers. Now, he had no real need of this undoubted fillip to a great reputation; but he was genuinely pleased, and did not attempt to conceal his pleasure. For some time he discussed whether he should be Sir Henry or Sir Honywood, but decided to be known by the same name as his father before him. He thus became one of the few practising barristers who had been knighted without reaching the rank of Law Officer. The only other circumstances in which a practising barrister is likely to be knighted is when he attains the rank of Senior Counsel to the Treasury at the Central Criminal Court or for some signal service to the State.

As early as the second week of February, big briefs came his way. The first was for Armstrong, accused of the Hay murder, and the other was to defend Captain and Mrs. Owen Peel, accused of inducing a village postmaster to delay the dispatch of betting telegrams. The case was known as the "Society Turf Sensation," for Captain Peel was well known on the Turf. It was heard at Bow Street and the Old Bailey.

The Police Court proceedings were followed by a fashionable society and racing crowd, and it was obvious that the limelight would play brilliantly on the principals. Briefly, the evidence for the prosecution was that Captain and Mrs. Peel went to the village post office just before a race at Kempton Park, and a telephone call came through for Mrs. Peel. Captain Peel had a sheaf of forty-six telegrams in his hand, ready to send off, involving a sum of £368 as stakes. It was alleged that he waited until after the telephone call had come through at three o'clock before handing the telegrams to the postmaster, and then suggested to this official that he mark the time received as 2:45 or 2:50. Both the accused denied these allegations; but, in spite of a strong plea by Sir Henry to show that the prosecution had failed to establish a *prima facie* case, they were committed for trial, bail being £1,000 each.

In his address, Curtis accused the Post Office officials of behaving unfairly, and made a great deal of a point he had established from the postmaster, when he said he had only agreed to ante-time the telegrams because he had had Captain Peel under observation the whole time.

Chief interest in the trial, however, was not on account of

the betting fraternity's close attention, but because the case brought up for review the whole question of whether the wife was under the coercion of her husband. Sir Charles Gill, K.C., who led for the prosecution, said it was a somewhat quaint presumption that a man and his wife were supposed to have but one will, but that all the authorities corroborated that opinion.

Mr. Justice Darling seemed to agree with Sir Charles, and although there was some lively discussion in the court at the beginning of the proceedings on this point, Curtis took no part, and at the end of the Judge's long dissertation outlining his final opinion he stood up and innocently remarked: "Do I understand your Lordship to say that the indictment against Mrs. Peel must be proceeded with?"

"Certainly yes," said the Judge. But he said that the defence could submit later that there was no evidence against the lady.

That day, Captain Peel pleaded "Guilty," and his wife "Not guilty." It was a curious situation. Curtis reminded the court that Peel had pleaded guilty only to ante-timing the telegrams, and not to the intent to defraud. He resisted any suggestion that, because Peel had repaid some £2,000 which he had won that day, it was a gesture of guilt; but in regard to Mrs. Peel, he said that neither she nor her husband knew the winner of the race when they persuaded the grey-haired rural postmaster and his assistant to accept the eight telegrams, which placed money on the three o'clock race.

The law that Curtis applied as exonerating Mrs. Peel, she being wife of Captain Peel, was that it was a presumption of law that, the defence being committed in the presence of her husband, she was under his coercion. The law could be traced back to King Ina, of the West Saxons, and King Canute. He did not mind whether it was a good law or a bad law, but reminded the Judge that it was the law. "The reason for that law has absolutely gone," said Mr. Justice Darling, "but I am bound to follow it. The doctrine of coercion is founded on the assumption that a woman would never dare to contradict her husband. It is absurd to say that the law is in accordance with modern circumstances." The legal point taken was successful and Mrs. Peel was not called upon to put forward any defence she may have had on the facts. Mrs. Peel was found not guilty and discharged.

Curtis had shown the absurdity of the law as it stood. And when the Press rumbled and thundered on the theme the next day, the judgment was also criticized as being an illustration of one law for the rich and another for the poor, since a month before, a labourer had been sent to prison with hard labour for a similar offence. The law, which Sir Charles Darling had called "a melancholy doctrine," was now called "musty and antiquated, a fly-blown legal doctrine."

The Judge indeed had gone out of his way to expose the folly of the Act which Curtis had resurrected from the dim past of wife-beating days, and had so determinedly pressed on the Court as inviolate. Curtis had bound the Court in what was the existing law, and incidentally had assured that in the future no other defender could drag King Ina's law out of the musty records, for a Committee of the House of Lords appointed by the Lord Chancellor duly reported.

The Criminal Justice Act of 1925 enacts that on a charge against a wife for an offence other than treason or murder, it shall be a good defence to prove that the offence was committed in the presence of or under the coercion of the husband. The Act, therefore, abolished the presumption that a woman was necessarily coerced. It is for her to prove it. The Peel case was the last, therefore, in which the doctrine was heard that a woman was inevitably under the influence of her husband. Not without some opposition in the Lords; for Lord Buckmaster gave it as his firm belief that the bulk of women acted under the husband's direction. But most people agreed that the Bench must be rescued from being placed in such an awkward predicament as to be obliged to follow a law that was classed as an archaic curiosity.

During the Peel case, Sir Henry had had his first long consultation with Mr. Thomas Matthews, Armstrong's solicitor in Hereford. The trial was to be held in the Shire Hall, Hereford, on April 3rd before the judge who had advertised the futility of the law so startlingly in the Peel case. Mr. Matthews found Curtis remarkably diligent. "The bulk of the work in connection with the case was done before he came to Hereford," he states. "He must have practically lived in the case for some weeks before the trial. Before receiving his brief, he wanted, week by week, the depositions and exhibits in the case then before the Justices."

Major Herbert Rouse Armstrong, a solicitor in the old-fashioned and sleepy town of Hay, just over the Welsh border, had been arrested on New Year's Eve.

Mrs. Armstrong's last illness had caused no suspicion at first. At the time of her death, the doctor had certified "natural causes," but several months later, on instructions from the Director of Public Prosecutions, the body had been exhumed; on examination by Sir Bernard Spilsbury, arsenic was found in the body, and it was suggested that during the last weeks of her life the poor woman had been treated to a course of poisoning. During her lifetime, Mrs. Armstrong had been frequently ill, and for one period had been treated in a nursing home and an asylum. During illness, she had betrayed signs of arsenical poisoning, and it had been discovered that her husband was in the habit of buying extensive quantities of arsenic as weed-killer. When she was away from home at the asylum, Armstrong had made strong requests for her to be returned to him; and when the asylum superintendent offered to keep her under control and supervision, her husband refused the offer. Soon after her return home, she began to show once again signs of arsenical poisoning; she had the "high-stepping gait" peculiar to the malady; she began to lose the use of her limbs; and on February 22 she died.

Armstrong, posing as the saddened husband, went to Italy; but soon afterwards he made up his mind to ask another woman to marry him.

It may seem strange that it was not for several months afterwards that the authorities became doubtful whether Mrs. Armstrong had died of natural causes. Their suspicions grew only because the Major tried to repeat his achievement. Also practising in the little town as a solicitor, there was a Mr. Martin; some aloofness had characterized relations between them, but there came a time when Mr. Martin was obliged to press Armstrong for the completion of a sale, for which he held large sums of money as solicitor for the vendor. Mr. Martin's repeated requests for a settlement had a curious result: the man who had seemed to shun his presence, now pestered him with invitations. And not only himself, but his wife.

Armstrong asked Mr. Martin to tea, and during the meal, a curious thing happened. There was a plate of buttered scones on the table; Armstrong took one up in his fingers, said "Excuse my fingers," and put it on his guest's plate. Mr. Martin ate it, and that night began an illness which lasted for some days. When better, Mr. Martin went to the police, and they advised him to say nothing, report all movements, and above all, to refuse all invitations to take food at Armstrong's house. Arsenic had been found in the contents of Mr. Martin's stomach, causing his illness. And when he was up and about again after his illness, the solicitor was amazed, when first meeting Armstrong again, to hear him say: "It may be a curious thing to say, but you will have another attack of the same kind . . ."

The invitations to tea were becoming more frequent here, in this little town, two men were watching each other, the one pressing the other to eat at his table, receiving every kind of excuse in reply. For the moment, the matter of the legal business was forgotten; matters of more grim moment were on hand. But for two months the police bade their man wait and watch. And not until New Year's Day did an Inspector of Police visit Major Armstrong and question him about that illness of Mr. Martin.

No mention to him yet of a suspicion that was growing in the official mind; merely a request for his own version of why Mr. Martin had fallen ill immediately after that tea-party. It was recalled, also, by the local doctor that long ago, while his wife still lived, Armstrong had asked what would be a fatal dose of arsenic. He was told it would be about two grains. "I thought that would be enough . . ." replied Armstrong.

Two days after the arrest for attempted poisoning, the police exhumed the body of Mrs. Armstrong. Local gossip had supplied many of the gaps, but it was Dr. Hinck's memory of the circumstances of the woman's death that resulted in the uncovering of one of the most cunning crimes of the decade.

A charge of murder was added to the charge of attempted poisoning. And it was this point, that suspicion of the major crime had come only from an alleged attempted crime later, that gave Curtis a ray of hope. It was working backwards to a crime. If Armstrong had been able to settle the comparatively trivial affair of the sale, the circumstances of his wife's death might well have remained uncovered. For many months there had hardly been a breath of suspicion in the village. The doctor had been satisfied that she had died from natural causes, and the neighbours had no reason to suppose that they were harbouring a murderer in the town. But perhaps it was that the vain man who always insisted on being addressed as "Major," who strutted a little before his friends, had found an easy way of disposing of all difficulties. . . .

Those tense weeks during which "the Major" was pressing Mr. Martin to visit him for cups of tea, were described in court by Mr. Martin himself. His descriptions reveal a strange, macabre situation, a grim shadow playing over an innocent tea-table, the English conversational institution. "I think I had about twenty invitations to tea altogether," said Mr. Martin at the trial. "Armstrong's house was about a quarter of a mile or half a mile from the town of Hay, and about three-quarters of a mile from my house. Subsequently I took my tea down to the office in order to have some ready excuse for not accepting his invitations. His office is just opposite mine, on the opposite side of the road. It would only have taken me a minute to go across. After I started tea in my office, Major Armstrong started having tea in his office, and he asked me over. I told him I was having tea at my office. . . ."

As usual, Curtis first studied the depositions, reading them through. Then he picked holes in the police case, running a red or blue pencil along the margin as he judged whether the point might be made favourable or not to the prisoner. He did not see Armstrong until just before the trial, and on Sunday morning April 2nd, the day after the Varsity boat race, he set out for Hereford in his open Rolls, a muffled figure driving the hundred-odd miles with the anticipation of the week's work ahead; he had his programme and his plan of campaign in his mind; he was taking matters quietly.

Even so it was something of a shock when he first encountered the urbane confidence of the meek, spectacled solicitor who insisted on his war-time title of "Major," and who had bombarded a frightened solicitor with invitations to tea, day after day, until he accepted.

Curtis walked with Mr. Matthews into the Assize Court. As Armstrong was shown into the room, he walked over to Curtis, his hand outstretched, a pleasant, conversational opening on his lips, as if the only matter in which he was interested was a race on the Thames at Putney.

"Were you at Oxford or Cambridge, Sir Henry?"
"Cambridge."
"They won the boat race and we will win this case. . . ."
For the prosecution appeared the Attorney-General, Sir

Ernest Pollock, K.C., M.P. (later Lord Hanworth, Master of the Rolls), Mr. C. F. Vachell, K.C., and Mr. St. John Micklethwait; for the defence, Sir Henry Curtis-Bennett, K.C., Mr. S. R. C. Bosanquet, K.C., and Mr. E. A. Godson.

During the first day's hearing Sir Henry made his vital submission against the admissibility of evidence tending to show that Armstrong had administered arsenic to Martin. This was to be the ground of his great battle in Court of Criminal Appeal—a battle which many legal authorities believed that Curtis had virtually won, though the Appeal Judges were against him. Briefly and simply, his point was that until the prosecution had shown that Armstrong had been concerned in an act which led to the conclusion that he had murdered his wife, it was inadmissible to give evidence that he had at a later date been concerned with an attempt to murder another human being. It was wrong, he held, to suggest "system" before it was proved that he had in fact administered arsenic —quite apart from the fact that the alleged "system" occurred at a later date than the alleged murder. The defence being, "I did not do it," that evidence was irrelevant to the present charge. It was clear to Curtis that, if that evidence were admitted, it would certainly weigh the scales down on the side of guilt.

Mr. Justice Darling, who from that date was much attracted to Curtis, and told him that he regretted that he was not a member of his own Inn, as he would have been able to welcome him as a Bencher, ruled against him. Curtis knew that he had lost the first—and the most vital—round in the Armstrong battle.

When the court adjourned a huge crowd had gathered outside the building in a snowstorm. In the court itself, women who had obtained seats after long hours of waiting in the cold, now produced packets of sandwiches and their knitting, chatting gaily of the sensations of this engrossing spectacle. The town was full of newspaper representatives and photographers, and during the trial every witness and official faced a barrage of clicking shutters as he left the court, while many cameramen contrived to take photos of the court in actual session, much to the anger of the Judge when he saw them in print.

During the first week Curtis suggested to Mr. Matthews that they visit the grave of Mrs. Armstrong. They went one cold afternoon when the snow was thick on the ground, and Curtis was fortunate in having chosen a moment when he was not pursued by newspaper men. Mr. Matthews stayed in the car while he wandered over to the snow-covered grave; he returned in a few moments white and shaken; and only to a few intimate members of his family did he tell what had happened while he stood in the snow at the graveside.

When he went there, he could see no sign of a living thing. The graveyard was empty and silent. But as he approached and stood near to the grave, he was suddenly confronted by a mongrel dog. The animal stood on the mound of Mrs. Armstrong's grave and snarled. Curtis, who knew and loved animals, saw that the animal would prove dangerous if he moved any closer: his hackles were up, and he appeared to be really savage; Curtis made a gesture of friendliness, but the mongrel bared his teeth. Curtis knew that he was making much out of an incident, but it struck him as peculiar that he, the defender of the man accused of murdering the woman whose body lay in that grave, should be forcibly kept away. He said nothing to any man at the time; but he asked in the town if the dog had been seen before in the graveyard, and was told that every other visitor had approached the grave without trouble. Nobody knew of such a dog; if Curtis had imagined for a moment, in his overwrought state of mind, that the animal was the property of Mrs. Armstrong, he soon verified that the dead woman had never kept a dog. The mystery remained; Curtis kept the incident to himself until long afterwards.

The case for the prosecution occupied the entire week.

Curtis decided to stay in Hereford over the week-end, since the threat of snow was still in the air, and he did not relish the prospect of a long journey. But the Sunday morning was bright and cheerful, and he knew how he could best prepare himself for the stiff work ahead after six days in the overcrowded court. At nine o'clock on Sunday morning, therefore, the leading counsel for the defence could be seen in his immaculate greatcoat, smoking an enormous cigar and preparing for a day's drive. He spent the entire day with a friend in the country, and drove back blithely at the stroke of midnight to his hotel, the only man hardy enough to withstand the intense cold in an open car.

The next day he spoke for four hours without a note. There was the usual half-page of note paper on the desk with a few lines scribbled that morning; he never looked at them. The speech in full was some twenty thousand words, sufficient to cover three entire pages of the *Times*.

The speech, which he always quoted later as the best he had ever made, began with a typical phrase: "At last I have an opportunity of addressing the tribunal which is trying Major Armstrong for his life. . . ." He exuded confidence and well-being, but he used a phrase that he often used in private conversations: "I have often wondered, and I have never wondered more than during the last three days, whether anybody realizes the terrible anxiety and responsibility which rests upon the shoulders of a member of the Bar when he is defending a man for his life. . . ."

Forty-eight times he had already appeared for men or women charged with murder; the agony of the responsibility was still with him, and always would be.

The case that Curtis had to meet seemed almost insuperable. It was a courageous man indeed who in face of the evidence which had been given could think, as Curtis thought, that Armstrong stood a reasonable chance of being acquitted. But, as he went through that four-hour speech, it was seen that he was destroying one by one the arguments put forward by the prosecution, and setting up other arguments in their place. He supplied a reasonable answer to every point made in the case for the Crown. On general grounds he said that there was a certain atmosphere of suspicion prevailing now they had a man in the dock charged with murder. "Every normal act seems in some extraordinary way to be made to assume a sinister aspect," he said. "Where there was no suspicion, there now is suspicion." His main defence was that on the evidence it was much more reasonable to assume that Mrs. Armstrong, a woman who had been certified insane and who had been declared to be suicidally inclined, had taken arsenic herself than that Armstrong had administered it to her. On this point Curtis recalled that she had been given arsenic every day in medicine during her month's stay in the nursing home. Curtis, therefore, promised to produce evidence that additional doses would have at least retarded her progress towards recovery.

He turned then to his second most important point. It was a Gilbertian situation, he said, when they had to consider the evidence concerning the alleged attempt to poison Martin, not with a view to finding a verdict on it, nor to express a view upon it, but for the purpose of throwing some light on whether or not Armstrong had already murdered his wife. "Even if there was arsenic in Mr. Martin," he said, "you have got to be satisfied that Armstrong put it there, and then you are not trying Armstrong for attempting to poison Martin. It is only put in as evidence to help you decide whether Armstrong had in fact poisoned his wife months before."

A further attack was made on the evidence regarding the attempted poisoning of Martin. The date of the attempt was said to be October 26th, when Martin had gone to tea with Armstrong and had been ill after dinner that night. Curtis said that he would show that it was far more likely that his illness was due to something he had eaten during dinner.

Another ninepin he knocked down was the prosecution's point regarding the alleged motive. It had been said that the motive was money. After her death, however, Armstrong had not spent a penny of the money his wife had left, and had made no attempt to do so until he needed money for his own defence—when an embargo was put upon it.

There was another curious point in regard to the search made by the police for small packets of arsenic. One packet was apparently missing, but when Mr. Matthews had made a search he had found it caught up at the back of the drawer. Armstrong had always said he bought white arsenic from the local chemist named Davies. The police had been unable to find a packet of white arsenic with this name on it. Curtis, however, produced with triumph the bureau and the packet, and Mr. Matthews in the witness box duly testified that Armstrong had been right.

One by one then, Curtis took hold of the various arguments ranged against the prisoner to make an apparently clear case, and destroyed their value. "There is not a scrap of evidence that Major Armstrong did administer arsenic, and why should you assume that he did?" he asked. "All the evidence is that he was the devoted husband doing everything he could for the wife who was sick and who suffered unfortunately from delusions. . . . Once a man is in the dock, then everything he does becomes a guilty act. . . . Let a man sit in the dock charged with murder, and his normal actions become suspicious and held up to scorn."

Armstrong was in the box for the rest of that day and half of the next day. He stood up to the cross-examination of the Attorney General well. But when Sir Ernest Pollock had sat down, and after Armstrong was reëxamined, there came probably the most dramatic incident in the whole of that amazing case. For twenty minutes or so Mr. Justice Darling in his quiet, level voice put to him question after question. He put them slowly one after another and they and their answers

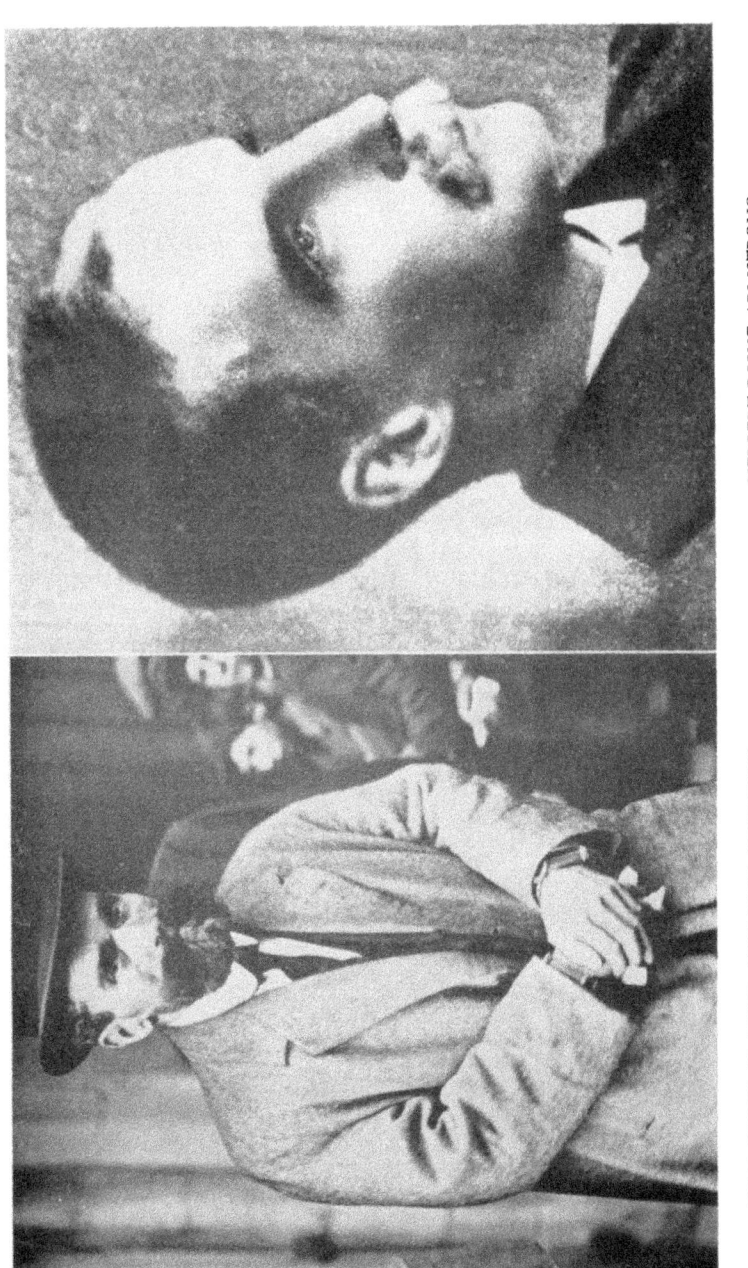

JEAN PIERRE VAQUIER, THE VAIN MURDERER
Photograph by London News Agency

HERBERT ROUSE ARMSTRONG
Photograph by Daily Mail

were very damaging to the defence. Sir Henry said he felt that they were like the words of Destiny. He well knew how much harm they had done his case at a time when he thought his client had come through more or less unscathed.

After calling the rest of the evidence for the defence Sir Henry began his closing speech on the ninth day of the trial. He apologized for the length of his former address, and he promised to be more brief; he congratulated the jury on their attention; and after the first few moments he rejoiced to find himself presented with a perfect opportunity for impressing the jury. The Judge, at the conclusion of his opening speech, had cautioned the jury not to discuss the case between themselves. Curtis said: "I must say I regret that that caution was not given at the end of the Attorney-General's opening for the prosecution; for, if it was a good exhortation at all, it was an exhortation which ought to have existed through a trial which has such nice issues as this trial has."

Mr. Justice Darling apologized. "I say at once that I regret I had not given the exhortation sooner," he said. "It is advice that I ought to have given the jury before, but I gave it the first moment it came into my mind."

Curtis hoped the Judge would not mind his saying what he had said. The Judge said: "Not in the least." Curtis went on with a new gesture of confidence, and was almost intimate with the jury, inviting them to share with him his gratitude to Mr. Matthews and "a number of loyal helpers." "Do not imagine that I am not grateful to those who have assisted me," he told them. The address lasted forty minutes, and though throughout he had been quietly advising the jury to look at the facts from a new point of view, he ended with something that was more like a stirring peroration than was usually to be found in his closing speeches. "The time is very near," he said, "when you will troop out of this court to consider your verdict, a verdict which, when you have determined upon it, and say 'Guilty' or 'Not guilty,' will be read by people who merely take interest in sensations, and pass on to the next sensation. But for the friends of Major Armstrong it means, I hope, his freedom; for his children, the restoration of their father to his home; and for Major Armstrong it means life."

The jury retired a few minutes after five o'clock, after a summing-up of more than an hour. Sir Henry had seemed confident enough. He knew that in Hereford they were betting five to one against a conviction, and he said to a newspaper reporter: "I have been in forty-eight murder trials, for and against, and I have never known the verdict so open." Mr. Matthews was impressed with his cheerfulness throughout the case. As usual, Curtis did not wait to hear the verdict. He could seldom bring himself to bear it. And now he walked along the road out of Hereford in the cold afternoon, and at six o'clock reached a village, and looked into the village post office. The woman behind the counter said that her husband was in Hereford, and was going to telephone her as soon as the verdict was made public. Curtis had only a few moments to wait before the telephone bell rang. The jury had said: "Guilty."

He walked back with a heavy heart, and the next night, when he reached London, he could not take his mind off the case. When he saw his family, he repeated the salient points of his defence as if he were still pleading before a jury for Armstrong's life.

"I shall never do a case like that again," he said. "I know that I have never done a case better and never will do. It was unjust—a poor show."

One incident connected with the case shocked Sir Henry. A London newspaper printed an interview with a juryman, in which there were said to be revealed the proceedings of the jury while they considered their verdict. Curtis later mentioned the matter at the Appeal Court, throwing doubts on whether the story was true, and receiving the agreement of the Appeal Judges that it was a shocking case of abuse of privilege. He did not suggest that the story was true, but heard also another and possibly more accurate version of what happened. Briefly, the story runs as follows: One of the jurymen had recently been involved in a civil action before Mr. Justice Darling, and had lost his case. He bore some resentment against the Judge because of this and, in a strange and irresponsible spirit of pique, imagined that one way in which he could show his defiance of the Judge was to resist the implications in his charge. When the jury retired, the foreman, who knew of this man's hostility to the Judge, passed round slips of paper to each member, suggesting that each write down, without signature, his own verdict. When he came to read the folded slips of paper, eleven of them read: "Guilty." The twelfth read: "Not proven." The foreman immediately looked at the juryman who nursed a grievance against Sir Charles Darling.

The juryman readily admitted that he was the author.

"You know about that 'Not proven,' " he said. "But all the same, I think he did it." With which he at once agreed to come into line with the others and find Armstrong guilty, having shown to his own satisfaction his ability to resist the implications of the Judge he disliked.

Curtis tried to take his mind off the great Armstrong trial with a motor tour in Devonshire. Notice of appeal had already been given, and he would have an opportunity of commenting on certain omissions in the charge to the jury, that he thought unfair.

But, before the appeal on April 20th, Curtis received the brief for yet another case that was to shake England. On March 6th, the police had found the dead body of a pretty young woman, battered and strangled in her Fulham basement flat. That night, they arrested, in a box at the Hammersmith Palace of Varieties, a young former flying officer who had spent the night with her. His name was Ronald True.

The accusation that it was his hand that had killed Olive

Young could not strongly be resisted, though Curtis, on his first examination of the case, hoped to be able to put forward that there was a doubt. But there was very obviously a far stronger defence. True was irresponsible, a dope-addict, insane. The defence was that True did not know the difference between right and wrong when, having been admitted with some reluctance to the girl's room for the night of March 5th, he had waked in the morning, fetched her a cup of tea, and struck her on the head four times with a rolling pin. She was dying, but True thrust a towel deep in her throat, wound the girdle of her dressing gown tightly round her neck, and strangled her. He dragged the corpse into the bathroom, leaving it lying on the floor. He then rifled her handbag but, curiously enough, did not make his escape, waiting until some time after the girl's maid had come, at nine o'clock.

"Don't disturb Miss Young," said True. "She is asleep, and I'll send the car round at midday."

He bought clothes at a shop where he was well-known, to replace those stained with the blood of his victim. He was affable as always, explained the stains by saying he had been in an aeroplane accident, and even showed the jewelry he had stolen, saying he had picked up the trinkets in France. He pawned the jewelry that morning, deposited the blood-stained clothes, bought a paper in which he read the screaming headlines of the "Fulham Murder," and threw it aside with the remark: "Nothing in the paper."

Sane or insane? On May 1st, before Mr. Justice McCardie, Curtis stood up at the Old Bailey to tell his client's strange life story. He knew that the prosecution was in a terrible difficulty. In cases when a strong defence of insanity is to be pleaded, the prosecution can call evidence to the contrary. The obvious witness, therefore, is the prison doctor: Dr. East and Dr. Young, the two doctors of Brixton Prison, however, were of the opinion that True was at any rate medically, insane. They agreed with the eminent mental specialists called by Curtis. The prosecution, therefore, consulted another medical man, Dr. Cole, who gave a guarded opinion that True was sane. Dr. Cole, however, was not emphatic enough to be a good witness for the prosecution; Sir Richard Muir, prosecuting, knew that Curtis would elicit from the witness grave doubts, and nullify his evidence. The alternative was to present no evidence that True was sane, and expect the deadly comment that the prosecution had been unable to produce a witness who would testify to his sanity.

The prosecution, therefore, was relying on a legal precedent, the "Rules in McNaughton's Case" of the date 1843, in which certain questions relating to the law of insanity are answered. Sir Henry had to fight against the application of those "Rules." He knew that, though he had the evidence regarding True's mental state on his side, he must obtain a direction from the Judge to extend the legal doctrines of insanity to embrace the evidence for the defence.

During the first two days, Sir Henry, in cross-examination, built up an atmosphere round Ronald True. Witnesses described how True had told remarkable stories of his experiences all over the world; how he had suggested starting a "Murderers' Club," members of which would commit murder for "a bob a nob"—a shilling each. He was leading the jury to look at this good-looking, neurotic young man as a creature tortured by his imagination; he established that, when True had bought new clothes, he himself had indicated the blood stains; that, when he had bought a paper, he had first asked for the *Sporting Times.*

Towards the end of the second day the case for the prosecution was ended. Sir Henry was direct in his opening address. He would call the prison doctors who would say that True was insane; he would call two other specialists who would say the same, and he would show that, from infancy, Ronald True was abnormal.

True's wife came to court to speak of his roving life. She

had first met her husband in New York, in 1917, and he had said that he was looking for another civil flying job. He had told her he had been wounded in France, and had brought down several German aeroplanes. "I afterwards found it was mostly imagination," she said. After a time her husband worked in a Government school in America, and was transferred to Texas and Mexico, where he was severely ill. But after the birth of their child, the wife accompanied him to the West Coast of Africa, where he was assistant manager of a mining company. The young flying man had tropical fever, and took drugs. "At times when he was under the influence of morphia, he was delirious," said his wife, "and he afterwards had no recollection of what he had done or said."

Always, Ronald True could get money from his mother—he was never stinted. But morphia dragged him down from time to time, and his wife had a difficult task in looking after him. Once, after receiving a letter from him to say he was about to commit suicide, she went to see him in London, and found him in a Soho café, a mental and physical wreck. He made a will in one of his fits of depression, and his wife saw it. It decreed that he wished to leave £100 to Dr. Barnardo's Home, and £100 to a Home for Lost Dogs. . . .

"People very frequently do strange things in mad fits," was the only thing he said to her when she reproached him.

Under the careful guidance of Sir Henry, Mrs. True revealed other strange characteristics of the twisted brain of Ronald True. He had a faulty memory, and for no apparent reason took books that he had not paid for from shops: the books were of no interest to him. Then came the final breakdown. He was operated on in a drug-home, and shortly afterwards disappeared. His wife took steps to have him found, for she knew that he carried a revolver with him, and she feared the worst if he came under the spell of another fit of forgetfulness. She went to Scotland Yard and orders were issued for his arrest; but the police could not find him. The next she heard of him was that he had been arrested for murder. So ended the testimony of the tragic woman who had stood by her husband through so many vicissitudes.

Curtis-Bennett had other witnesses to give further details of the strangeness of the man who stood smiling in the dock on the charge of murder. A war-time companion told of his most serious crash, when he was pitched on his head from a wrecked plane. After that, he seemed queer and shaky and erratic, said he could not bear to wear a hat on his head; when he earned his "wings," he had a special badge made to wear on his tunic, the wings three times the size of the regulation issue, picked out in various colours.

Another war-time comrade came to tell the Court that after his crashes True was unstable, feverish—"always rushing about and laughing in a loud voice." "He made an impression on me that lasted six years."

Possibly the worst place for a man of True's temperament was the West Coast of Africa, the "White Man's Grave." But it was here that he obtained one of his best positions, and it was here that his eccentricity and his habits became most marked. He became known by the natives as "the massa what live with his mammy [meaning his wife], and who is sick by the head." He was seen to walk about hatless, and in his pyjamas. He made bombastic threats and bets; said he was going to fly over the Sahara; it was the first time he had been in a country where whites governed blacks, and he committed the unforgivable sin of "hobnobbing" with natives.

But the most curious sidelight on this man's mind was given by a chauffeur whom he had employed to drive him in and around Portsmouth, saying that he wished to have a driver because he knew his mind was often a blank. True was then partly confined to a Bath chair: a pitiable figure in many ways, well known about the town, for on the Bath chair were little toys, such as might amuse a child, but which afforded satisfactory amusement for this good-looking young man who was known to have suffered mentally from his war experiences.

"One toy was a monkey with an Irishman's green hat tied up with little ribbons," said a witness. "Another was a black retriever dog. You squeezed it, and it would 'talk.' There was a cat with a long neck, a hooter, and all sorts of things . . ."

Then one day True ordered the chauffeur to drive him to the races at Newmarket in time for the first race—a journey quite impossible in the time. But the chauffeur, perhaps humouring his master, started out on the journey. Not knowing the road, he took a corner too fast on the hill overlooking the notorious Devil's Punch Bowl. The car skidded round three times, and for a moment it seemed that it would crash off the road to the bottom. The chauffeur and his companion in the front seat flung their weight forward to keep the car on the road as it stopped on the very brink of the precipice. And, as they sat white-faced and shaking, they were amazed to hear peals of laughter from the back seat, where Ronald True lay back at his ease, his warped sense of humour tickled by being in such a position. . . .

And through all these months when he was virtually a cripple, chained to a Bath chair, under medical supervision, he was calling on local chemists, buying small quantities of the drug that brought solace to his tattered nerves. In five months, he had secured from chemists 4,000 half-grain tablets of morphia, and he was always trying to obtain more.

Nineteen witnesses came to tell similar stories of the eccentricity of this young man whom they had always pitied as a victim of the War, but whom they had often referred to as "the madman." The prosecution for the most part attempted no rebuttal of their evidence, Sir Richard Muir contenting himself with a few questions to each. It seemed indeed that Curtis-Bennett had made certain that no man in that court could call upon Ronald True to answer for his actions as a sane man.

True's aunt said that as a child he tortured rabbits, burying them with their heads above the ground, so that they died of starvation, while he watched them. He ill-treated a favourite pony; when he grew up, he took drugs. The Brixton doctors duly gave their opinion that he was insane. They were cross-examined at length, but Sir Henry was satisfied; and when towards the close of the fourth day, he asked for a direction from the Judge, he put forward very strongly his opinions of the McNaughton Rules, which, he said, were no longer in line with medical knowledge. Now Curtis showed the deep study that he had made of his subject. He produced many other authorities to support his own condemnation of the McNaughton Rules, and in asking for the question for the jury to be put in a particular form, suggested that it should be, "Was True deprived of the power of controlling his actions?"

This debate on the form of the question to be put to the jury lasted over an hour that day; and again on the fifth day Sir Henry was quoting other cases for an hour before beginning his closing speech for the defence. He assumed that the jury would conclude that it was True's hand which killed Olive Young. That admission was contained in one phrase, and he passed to the main point immediately. He spoke for a few minutes only: Was there ever such a case in which abnormality had been so clearly shown? People had come forward from all parts of the country to testify to True's drug-taking and his eccentricity.

"I am sure," he concluded, "that the jury will not allow a human being to be made a pawn in a great legal game. . . ."

It was the shortest speech for the defence he had ever made in a murder trial. But he was confident that the doctors' evidence could not be ignored, and he had already made his great effort when he had debated with the Judge on the form of the question to be put to the jury. He was confident and assured. And indeed, he made only a passing reference to the fact that the prosecution had not produced medical evidence to rebut his strong—seemingly invincible—proof that True was a maniac with homicidal tendencies.

Sir Richard Muir was equally brief, but when Mr. Justice McCardie was well embarked upon a lengthy summing-up, Curtis' heart sank within him; the Judge was giving no suggestion to the jury that True was insane, and was, in fact, making it clear that they must decide on the question as to whether True's delusions and peculiar character did in fact cause him to have no knowledge of what he was doing when he struck Olive Young—not once, but four times. "All the doctors say that the prisoner did know what he was doing at the time," said the Judge. "And if you ask yourselves what was the nature of the crime, you may well say, How is it possible to think that he could not be aware of it? . . . You will probably feel that the prisoner did know at the time the physical nature and quality of the acts he had perpetrated."

This was the death sentence, Curtis knew. He was surprised that the jury were out for an hour and a half.

Chapter Ten

THE GREATEST YEARS—2

For the next ten days he switched his mind from the True appeal, already lodged, and grappled again with the Armstrong appeal. He again contested the advisability of evidence regarding Armstrong's alleged attempt to poison the solicitor Mr. Martin, and attributed to Mr. Justice Darling a misdirection of the jury. He made considerable capital out of the curious incident of the missing packet of arsenic, found by Mr. Matthews, and said that the Judge had represented this to the jury as a point against the prisoner, whereas he submitted that, if put in the proper light, it would be in his favour. He was biting in his irony: "If a man is accused of murdering his wife," he said, "and there is poison in the house, if he does *not* go into the room, people say he is keeping away to divert suspicion, and if he *does* go in, then that in itself is put against him."

His main point, however, was regarding the admissibility of the Martin evidence. It was on this point that he had made a complete survey of murder cases over the last seventy years, quoting precedent after precedent to support his claim; he went to Australian, Canadian, and American law for his instances, and received the admiration of all who followed him for his forceful battle. He had thought that he would be in the Court of Criminal Appeal for one day; he had made other arrangements. But there were so many questions from the Appeal Judges, and their opinions were expressed at such length, first on one side and then on the other, that the hearing lasted over four days. It is worth noting that, though his argument has had so many supporters, the decision of their Lordships in the Armstrong Appeal, stands today as good law.

The appeal failed, and despair fell once again upon the man who had promised himself, some years before, that never again would he take a case too much to heart. He could not get Armstrong out of his mind and determined that, if possible, the case should be taken to the House of Lords. For such a course the "fiat" of the Attorney-General is required, and it must be shown that the final appeal is being made "on a legal point of public importance." Curtis thought that he could fulfil that proviso, and made his application to Sir Ernest Pollock. Although he did not question the good faith of Sir Ernest in this matter, he did feel that it was unfortunate that his application must be considered by the very man who had been counsel for the prosecution.

Permission was refused. Armstrong must be hanged.

Then, and not till then, could the public be told facts which were known to every newspaper: It was said Armstrong was afflicted with a poisoning mania. Curtis himself had the opinion that a poisoner, after his first victim had died, must repeat his crime; Curtis knew that the Home Office had considered exhuming the bodies of three other local people, and were ready to authorize the exhumation of the bodies. Reporters during the trial spent every night waiting at the churchyard for police officers to begin digging. But it seemed moderately certain that Armstrong would be convicted on the evidence of the exhumation of his wife's body.

But, on the facts presented, Sir Henry believed that his client was wrongly convicted. More than in any of his other cases, he felt that he had not deserved to fail. "A poor show," he said.

The phrase concealed a crushing despair. Before Armstrong hanged, on May 31st, he was again in the True case. But reminders kept coming to him of that meek, somewhat sinister country solicitor whom he could not help liking. From the jail there came a note of gratitude, and with it a diamond tiepin "as a memento of the trial." Mr. Matthews, at the public auction of Armstrong's goods, bought for him, against fierce competition, a medicine chest which had figured largely in the trial and been exhibited in court. And years afterwards, Curtis used to visit Hereford, where he would discuss again the great trial which had been his first outstanding defence, and his best.

On May 25th, Sir Henry appealed for True. Were the jury to disregard the evidence of doctors? The McNaughton Rules were old-fashioned, and had been suspended with the advance of medical knowledge. The appeal was dismissed, but meanwhile Mr. Justice McCardie, as was his duty, had drawn the attention of the Home Secretary to the medical evidence. Three eminent medical men were appointed to examine True, and found him an undoubted lunatic. He was reprieved. This perfectly ordinary sequel of events drove the Press to fury. It was recalled that, a month before, one Henry Jacoby had been hanged, in spite of a jury's recommendation to mercy, for the murder of a knight's widow: "Trial by Harley Street," it was called, and in the House of Commons the Government was plied with questions. True, it was said, was the illegitimate son of a well-known peer, and strings had been pulled in Government circles. Even the legal profession resented the overriding authority of three doctors over Judge, jury, and Court of Criminal Appeal.

Actually, of course, the sequence of events had only been in accordance with common law, and the Home Secretary, Mr. Shortt, read the House a lecture on the subject and reminded the country of this fact. Lord Birkenhead appointed a committee to report on the insanity laws; but their recommendations brought the code no closer to modern medical opinion, and the McNaughton Rules still stand—the reason being that, before insanity can become a defence to crime, it must be taken to extreme limits and, above all, must be proved by the defence. But Curtis, though he had himself failed to save

Ronald True from the gallows, knew that justice had been served by his life detention in Broadmoor. True was undoubtedly mad. A letter from jail, written before he knew he was saved, read as follows: "Cheerio old nut! And if you come to the place I'm going to, I'll have a nice cup of cold water ready for your arrival."

Even in the "roaring twenties," of which strange excitable decade Ronald True was a distorted victim, that letter is eloquent of a callous irresponsibility that was first shown when he watched his pet rabbits starve to death, and was shown again when he belaboured a naked girl with savage blows and rammed a towel down her throat—for a few pounds of ready money.

In September, Curtis went abroad for a fortnight. It was his custom to motor to Boulogne and stay the night. But for some reason he arrived in London on Friday September 29th. The fact that he had cut short his tour by a week-end resulted in one of his successes in an appeal case. For at half-past nine that Friday evening, two police constables in Hyde Park began to follow a tall soldierly figure in a trilby hat and evening dress whom they suspected of annoying women. They thought they saw him talk to three women in the course of several minutes, and when he was sitting on a park bench they approached him and told him he would be arrested for annoying persons using the Park. The man repudiated the charge with anger and, it was said, used violence on the police, who took him to the police station. He then gave his name as Sir Almeric Fitzroy, Clerk of the Privy Council.

That night his solicitors telephoned Curtis-Bennett and asked him to appear for Sir Almeric at Marlborough Street Police Court the next morning. There would be time for a consultation first and the brief was marked "50 & 2." The magistrate waited until the end of his list before hearing the charge, and, the defendant pleading not guilty, remanded him until the following Saturday. In the interval, Curtis-Bennett had several consultations and a view of the scene of the alleged offences.

But in the meantime, while he was putting all his energies into the examination of that case, there occurred, on the Tuesday following Sir Almeric's arrest, a drama that is destined to live in the annals of crime in England for many years to come. Frederick Bywaters, a writer on the P. and O. steamship line, had struck the blow that was to bring himself and his mistress to the scaffold.

The history of the relationship of Bywaters and Mrs. Thompson is as follows. Seven years before, Mr. Thompson, a clerk in a shipping office, had married Edith Graydon, several years younger than himself. Edith was in a good employment, and had proved herself a conscientious and skilful worker. Perhaps because there were no children, and she intended that there should be none, she remained in her employment long after the time when most wives retire. They lived in Ilford, and seemed a perfectly happily married couple until Bywaters, a young and good-looking man who had recently lodged with Mrs. Thompson's mother, made their acquaintance. Unsophisticated and inexperienced, Frederick Bywaters found an immediate attraction in the intelligent woman who made her own way in the world; and she, on her side, found him fresh and romantic, an ideal companion in contrast to her somewhat humdrum husband. Bywaters became closely associated with their lives; he proposed that he should become a lodger in their house; and in June of 1921 he went with them on a holiday to the Isle of Wight.

It was probably during this month that the two became lovers. At any rate, in subsequent correspondence, the date of June 27 earned considerable emphasis. In August he quarrelled with Mr. Thompson, who asked him to leave the house, and in September he sailed in the *Morea* for the East. But the woman followed him with her love; her letters were eloquent of her longing for him. She wrote at length and picturesquely, giving the young man a detailed picture of her thoughts and her heartaches. Bywaters kept them in his ditty-box, unwilling to destroy them, though she frequently reminded him that she kept only one of his at a time, destroying previous letters as new ones arrived. She did not know that her own letters were bound in an ever-growing bundle; that one day they would be read out to the world, and that new interpretations would be put into such sentences as, "Yesterday I met a woman who had lost 3 husbands in 11 years and not thro the War, 2 were drowned and one committed suicide and some people I know cant lose one." She called her lover "Darlint," and signed herself "Peidi"; for pages and pages her pen ran on, day after day, telling him of every circumstance of her life, the bets she put on horses, the theatres she saw, the conversations of her relatives. But very soon, in those letters, there entered a new note; her mind began to dwell on the happier prospect ahead if her husband were to die. There were times when she refused him his marital rights, and Mr. Thompson knew that he must blame the memory of Bywaters for her attitude. "On Wednesday we had words—in bed—Oh you know darlint—over that same old subject, and he said—it was all through you I'd altered."

During the night her husband had felt unwell, after taking a cure for insomnia. And when she told her lover of the illness, she put it this way: "I told Avis about the incident only I told her as if it frightened and worried me as I thought perhaps it might be useful at some future time that I had told somebody. What do you think, darlint."

And at the bottom of the letter, there was this postscript: "It would be so easy darlint—if I had things—I do hope I shall."

Bywaters came home for two weeks, and sailed away again. And if ever his shipmates caught sight of his mail, they must have been surprised at the contents of the regular letters that he received in the same rounded handwriting. For there were piles of newspaper cuttings included with the letters, and they were all on one subject: "POISONED CHOCOLATES FOR UNIVERSITY CHIEF," "BEAUTIFUL DANCER DRUGGED." And when she read of a poisoning incident in a book or a magazine, she wrote it out at length for her lover. She wrote frequently of using powdered glass, and poison; and always, a rising and more urgent strain ran through all her letters: "There will be no failure this next time, darlint—there mustn't be. If things are the same, then I am going with you—wherever it is—if it's to sea—I am coming too and if it is to nowhere—I'm also coming darlint. You'll never leave me behind again, never, unless things are different."

Letters written over a period of one year, packed with extravagant similes to show her devotion; short scribbled notes arranging an appointment when he was in England, long, pathetic protestations of her loneliness when he had sailed away again. Frederick Bywaters tied them all together for the solace of his lonely hours at sea.

On October 3, 1922, a week after his ship had reached Tilbury, Bywaters and Mrs. Thompson had tea together at a café. He knew that Mrs. Thompson had to go with a family party to the theatre that evening, accompanied by her husband. He spent the early evening with Mrs. Thompson's parents; at about the time when the Thompsons were leaving the play, he left the house.

Mr. and Mrs. Thompson, to reach their home from the station, had to pass through a dark road. According to Mrs. Thompson, they were walking in silence when a man rushed out from the Gardens and pushed her away from her husband. She saw the man was Bywaters; the two men scuffled, and Bywaters ran away, leaving her husband collapsed on the road. She ran for help, obtained a doctor, and was told that her husband was dead. This statement was only made to the police after she had made several statements to the effect that she had seen nobody on the road, and that her husband had slumped down suddenly, as if stricken with illness.

The next evening, the police arrested Bywaters and charged him with murder. His version of the scuffle, given more fully at a later date, was as follows: "I went to see Thompson to come to an amicable understanding for a separation or divorce. I had spoken to him about this on two occasions previously. I saw Mr. and Mrs. Thompson walking along the road. I overtook them, and pushing Mrs. Thompson with my right hand, with my left hand I held Thompson, and swung him round. I said to him, 'Why don't you get a divorce or a separation, you cad?'

"He said: 'I know that is what you want, but I am not going to give it to you; it would make it too pleasant for both of you.' I said, 'You take a delight in making Edie's life a hell.' Then he said: 'I've got her, I'll keep her and I'll shoot you.' As he said that, he punched me in the chest with his left fist and I said 'Oh, will you?' and drew a knife and put it in his arm.

"I thought I was going to be killed. I thought he was going to shoot me if he had an opportunity. All the time struggling, I thought he was going to kill me. . . ."

The police took the letters from his personal luggage in his cabin on the *Morea*, identified a knife found near the scene of the struggle as his, and framed the charge of "incitement to murder" against the woman.

Sir Henry Curtis-Bennett, briefed to defend Mrs. Thompson, first met her on October 6th, and was immediately impressed by her personality and by the changing sides of her character.

Once he had heard the case for the Crown, both he and Mr. Walter Frampton, his junior in this case, formed the view that, if Mrs. Thompson acted on their advice, she would not go into the witness box, their view being that, though the letters were strong evidence against her without explanation, it would be fatal to submit her to cross-examination.

"In my view," Curtis said, "the best line to take would be

that, while there may be sufficient *prima facie* evidence against you, there would not be sufficient for any jury to convict you. I take it that the physical action of the stabbing by Bywaters will be admitted; the only possible connection that can be made between yourself and the actual committing of the crime, is an interpretation that may be put on the letters found in Bywaters' possession; but, on the other hand, I hope to obtain a refusal of their admittance as evidence on the ground that until the prosecution can show that you took some active part in the murder—if it was murder—then they are inadmissible."

To Sir Henry's great surprise, Mrs. Thompson said: "I wish to give evidence."

Sir Henry realized that Mrs. Thompson had no inkling of the danger in which she stood. She was content to have the letters read—this being perhaps yet another aspect of her remarkable love of the limelight. Her wish to give evidence—indeed, her insistence on entering the box—may have been another indication of this anxiety for notoriety. But Sir Henry pressed her—pleaded with her—to change her attitude.

"My most earnest wish," he said to her, "is that you should take the advice of those who know legal procedure. I cannot put it too strongly that there is a risk, a risk that you yourself cannot appreciate, in your submitting yourself to cross-examination on these letters, if they are admitted. I am keeping in mind the possibility of the Judge remarking adversely on the fact that you do not go into the box; I have that ever in mind; but I wish to put to you as strongly as I am able, my opinion that on the evidence produced by the prosecution, no comment made by the Judge in this matter will be as dangerous as if you submit yourself to cross-examination."

It was apparent to all students of the barrister's art that his advice should have been opposed to his client's undergoing cross-examination, and himself submitting to the jury that the evidence produced was not sufficient to warrant a conviction.

Indeed, every legal authority who has discussed the case has emphasized that Sir Henry's advice was sound. Mr. Filson Young even suggested that Sir Henry should have returned the brief when he was faced with the adamant attitude of Mrs. Thompson. "I should have asked her to brief another counsel," said Mr. Young, in his "introduction" to the "Famous Trials" report of the hearing. "An experienced lawyer could have foretold, and must have known, the very great difficulty that the prosecution would have in getting a conviction against Mrs. Thompson if she herself did not give evidence. . . ."

Sir Henry was grieved at the suggestion that he should have thrown up the case. "I never considered—nor would I be entitled to consider—taking such a step," he said; "but being convinced that such a course would have prejudiced her case, and being also assured in my own mind that Mrs. Thompson would not have altered her attitude if I had done so, I came to the conclusion that I had done my best with her. If the letters were admitted, as I feared they might be, then I had ample evidence of the imagination of my client, of the way in which she allowed herself to be swayed by fantasy, and I could truthfully represent her—and prove my contention—that she was a woman who had but to read of a character which she admired or in which she was interested, to straightway surround herself with the environment of that character."

There was almost a scene when Mrs. Thompson refused to accept the advice of her counsel. Sir Henry still tried persuasion, but without the slightest effect. He realized that she felt herself in no danger; she thought she could save Bywaters by giving her explanation of the meaning of those letters, though, since the defence of Bywaters was not a denial that he had struck the blow, but that he had struck fearing an attack from Mr. Thompson, it was difficult to see how the explanation of the letters could help her lover, save by making it clear that the murder was not long premeditated.

There was another difficulty presented by Mrs. Thompson's

explanation of the letters, if the letters were admitted as evidence. Certain passages might well be quoted by the prosecution as evidence that the woman had put into the mind of her nineteen-year-old lover the thought of murder. There was a perfectly simple explanation. Mrs. Thompson, infatuated, as she was, with Bywaters, and being terrified of losing his love, and fearful lest he should turn his attentions to another, perhaps unmarried, and therefore less complicated source, thought that she could best retain his love by *pretending* that she would go to any length, even to that of destroying her husband's life for love of him. Could Sir Henry persuade the Jury to accept that explanation? Could he make the Jury realize that they were dealing with no ordinary woman?

This also Curtis-Bennett put to that handsome, self-possessed woman, who discussed with him the smallest details of that love story which was soon to become public property. Still she refused to renounce her intention of going into the box. Was it vanity and a love of the limelight that influenced her? Curtis-Bennett was able to show that she revelled in the dramatic, that she exaggerated every incident to reveal its drama; that she was not above writing fiction as the sober truth. Her solicitor, Mr. F. A. Stern, lent his influence to that of Sir Henry and Mr. Walter Frampton, pleading with her to realize the danger in which she stood; she would have none of it.

The letters themselves, which were read with avidity throughout England, were remarkable. They revealed, as Sir Henry put it, a woman who lived a commonplace life of hard work, for which she was amply paid, who was part and parcel of a workaday world, and who yet had a secret life of her own. Highly imaginative, romantic, almost visionary, she poured forth her soul to that young man and set him afire. When, halfway to the other end of the earth on his ship as clerk, he tired of her image and suggested half-heartedly that in future they might only be friends, she revived his love with more ardent promises and protestations. She told Bywaters of occasions when she was approached by other men, suggesting to him that she was a superlatively desirable creature who had difficulty in resisting the blandishments of others, but who favoured him only because of her love for him. Sir Henry knew that the verdict lay in those letters, and studied them intently, arriving at an opinion of the writer that made him fervent in his appeal for her life. Edith Thompson never knew that her life was at stake; indeed, Sir Henry considered that she regarded his efforts on her behalf as a mere formality....

He was always angry when this love between Edith Thompson and Frederick Bywaters was referred to in court as a tawdry passion. The Judge, indeed, used the words "insensate silly affection" and "silly but at the same time wicked affection." Sir Henry regarded Edith Thompson's love for Bywaters as a great and sincere passion, a love capable of sacrifice and suffering. He thought the letters contained passages of real beauty and said, "I wish I could write love letters like that." In this opinion he is supported by Mr. Filson Young, who writes, "To find their match you would have to look in the letters of people far above her in poetic and literary attainments." Mr. Justice Shearman, in his charge to the jury, quoted the following passage written by Mrs. Thompson about her husband: "He has the right by law to all that you have the right to by nature and love," and said of it: "If that nonsense means anything, it means that the love of a husband by his wife means nothing because marriage is acknowledged by law. I have no doubt that the jury and every proper-minded person is filled with disgust by such expressions." Again, in the Court of Criminal Appeal, the Lord Chief Justice referred to the trial as "this essentially commonplace and unedifying case." Though it was not his duty to stress his opinion in his speech for the defence, Sir Henry held diametrically opposite views, and it was the fact that this great and sincere love had been portrayed in such slighting terms in court that caused him to say emphatically, long after the trial was over, "Mrs. Thompson was hanged for immorality. . . ."

So much for the preliminary work that Curtis-Bennett expended on the remarkable case of Edith Thompson. She was committed for trial with Bywaters on November 3rd, but in the meantime Curtis had had his name and his photograph under staring headlines in every newspaper in the country over the sensational Fitzroy conviction and successful appeal. On October 7th, the Saturday following his first appearance in court, Sir Almeric again appeared before Mr. Mead at Marlborough Street, with Mr. Herbert Muskett prosecuting, and Sir Richard Muir as junior to Curtis-Bennett for the defence. Most of the hearing was taken by Sir Henry's probing questions to the police constable on the time factor, and when there appeared before him the woman, Mrs. Dorothy Turner, who was alleged to have been annoyed by Sir Almeric he confessed that he was not yet in a position to cross-examine her very fully, and only asked questions about her movements during that evening. Mrs. Turner said that she had an appointment, but preferred not to write down the time or the name of the gentleman she was to meet; "There are posts," said Sir Henry. "You have not heard from him since?" Mrs. Turner admitted that the gentleman had not corresponded with her at all.

Mr. Mead heard the case again the following Saturday, remarking that it must be completed during that day. And, during the first hour, it certainly seemed as if Sir Henry needed no further adjournment to wreck completely the case for the prosecution. For now it was learned why Sir Henry had confessed that he was not ready to cross-examine Mrs. Turner the preceding Saturday. She had proclaimed herself a lonely widow, in receipt of a pension, employed at two Brighton hotels. During the intervening week Sir Henry had checked this description. First, he asked her once more to give the name of the man she was going to meet that night. Again she refused, though she said she had a letter from him. When was she married, what was the name of her husband, when did he die, and where were they married? Mrs. Turner told him, with some hesitation.

Then he changed his line of questioning, without warning. She said she had been employed at two Brighton hotels.

The last of them being the Queen's?—Yes.

She had not smiled at Sir Almeric?—No.

She had been living in Kennington?—Yes.

Alone?—Yes.

"Be careful," said Sir Henry. "I suggest that you are living there in two rooms, a bed-sitting-room with a double bed in it, and a kitchen, with a man who goes by the name of Turner?"

"No."

"I think it is fair to remind you that you are on oath. Did you not take this room for yourself and your husband? That will give you a chance to tell the truth about it. Did you?"

"No."

"I have the landlady here," said Sir Henry wearily, and a woman entered the court. Mrs. Turner collapsed in a faint, and when she had recovered, Sir Henry continued relentlessly.

"I put it to you, to give you an opportunity of withdrawing now, while there is time, the answer you gave when you said you were not living there with a man who gives the name of Turner, right up to this morning?"

Mrs. Turner was silent. And it was at this period that Mr. Mead suggested that she need be troubled no further.

"To save time," said Mr. Mead to Mr. Muskett, "have you any further corroboration of the police evidence?"

It seemed that after the destruction of the evidence of the chief witness, Sir Almeric would soon walk from the court with his honour vindicated.

When, therefore, further evidence was taken for the prosecution, and Mr. Mead intervened during his cross-examination, Sir Henry could not prevent himself showing his impatience by a gesture. "It is hardly worth while being so petulant," said the Magistrate.

"I am not being petulant at all," retorted Curtis, and when Mr. Mead later interrupted his speech for the defence, he protested strongly at the "attitude being taken here."

"I did think," he said, "that when I was stopped in my cross-examination, that you had made up your mind that this charge was an ill-founded one, and could not be substantiated; otherwise I suggest I ought to have been allowed to continue my cross-examination. . . . I had much more to cross-examine her upon, and one never knows whether the woman would not have realized that truth is the best thing to tell. . . ."

His address on opening the case for the defendant was scathing in its irony and its revelation of what the police had not done to verify their evidence. He pointed out that in most cases of similar character, the woman who could be chief witness would not give evidence. "Thank goodness," he said, "we have the woman here. . . ."

He told how he and Sir Richard Muir had been to Hyde Park the night before, and suggested that it was impossible for the police officers to see what they professed to have seen. He suggested that a tribunal should enquire into such evidence and averred that the whole police story would not hold water.

Sir Almeric and Lady Fitzroy were both called, and gave a reasonable version of their actions that night. Yet, in the first few words of his decision, Mr. Mead announced that he would find Sir Almeric guilty and imposed a fine of £5 and £10.10s. costs. "One must not make too much of this matter," he said. It was a mild offence. . . . The evidence of the constables had not been prejudiced at all by the evidence of Mrs. Turner, and he could not disregard the police statements.

"It is quite obvious you don't appreciate what the defendant's evidence is," said Sir Henry, and indeed Sir Henry and Sir Almeric were quite astonished at the decision. For some considerable time, magistrate and counsel argued, Sir Henry saying that, after his cross-examination of Mrs. Turner had been stopped, he was of the opinion that Mr. Mead had made up his mind in favour of an acquittal.

"I regret the misunderstanding, but I am not responsible for it."

But if Mr. Mead considered that "too much must not be made of this matter," the Press of the whole country in the days following evidently disagreed. The newspapers saw a "peril to everyone" in the conviction, and said the whole country was astounded by the action of Mr. Mead, "whose decisions during the past year or so have attracted widespread attention." It was recalled that Mr. Mead had fined an eminent clergyman in the preceding year and had seen the sentence quashed on appeal; a hawker, sentenced to imprisonment for a trivial offence, had been released by the Home Secretary.

"This magistrate is now in his seventy-sixth year," said the *Daily Express,* and a correspondent asked: "What are we to do to be safe in the Park? Wear blinkers, a gag, and a gas mask? Is the Park open for the public pleasure, or is it a happy hunting ground for the police?"

"If Mr. Mead be allowed to regulate our lives, it will be dangerous to ask permission to lift a bag on a railway rack," said another. Arnold Bennett wrote, "When immorality decreases in Hyde Park, the reason is not the ardour of the police but the coldness of the weather."

"Mead must go!" was the chorus taken up in the Press, and not a few cartoonists drew him with cruel lines of senility, Strube in the *Express* picturing "The Freedom of the Parks," with men and women shepherded along different paths by the police, barbed-wire entanglements to keep the sexes apart, and police making arrests for omissions to wear blinkers.

"Freddie" Mead, as he is affectionately called by all who know him, did not "go." Years later he retired from the Bench which he had adorned since 1889, an aged man, but in full vigour of mind and spirit. The Court at which he sat for many years, Marlborough Street, is, by reason of the district within its jurisdiction, apt to be visited more frequently than other police courts by people of note, and any mistakes which a magistrate may make there attract more publicity, and therefore more blame, from the Public Press than when they take place elsewhere.

"It is an outrage!" wrote James Douglas in the *Sunday Express*. "The villain in a melodrama always wears evening dress and has a name like Almeric Fitzroy!" And the *Pink 'Un* reported that the latest cry from the nursery was: "Don't go into Hyde Park, Daddy!"

It was generally admitted that Hyde Park was immoral, but there is little danger in saying that, had Sir Almeric not succeeded in his appeal, a storm would have arisen throughout the country that would have eclipsed his preliminary "acquittal" by newspapers. Long years before, when Curtis was first briefed in a "Hyde Park Case," he said that he had been advised by his father never to cross the Park at night. As the Park Regulations were read by Sir Edward Marshall Hall for the respondent at the Appeal Court, it did appear that Sir Almeric had been guilty of a technical offence in speaking to a woman, but the whole country demanded that a commonsense view should be taken of such cases, and that a man who was actually walking to meet his wife by appointment, should not be convicted.

Sir Almeric's character was vindicated on November 10th by Sir Robert Wallace at London Sessions. The evidence of the constables, that Sir Almeric had spoken to a woman, was not in dispute, but it was Sir Henry's challenging phrases regarding Mr. Mead's stopping of the cross-examination of Mrs. Turner that gained Sir Almeric a proportion of the costs. These amounted to some £500—a record for a hearing that had taken only three days in all.

It was an unusual step for the Bench to take, and Sir Robert Wallace himself expressed doubts as to whether it was in order. But Sir Henry had flung one criticism after another at the manner in which the whole case had been conducted. Why had not the police checked the evidence of their witnesses, he asked. Why had it been necessary for Sir Almeric to spend a large sum of money in proving facts that the police could easily have done? Why had they not verified Mrs. Turner's statements? If they had gone to her lodgings and put one question to her, they would have found out beforehand the value of her evidence. If they had telephoned the Admiralty, they would have discovered that she was lying about her pension. What would have happened to a poor man who was charged with such an offence? Her evidence would have been accepted.

Once more the Press thundered its denunciations of Mr. Mead. James Douglas wrote, "Let us all combine to put and keep the police, the magistrates and the Home Office in their proper place."

Four days later, while the Press still raged, Curtis-Bennett was briefed at short notice to represent an elderly doctor, who, in the words of the Judge, "passed through the fires of hell" through the tittle-tattle and the pesterings of the newspapers. He had been called in to give an anaesthetic to a rich widow in Chiswick. The widow died soon afterwards, and two months later her body was exhumed for an examination by Home Office experts. At her funeral, suggestions had been made by relatives that it was curious that the doctor had been the only medical man in attendance, and one of the dead woman's relatives wrote to him making certain suggestions. From every newspaper placard in London, the doctor was faced by phrases recalling the tragedy to his mind. Distracted with grief and harassed by publicity, the doctor went to the Russell Hotel, wrote a letter to his wife and one to the Coroner, and took sulphonal. He was on the point of death when they found him. And there then began the ordeal of an inquest and a trial for attempted suicide that were considerably less painful to him than the "trial by gossip" that had already convicted him.

The exhumation had been ordered after receipt of anonymous letters, and when it was revealed that the doctor benefited to the extent of some £13,000 under the will of the widow. In his first letter of explanation to the Coroner, he had referred to this fact. "I can be shown to be interested in the death," he wrote, "but was more interested in the patient's life, for it is known to others as well as myself that the lady was on the point of making a new will, leaving out certain legacies of the present will, and thus to my advantage."

The resumed inquest lasted only a few hours, and Curtis saw that the Coroner was likely to advise the jury that there was no evidence that the doctor was in any way to blame. He therefore said little, and after only fifteen minutes absence, the jury duly declared that death had been due to misadventure, and completely exonerated the doctor. Two days later he appeared at the Old Bailey on the charge of attempted suicide, once more to be vindicated by Sir Ernest Wild, the Recorder, who went out of his way to refer to the "vulgar tittle-tattle" in the case, ending with the words, "You have come through hell unsullied and nobler."

There was no denial of the attempt to commit suicide, but Sir Henry dwelt at some length on the "inevitable" publicity attending the exhumation. "The result was that this gentleman found he was being pointed at as a probable murderer; there was not one scrap of evidence that he had done anything improper." Sir Henry read out the doctor's pathetic farewell letter to his wife. "My love," he wrote, "has been in increasing ratio, and was never so fond as now."

The sentence was a curious one. "I will not say your character has been reëstablished, it has been doubly established. But I have to consider the offence against society," said the Recorder. "The sentence I pass on you is four days' imprisonment, which means that you will be immediately released."

Chapter Eleven

THE GREATEST YEARS—3

THROUGHOUT these days of hard work, Sir Henry had on his mind the great case that was pending. During another full week, he was engaged at the Hertford Assizes; and as December began he refused briefs so that he could concentrate for the Old Bailey trial of Mrs. Thompson on Wednesday the 6th. Edith Thompson was still adamant; there was no hint that she would allow herself to be guided by the advice of her counsel. The two months which she had spent in prison had not influenced her determination, and long before the first day's hearing, Curtis knew that he had one of the most difficult defences of his career. He feared the worst; yet he could never succeed in instilling in the mind of that determined woman a fraction of his own concern. He could only hope to prevent the letters being admitted in evidence.

On the first of those five gruelling days, Curtis-Bennett attempted the refusal of the letters as evidence. As was expected, the application for a separate trial was refused, and Curtis suggested strongly that the letters should not be admitted until the prosecution had shown that Mrs. Thompson was present when the fatal blow was struck, and further, proved some act showing she was party to the crime. He quoted the Armstrong case to strengthen his point, but, as he feared, Mr. Justice Shearman would have none of it. The first point was against Mrs. Thompson. Curtis knew, at the end of that first day, that already she stood appreciably nearer to the gallows.

He knew that he could safely rely on the wide experience of Mr. Walter Frampton for the examination of Mrs. Thompson, and not until the fourth day of the trial did he reëxamine. There was little to do save clear up some of the matters that had sounded so ominous when detailed by the prosecution. An example of his methods, and a very typical one, was his patient correction of a hostile impression caused by the reading of extracts from one of her letters to Bywaters. She had been reading "Bella Donna" and it was suggested that her interest in the book was due to the similarity of Hichens' characters with her own domestic triangle. To the Solicitor-General she had acknowledged that the woman in the story planned to poison her husband in order to go to another man.

Curtis destroyed the appearance of similarity with a few questions. Was the husband in the book wealthy? Yes. Was the lover a wealthy man? Yes. Was Mr. Thompson wealthy? No. Was Bywaters wealthy? No. Did she in fact support herself? Yes.

The only two witnesses called for the defence were the sister and mother of Mrs. Thompson. Curtis confined himself closely to questions of fact that he wished to emphasize in his closing speech.

And then: "That is the case for Mrs. Thompson."

How earnestly he wished that he could have said that earlier. If Curtis had had his way, he would have called no evidence. He dare not have submitted that there was no case to go to the jury, for the Judge would certainly have overruled his submission. But, in the absence of her testimony, he could have said that the actual evidence of her behaviour after the crime supported the theory that she knew nothing about Bywaters' intention.

To the day of his death Curtis insisted that he could have saved that woman. But there it was; he must fight for the life of a creature who did not know herself to be in danger. He must fight with her weapons—the second-best weapons—rather than with his own. The ground had been taken away from under his feet.

It was Saturday morning, and in his pocket were tickets for the Rugby Trial Match at Twickenham that afternoon. There was some question whether Mr. Cecil Whiteley would finish his closing speech for Bywaters that morning in time for Curtis to begin his speech for Mrs. Thompson. In any case, he welcomed the delay until Monday for the conclusion of his speech, and would have been unwilling to leave the verdict in the mind of the jury over the week-end. He believed that his eloquence would be more powerful in effect if his voice still rang in their ears as they deliberated. And although the prosecution must have the last word, he treasured the slender hope that his words would linger in their minds.

He spoke for only half an hour—a condensed and unemotional attack on the theory of the prosecution. He "supposed" the case was founded on nothing but the letters, and, outside that, on nothing but guesswork. He asked the jury if they did not consider Edith Thompson to be one of the most extraordinary personalities they had ever met. He built up her character for them: the imaginative, fanciful woman living in a world of make-believe. He was leading them to look at Edith Thompson in a new light, so that they could bring themselves to believe that when she put pen to paper, it was to record thoughts and suggestions that had no relation to her everyday life. "Have you ever read more beautiful language of love?" he asked. "Such things have seldom been put upon paper. This is the woman you have to deal with, not some ordinary woman. . . ."

There were some typical examples of his style in the address. He had begun with the familiar "At last I have an opportunity of putting Mrs. Thompson's case to you." He said: "You are men of the world, and happily your body includes a member of the other sex, so that you will be able to discuss the matter from both points of view. . . ."

That morning's speech ended on a low note dealing with the facts. But when Mr. Justice Shearman gave the indication that the court would adjourn, he was crushed by the Judge's last words of admonition.

"This was certainly a great love," Curtis had said.

"You should not forget that you are trying a vulgar and common crime," said the Judge.

From that moment Curtis knew that he had the Judge against him. He had lost most of the ground gained that morning.

Twickenham that day had lost its old appeal. The agony that he always felt was with him, but he showed no sign of the strain that wore him down during every murder trial. And on the Monday morning he stood up fresh and confident, to make a speech of only half an hour, which, however, stands today as a classic combination of straightforward appeal and cold simple logic.

He had many of Edith Thompson's letters to read, and it was a difficult task. But he had the voice for it. "Darlingest lover of mine, thank you, thank you, oh, thank you a thousand times for Friday—it was lovely—its always lovely to go out with you. And then Saturday—yes I did feel happy—I don't think a teeny bit about anything in the world, except being with you . . ." Difficult to invest those repetitions with feeling and sincerity in the cold atmosphere of a court of law. . . .

He made heavy play with a theory of the prosecution that one of Edith Thompson's letters referred to her husband, whereas he had been able to prove that she was writing about a bronze monkey. "Does not that show the danger of guesswork?" he asked. "There is not one reference in the letters which anyone in this court dare say shows that the suggestion made by the prosecution is true."

Then he ended: "I am loath to leave this discussion, because I am anxious to feel and know that I have dealt with the whole case as it is put against Mrs. Thompson. I know I have risked your displeasure in taking up your time at such length, but you do not grudge a few hours one way or the other spent on something which means eternity. Of course, I cannot see what is in your minds, because I cannot tell whether the matters I have been discussing are matters that you don't want to discuss because you have made up your minds. But in asking this question I know one thing: I shall get your answer, and the answer to the question I have put is that Mrs. Thompson is not guilty."

There was no peroration, no elaborate turn of a phrase that might haunt a jury; he wished only to exude a confidence which he did not really feel—which he had not felt since the Judge's bitter valediction two days before.

The Solicitor-General had finished his closing speech some time before the luncheon adjournment, and Mr. Justice Shearman had had time once more to destroy the idea of the "great love" in the jury's minds. "We have heard flights of fancy in this case," he said, and emphasized again that it was an extraordinary charge, that the circumstances were ordinary. He criticized Curtis-Bennett for remarking that he "thanked God that the jury had to decide and he had not." "If that remark was intended to frighten you, I hope it will not," said the Judge. "Let us get rid of all this atmosphere. You are told that this is a case of a 'great love.' If that means anything, it means that the love of a woman for her lover, illicit and clandestine, is something great and noble. I am certain that you, like any other right-minded person, will be filled with disgust at such a notion. . . ."

The Judge proceeded to kill outright the glamorous aura that had been woven round the love story of Edith Thompson and Frederick Bywaters—much to the disadvantage of Curtis-Bennett's case. "She was involved in a continual practice of deceit—the letters only breathe this insensate silly affection . . . they are the outpourings of a silly and at the same time wicked affection. . . ."

Sir Henry's client sat in the dock unmoved. But when he left the court with the retirement of the jury at half-past three

"A DOMINATING PERSONALITY IN COURT"
Photograph by Keystone

to wait in an anteroom of the Old Bailey, unable to bring himself to hear the verdict, Curtis feared the worst. Before six o'clock his fears were confirmed. That night, as he walked home, the evening newspapers blazed the news of Mrs. Thompson's guilt. A cigar merchant, an old friend of his, looked out of his shop and saw a familiar figure approaching. Curtis walked with his hands behind his back, deep in thought. "But how different he looked from the fine erect figure I knew!" writes the cigar-seller. "He was walking along slowly with his head bent down, umbrella under his arm. I opened the door of my business and greeted him: 'Good evening, Sir Henry.' Almost in a whisper came his reply. 'Good evening, Mellor. I am very, very tired.' . . ."

Ten days later he appealed on the grounds that the Judge misdirected the jury, and that the community of purpose between Edith Thompson and her lover had not been shown up to the moment of the crime. The appeal met with failure.

Curtis had in his mind a curious, illuminating remark Edith Thompson had made to her mother.

"How could you write those letters?" the latter asked.

"Nobody knows what kind of letters he wrote to me," was the reply.

Among the many fallacies that found publicity after the failure of the appeal, none made Curtis so angry as one theory suggesting that the reprieve of True had made the Home Office determined to refuse mercy because of the castigation of the Press. Bywaters could not be reprieved on the facts. The reprieve of Mrs. Thompson would have caused another storm, for public opinion, led by the Press, had hardened in favour of a condemnation of the woman and forgiveness of the youth because he was a weak and often unwilling slave of her stronger will. (Was it not proved, said Curtis, that she had *posed* to him as a woman capable of doing anything—even murder—to keep his love? She had to: Bywaters wanted to get away from her.)

There was no reason why Bywaters should not be hanged; could the woman be hanged, and not the man? Again, another section of public opinion would have been outraged, and it was absurd to suggest that the convicted instigator and not the actual murderer should pay the extreme penalty. But many put forward this theory; the law is that, if there is incitement to murder over a long period, then the instigator may be responsible for the consequences of that incitement and can be charged with the murder. If Mr. Thompson had walked home from the theatre alone that night, and met his death at the hands of Bywaters, would the letters found in his possession have convicted Edith Thompson on a charge of murder that she had not even witnessed?

Bywaters and Edith Thompson, whom Curtis had called great lovers, and whom the Judge had dismissed as paltry deceivers, never saw each other again, but died at the same moment on January 9th. But for years afterwards, indeed until the last years of his life, Curtis claimed that Edith Thompson, the woman who would not save herself, "paid the extreme penalty for immorality." He said to Mr. Stanley Bishop, the journalist: "I know—I am convinced—that Mrs. Thompson would be alive today if she had taken my advice. She spoiled her chances by her evidence and demeanour. I had a perfect answer to everything which I am sure would have won an acquittal if she had not been a witness. She was a vain woman and an obstinate one. She had an idea that she could carry the jury. Also she realized the enormous public interest and decided to play up to it by entering the witness box. Her imagination was highly developed, but it failed to show her the mistake she was making. I could have saved her. . . ."

The biggest case in which Sir Henry was concerned in 1923 was the Fahmy shooting tragedy at the Savoy Hotel. It will be remembered that during a sensational storm that broke over London on the night of July 9th–10th, a porter in the hotel had heard three pistol shots fired in quick succession. Prince

Fahmy Bey, the rich son of a rich Egyptian engineer, was found shot. His wife, a fascinating and sophisticated Parisian lady named Marguerite Forente, was in the room with a pistol in her hand and in a state of great excitement. She was alleged to have said in French: "I have pulled the trigger three times."

After her arrest she sought the advice of Mr. Freke Palmer who immediately retained the services of Sir Henry and Mr. Roland Oliver. At the desire of Madame Fahmy and her friends Mr. Freke Palmer later retained Sir Edward Marshall Hall to lead for the defence.

The trial, which began on September 10th, at the Old Bailey, was one of the sensations of the year. Marshall Hall was at his brilliant best. The defence, which was successful, was that the pistol had accidentally gone off as Madame Fahmy did not know it was in a condition to be fired. She was in possession of the pistol at that moment because she was defending herself against an attack by her husband.

After the acquittal, when Sir Henry and his wife were driving to Boreham, a woman stepped out behind an omnibus. Sir Henry cleverly avoided her; but she was wearing rubber shoes and, the road being wet, she slipped against the car and suffered a severe injury to her head from striking the rear part of the car. She died shortly afterwards.

As one would expect from a driver of his experience and skill, he was absolved from all blame at the subsequent inquest. But his relief and pleasure at the acquittal of Madame Fahmy were rudely shattered by this tragedy and by his sorrow for the relatives of the unfortunate woman.

Chapter Twelve

TRUE STORIES

Sir Henry's life was a series of contrasts. He switched apparently easily from farce to tragedy, from personal grief to the rôle of public jester. And it was in conformity with this rule that the jest that was most often on his lips, and in the speeches of others, was in actual fact his own most serious handicap; the doctors had given him warning.

His father had been of slim build to the end of his days. When Curtis was a young man, in training for the cycling track, he had shown few signs of putting on weight. Before the War, he increased in weight, then took it off as a result of the change in diet during the War. But after the War he found himself adding a stone every year. He was always agile and brisk in his movements, and he wore his immaculate clothes well, but he could not ignore the warnings of his heart. He was already caught in the vicious circle of weak-hearted men who are fat; his corpulence added to the strain on the heart, and the weak heart prevented him taking exercise to reduce his girth. He liked to be called the "Falstaff of the Bar," but he knew that those who chaffed him did not realize they were joking of his nemesis.

There was only one attitude for Curtis to take. He capitalized his generous proportions. In time he used every well-known story of fat people—always with the solemn assurance that the hero was himself—and was reduced in his latter years to recounting true stories. The last story he ever told was of his own weight, and was true. But before that time came when he was telling true stories to every banquet audience, he had become the principal figure of every incident told of every fat man at the Bar, and of a great many others, witty and wise, foolish and trivial, that have ever been invented by a world that looks kindly on a Colossus in their midst.

> Let me have men about me that are fat,
> Sleek-headed men, and such as sleep o' nights.

Curtis thought that Caesar's was the average opinion of the world, and he was right. And he judged that the only fat men who cannot be abided are those who pretend they are thin. Henceforth, Curtis would never let a Judge, jury, a public meeting, or a dinner audience forget that he was the Triton among the minnows of the Bar. Judges fed him with cues for a joke on it; his learned friends gave him opportunities that he never missed; witnesses unconsciously gave him slender, unintentional hints, on which he hung the fact of his weight with a mental agility that was in direct contrast to the ponderousness of which he joked.

Perhaps the earliest legal witticism on the subject of fat which Sir Henry inherited by natural right was that which concerns the question of a Judge to a barrister: "Do you move?" The classic reply, from the gargantuan barrister, is: "With difficulty, m'Lord." The story has been told as originating from Sir Henry. Probably he would have said it if it had not been a hoary jest in legal circles since the twenty-stone Mr. Murphy said it. Or, it may be that Mr. Danckwerts first offered this extremely obvious riposte for a man of immense proportions. But since the story was told of Curtis in his obituary notices, there is no knowing whether Murphy and Danckwerts had not also inherited the response. Curtis, at any rate, never claimed it as his own. He had to find new stories of fat men, and to give utterance to them as they occurred.

Certainly, some of his stories were old, but little known;

he told them, however, because they were good, and they sounded well as told by a fat man about himself after a good dinner. His favourite story went that he had recently been to the seaside and, stopping on the pier to inspect a penny-in-the-slot weighing machine, had wondered what this particular sample of a notoriously fanciful breed might show his weight to be. As he put the penny in, he noticed that two urchins stood behind him, entranced at the prospect of seeing what the portly gentleman with the cigar might weigh. The needle swung round wildly, and settled at six stone ten. Sir Henry, knowing the vagaries of these machines, was unsurprised. But there was a voice from behind him of awe and wonder.

"Coo, 'e must be 'oller!"

Another version of the same story told by Curtis was that he and his son, daughter-in-law, and granddaughter tried their varying weights upon a pier weighing machine. This, however, was one of those newfangled machines which announce the weight by means of a gramophone record. The machine duly announced "3st 5lbs" for Susan Curtis-Bennett; "8st 1lb," it announced for Margot Curtis-Bennett. Sir Henry put another penny into the machine and stood on the step: "One at a time please, one at a time," came a stentorian voice. . . .

Shortly after Bottomley's release from prison, Curtis was lunching at Romano's in the Strand when he saw Horatio at another table. When he finished lunch, he went over and greeted him saying how well he looked.

Horatio looked him up and down solemnly for a moment or two. "Yes—it saved my life," he said. "And it looks as if three years wouldn't do you much harm. . . ."

In court, he took every opportunity of referring to his weight. When he and Mr. Walter Frampton were in a case together, there was always sure to be a muster of members of the Bar and spectators, for both were of a similar build, and each was likely to draw a laugh from the court at his own expense. Owing to the number of counsel present on one occasion, there was real difficulty for both of them, and Sir Henry remarked that they dare not turn to face each other "in case we cannoned off the cush."

When Curtis had a smaller colleague at his side or behind him, he seldom failed to draw attention to the difference in their figures. Once, a very slim colleague was sitting behind him, and the Judge asked: "Is there no one on the other side, Sir Henry?"

"Yes, m'Lord," said Curtis—in the very voice and intonation of the vast Murphy whom he had succeeded as the Falstaff of the Bar. "Yes, m'Lord. My learned friend is obscured by my body. Not that I offer any apology for my size, m'Lord, because I sometimes make a good impression upon juries by virtue of it, as well as by my forensic eloquence."

Apart from the jest, this was by no means untrue. There was a good deal of truth behind the remark of a Judge to Sir Henry when he told him—quite inaccurately—that he was losing weight. "When you lose half your weight, Curtis, you will lose half your practice...." Clients seemed to like a weighty, well-dressed confident advocate.

In licensing cases particularly, a jest about his girth immediately changed the atmosphere of the court, and Curtis had the Bench friendly to him. When he appeared, there was sure to be a full muster of J.P.'s, most of them sure of a day's enjoyment when they saw Curtis was there. Accommodation was not always adequate for the big muster of barristers and solicitors. Often enough, the courts were stuffy and overcrowded; and when comment was made on the discomfort Curtis never failed to take his chance. When the Chairman of the Bench once remarked on the lack of ventilation, he said: "Yes, I quite agree it is very hot, but I am hoping that you will not be long in deciding in favour of my application, and then there will be very much more breathing space in the court."

There were times when he actually had to move the furniture in rural courts, to give himself room to move when he stood up. Curtis always helped to rearrange the furniture himself, making the best of the occasion and ensuring the friendship of every minor court official. He made it appear that he was proud of being the heaviest man at the Bar; and never, even to his most intimate friends, did he reveal the fact that he knew his weight was shortening his life.

One of his great friends, for whom he had a sincere admiration, was Mr. George McClure, now Senior Treasury Counsel, who often appeared with him as his junior, and provided a complete contrast in physical stature. Curtis and McClure once appeared in a case concerning a tubercular cow.

"What I want to know," said the magistrate, "is how tubercular cows can be recognized. How is one to tell whether a cow is tubercular or not?"

"So far as I can make out," said Curtis, "a normal cow is built somewhat on my lines, whereas a tubercular cow is built on the lines of my friend Mr. McClure!"

But his humour was not confined to this personal subject. His brain leapt to the ridiculous and the grotesque, and it could be seen that he could no more restrain himself than he could reduce his weight. In a case in which there was an allegation of appropriation of money from the servants' box "For the Unseen Staff" at an hotel, Curtis kept the court on a level of joviality that must have been unique. Throughout the case he was in a mood when he could not help commenting on the appearance of witnesses. The "Unseen" staff appeared to give evidence—a raggle-taggle crowd of nondescripts, all shapes and sizes. It took some time for these witnesses to give their evidence, and before they had finished, Curtis leant over to the jury to make a small point and began: "Members of the jury, we are still in the Presence of the Unseen...."

Country Justices of the Peace were not proof against his whispered comments. When an old and bearded patriarch appeared from the door at the back of the bench, and the court rose to do him honour, Curtis convulsed his fellow counsel with a remark that might easily have been heard by the old man. "It appears that Santa Claus has decided to pay us an early visit this year," he said.

The manner of his replying to questions, in a solemn voice without the vestige of a smile, lent piquancy to his wit.

His wit was never directed against ignorant witnesses who appeared in court suffering from nervous strain. He was especially tolerant of their mistakes, and would never take advantage of an obviously shaky witness who was uncomfortable in the unfamiliar surroundings. As Chairman of the Essex Sessions, he had many opportunities of showing this kindliness in a practical way. One old country couple were once charged with "harbouring thieves." They had no legal aid, and were baffled and overawed by the atmosphere of the court, so that the prosecution seemed certain to secure a conviction. Sir Henry saw that this would be a travesty of justice, and from the Chair subjected the prosecution to a searching cross-examination. The result was an acquittal. He had shown his own broad and elastic view of the meaning of the word Justice.

Many times he sent money to poor people who had come under the notice of the Law, and they never forgot him. But there were times when his friendliness with all and sundry had some strange sequels. In a murder case, he was rather surprised to obtain a verdict of acquittal, the jury having been sent back several times after declaring that they could not agree. Curtis knew that he had one or two of them on his side, but he was amazed when they seemed to have been able to sway all their colleagues. Years later, he defended a client whose face he seemed to remember. The man said: "I know you will do your best for me, Sir Henry. I did you a jolly good turn in that ——— murder trial. I told the jury I wouldn't agree if I sat there all night, and in the end I won the whole lot over and got you a verdict of 'Not guilty.'"

His generosity was also extended to colleagues and clerks. On the death of Mr. Allen Laurie, one of Sir Henry's oldest friends, he noticed at the Quarter Sessions, where Mr. Laurie had been deputy-Chairman, that his clerk stood in the background. Sir Henry wondered whether he would have another position. He found one for him within a week; and the letters of gratitude he received from men for whom he had found a post formed an appreciable part of his mail.

His heart, indeed, dictated his actions throughout his life. He could not bear to see suffering; it was ironic that this emotional man should have chosen a profession which brought him into close contact with so much of the seamy side.

Chapter Thirteen

A BARRISTER IN THE HOUSE

In January, 1924, Curtis was asked if he would stand for Parliament. The Rt. Hon. E. G. Pretyman, who had been conservative member for Chelmsford for fifteen years, had lost the seat at the last election to the Liberal, and decided not to stand again. The choice of Curtis was fairly obvious, although during his earlier years he had not taken much active interest in politics, and was not fond of the idea. Indeed, his old friend Marshall Hall had continually said to him: "Don't be stupid, Harry. You won't like it. You'll find it too much for you. Don't say I haven't warned you."

But Curtis considered it his duty to stand for a division where he had lived so long and in a county which had so long been the home of his ancestors. The seat had been lost to the Liberals mainly through the apathy of the Conservative voters, and there was a vast amount of work to do in visiting the small villages and towns in the countryside to revive enthusiasm. Every village considered itself to be of supreme importance, and Curtis determined to visit all of them; at week-ends he often worked harder than during the week, having high tea at six o'clock in the afternoon, travelling to two or three villages in the evening, and returning exhausted to a cold supper near midnight. He had, however, the support of his family. His wife was an excellent speaker and addressed many meetings: his daughter Ann took the greatest interest in his speeches, and although his clerk John Winkworth professed to be at a loss to understand why Curtis made so many speeches without fees, he also put his shoulder to the wheel.

Curtis hoped he would be the exception to the tradition that barristers make bad politicians. A quarter of a century before, Marshall Hall had given proof that there was some substance in the belief, but Curtis had a better manner with a meeting and a readier reply for a heckler. Throughout 1924, therefore, while in the courts of justice he was fighting for the lives of men in three of the most famous cases of his career, in the villages of Essex, he was attending garden parties, fêtes and bazaars, rummage sales, political socials, smoking concerts, and dinners, and at least one "tremendous mass meeting in the village hall."

He made himself hail-fellow-well-met in every corner of the constituency, became a familiar figure at the wheel of the open Rolls, and obtained a truly magnificent Press. The Liberals had got in by some three thousand votes, but for the election fight at the end of October Labour put in another barrister as candidate, Major N. H. Moller, and the sitting member, Mr. S. W. Robinson, was likely to lose the Labour votes that had undoubtedly put him in some years before.

It was the "Zinovieff Letter Election," and the *Daily Mail's* publication of the famous letter of the Premier, Mr. Ramsay MacDonald, had given Conservative candidates an excellent talking point. The withdrawal of the Campbell prosecution and the proposed Russian Treaty were other matters which village electors were asked to consider, and, without having read a single line about either, were expected to denounce with indignation. Curtis made great play with both points in the usual vein of a candidate who has every confidence of victory. The usual allegations were made that he was standing for Parliament in order to better himself, and he made the usual capital out of them by a vigorous and indignant denial; he had a perfect platform manner and a ready wit. For the two hundred meetings that he addressed shortly before polling day, when he drove from village to village throughout the evening, he had three speeches in readiness, the subject of considerable chaff from his family. And he used his daughter's idea for an election poster that became very familiar. Chelmsford Radio Station was then called 5XX. Curtis had hundreds of posters made with the inscription: "5XX CALLS 4C-B."

He noted with interest in his press-cuttings how the Press of opposing interests can deal with one subject. A photograph was taken of Curtis, looking very prosperous in a huge overcoat, talking to a poorly dressed roadsweeper. The *Daily Mail* headed it: "Sir Henry solicits the support of a roadman." The *Daily Herald* ran the caption: "Thoroughly comfortable; will you vote to keep me thoroughly comfortable while you keep your old hat and old boots and go on sweeping the roads?"

But it was a clean fight, and Curtis loved it. He was proud of one peroration that he kept for the final day's canvassing, in which he verbally waved the Union Jack with great vigour, spoke of the "thin Red line," and was, of course, rewarded with terrific enthusiasm, while women in the audience showed their approval with their tears. And there was always the "little story" that sent the audience away happy, the best of which concerned the simple old cockney shopkeepers who were arraigned for the offence of selling cigarettes after eight o'clock. They were tried by a venerable magistrate with a bald head, and during the case it was obvious that the old man felt the draughts in the court very keenly. As the prosecution ended, he realized that he stood in danger of contracting a severe cold, and dragged from his pocket a black silk skullcap. As he fitted it on his head, one of the defendants stiffened with horror, and said in an audible whisper: "Lumme, 'e's going to sentence us to death!"

He was good too at the riposte that brings a laugh.

"If you are elected," shouted one heckler, "will you defend us for nothing?"

"That depends exactly on what crime you are thinking of committing," said Curtis.

"Never has Sir Henry conducted a case more skilfully than

the case against Socialism," wrote a national paper. "His wonderfully mellow voice can swell to a rushing cascade of fierce intensity, and then sink to a quiet coaxing, cajoling tenderness. Interrupters do not trouble him. The man whose cross-examination has brought clever criminals to punishment can kill the average political heckler with one retort."

He was returned with a five-thousand majority in the Labour landslide of 1924. His was the largest individual poll ever returned, in the largest general poll in the history of the division, Essex being one of the twenty-one counties in which the Conservatives won every seat. And the *News of the World* depicted Sir Henry and Sir Henry Slesser, the two legal victors, with the caption: "Where there is no moaning at the Bar."

During the year, he resolved to move more freely in social circles. He spoke at the Press Club on a singularly brilliant "Criminal Justice Evening," with Lord Darling and Mr. Travers Humphreys and Mr. J. D. Cassels among the guests, and at the Stage Golfing Society Dinner.

But his career in the House of Commons was destined to be of short duration. During the election campaign, Sir Henry had been warned by the doctors that he was taking a risk if he intended to increase his hours of work. But he made a resolution to speak once a fortnight in the House if it were possible, and though he had a contempt for the forensic ability of most of the Members of the House, he liked the atmosphere, and he liked the informality of the Commons smokeroom. On April 1, 1925, soon after coming from a big murder case, he was due to make his maiden speech. It would be thought that for this important occasion, and to honour a newcomer to the House who came with a great reputation in another sphere, a subject would have been found for him that suited his nature and his gifts. He could have made a "human appeal" to the House better than any other member. He might, with the proper subject, have filled the house to the doors on every subsequent occasion, and made his mark as a Member to be listened to.

But for his maiden speech, Sir Henry was asked to move an amendment to the Widows Pensions Act. He could arouse in himself only a slight interest. The House was conscious that this was merely a formal maiden speech, on a subject of which the Honourable Member for the Chelmsford Division knew very little from his own experience. Curtis had read it up and written copious notes—a fatal procedure. His hands were encumbered by several sheets of paper at which he was expected to glance for every sentence. He was uncomfortable and fidgety, unlike his usually confident self, and though he warmed to his task, it was obvious that he was not happy. He was guilty of switching from the dramatic to the commonplace in a manner that had never been known in his addresses in a court of law. At one stage he said: "Then we are left with the death of the breadwinner—death, the summons for which comes quite unannounced, the summons against which, when it comes, there is no appeal." Then he dropped from that dramatic theme and continued without an interval: "It is only right, in my opinion, that the weekly contribution should cover, for the man who is paying it, the pension of the mother of his children."

Curtis was perturbed and dispirited. His wife had watched him from the gallery and knew that he had never been so nervous in his life. People said that his speech was excellent and the Press remarked the following day that he was an exception to the oft-repeated rule. But those who knew him, realized that he had spoken far below his capabilities. "It's only because the average in the House is so low that anyone thought anything of my speech at all," was Sir Henry's own comment. He never spoke again, for he had the uncomfortable and unfamiliar feeling that no speech of his could make any difference to anyone. Hitherto he had always known that every word of his might influence someone: speaking on the side of the Conservative party in the House, he felt that nothing he could say would make an iota of difference for the Government which had such a huge majority. He often said: "How I wish we were in opposition!"

Sir Henry's first case of interest in 1924 was the Rodeo prosecution. Mr. Charles B. Cochran had brought Tex Austin's rodeo from America as an entertainment for the British Empire Exhibition at Wembley. It was the first time that English people had had an opportunity of seeing the great cowboy sport that is so popular in America, and with his usual flair for publicity, Mr. Cochran had made the entire nation conscious of the picturesqueness of some score of cowboys who rode through the streets of London in motor-coaches lassooing the top hats of city men, whooping through the restaurants and theatres, and generally providing their own advertisement. They were excellent showmen, and brave and clever men. But when, at their first appearance at the newly opened stadium, there was an ominous and sickening crack of a broken limb as the lasso curled round the leg of a steer, the Press of the country doubted whether such entertainment would be tolerated by the British public. The R.S.P.C.A. had its inspectors watching the spectacle, and summonses soon followed. Curtis was briefed for the R.S.P.C.A. and Marshall Hall was briefed for Mr. Cochran, while Tex Austin was represented by Mr. Walter Frampton.

Mr. Cochran possibly found some benefit through the publicity given to the case. He announced that the show would go on, but with the omission of the steer-roping contests in one of which the accident had occurred. Meanwhile the cowboys had lost half their number, incapacitated and in hospital, in the excellent bulldogging contests in the course of which the rider of a horse throws himself round the neck of a galloping steer and drags it to the ground. They were cheerful invalids, and took their injuries purely as a matter of course. And the majority of the public found vast entertainment in the new spectacle that they provided at Wembley—so long as there was no obvious cruelty to the animals.

The summonses, which were heard by the Wealdstone magistrates, referred to the "cruel ill-treatment of a number of steers during a steer-roping contest," and were against Mr. Cochran for "keeping a place for the purpose of fighting certain animals, to wit, steers."

Outside the court the cowboys sat on the curb before a large crowd, twirling their ten-gallon hats. Tex Austin was besieged by autograph hunters, and it was evident that although many thousands of people believed that cruelty to animals resulted from their performances in the arena, the cowboys themselves had become public heroes. Curtis, opening the case, spoke of their performance as an "entertainment." Marshall Hall would have none of this, but Curtis replied: "You can call it what you like, Sir Edward Marshall Hall, but I am going to call it an entertainment." After describing the incidents, Curtis said: "The animal comes in for the purpose of bringing money into the pockets of Mr. Cochran and, possibly, Mr. Austin. I do not know if it is going to be suggested that Mr. Cochran is not responsible, but perhaps some people will think that Mr. Cochran is far more guilty than the cowboys themselves of cruelty to these animals. I wonder what sport it is to the animal which has its legs broken. . . . You do not get out of this what is known by the Englishman's love of sport."

There was a great deal of prejudice shown by the public towards the case, and Marshall Hall himself had received letters charging him with being a "dirty traitor" because he had formerly spoken on behalf of the Dumb Friends League. "I deeply resent the suggestion that I have no sympathy with animals," he said; "I regret very much the fanatical feeling that has been broadcast condemning everybody before they have had a chance of replying."

Sir Henry could do very little against the many witnesses called by the defence. Sir Edward Marshall Hall's clients had advertised for witnesses of the spectacle, and had received the offers of several volunteers, many of whom said they had observed no cruelty. Tex Austin himself, who said he had been prosecuted in America by "a similar bunch of people," proved a difficult witness. "The steer was quite happy with its broken leg?" asked Curtis. "I never asked it," said Tex. And the case came to a somewhat tame ending on its third day, the Bench being of the opinion that there had been no cruelty in the exhibition and the summonses were therefore dismissed.

The final day's hearing of the rodeo case seemed to Curtis merely like a light interval between two cases of grim and terrible drama. Only four days before, he had heard Jean Pierre Vaquier sentenced to death and seen him dragged screaming from the dock. And a week later he was to appear for the Crown against Mahon—in one of the most gruesome and eerie murder trials that he had ever attended.

The details of Vaquier's love story with the wife of the proprietor of the Blue Anchor Hotel at Byfleet, and his carefully planned murder of her husband, make a case of obvious appeal to the student of criminology and to the seeker after sensation. Sir Henry did not like the case. When he first saw Vaquier, after he had made no less than five statements to the police, he indicated that he believed a certain line of defence would be advisable. Vaquier agreed. At their next meeting the excitable, bearded Frenchman indicated that he wished to change his mind; he preferred that an entirely different defence should be put forward. Curtis protested. Vaquier could not speak English, and Sir Henry's French was inexpert, so that their consultations were further complicated by the necessity of having to employ an interpreter. And after that second meeting, Curtis would have thrown up the brief had he not known that it was his duty to continue rather than prejudice the defence.

The brief points of the charge were that while in Biarritz, Mrs. Jones, the wife of the owner of the Blue Anchor Hotel, had become friendly with Vaquier. When he followed her to England, she made him welcome in her husband's hotel. Two weeks after arrival, he went to a chemist in London and bought strychnine. And at the end of the month, the hotel proprietor was found dead from strychnine poison administered in a dose of bromo salts. Vaquier was questioned that night, gave three other statements during the next eleven days, and was arrested nearly three weeks after the murder, following a statement to the police by the chemist who had sold him the poison.

It was a strange love story that was told to Curtis in his chambers. Curtis could not forget that these two creatures, whose paths had accidentally crossed in an hotel in Biarritz, could speak hardly a word of a common language; they made love by dictionary, and in other circumstances their difficulties might have been farcical. Jean Vaquier always addressed her as "Madame Jones"—even on the most intimate occasions. He preserved a courtly attitude towards her, and it was perhaps part of his charm for the opposite sex that he was such a vain and flattering courtier. He wept when she left him for the first time in the South of France; he begged her on bended knees to return and become his mistress. He showered compliments on her with true Basque impulsiveness and skill. It must have been a source of sorrow to him that when he came to England, to get in touch with her within two days of arrival, he must come, not in the guise of a faithful knight, but as the hopeful vendor of an apparatus for treating sausages.

Mr. Jones, the publican, was a mild drunkard. He frequently suffered the next morning from his excesses, and was in the habit of taking salts in an effort to recover. A fortnight after the Frenchman's arrival at the hotel, there was a party at which several of the guests were drunk. Mr. Jones, although he had obviously drunk a great deal, seemed unaffected, but the next morning he wished to have his drink of salts. He found that Vaquier had been down before him; he took his salts, took also an emetic that made him sick, and sat down opposite the Frenchman. Jean Pierre Vaquier was waiting for him to die.

He was already dying when the doctor arrived just before midday. Half a grain of strychnine was found in the body; and he died from asphyxiation—the usual result of taking the poison.

Vaquier made a statement to the police the next day. And when Mrs. Jones said to him, "You have assassinated Mr. Jones," he replied: "Yes, Mabs; for you." A few days later he moved to another hotel in Woking, and from time to time volunteered new statements to the police. Why did he do that? Curtis had the explanation: it was because, according to the laws of his own country, he must prove himself innocent of the crime.

The trial was held on July 2nd at the Guildford Assizes. The courtroom in those days was no more than a village hall used throughout the year for dances and other festivities. Next door was the local theatre, and the whole appearance of the court was that of scenery roughly bolted together for the court scene in a stage drama. When the Judge opened the door leading from his retiring room, he was using the same corridor through which the theatre stall-holders passed, and in the brief moment that the door was open, there could be seen the notice: "Stalls this way." For that week the theatrical engagement had been cancelled and dances were held elsewhere: in the real-life drama that was now being enacted, however, there were some famous actors: Mr. Justice Avory as the Judge; the Attorney-General (Sir Patrick Hastings, K.C., M.P.), Sir Edward Marshall Hall, K.C., Mr. H. D. Roome, and Mr. George Ansley for the prosecution, Sir Henry Curtis-Bennett and Mr. A. B. Lucy for the defence. And to continue the illusion, the most imaginative novelist could hardly have depicted a character more fanciful and vain than the prisoner.

Vaquier was careful to pomade and scent his hair and beard

before he appeared in court every day; he was vain about his clothes, and it was obvious that he wished to be well in the limelight and to gain a reputation as a wit, even though that reputation might bring him nearer to the gallows. He posed and postured, and his chief objections to the methods of British justice were that he was not given the opportunity of being confronted with his accusers as is the custom of France, and that there was no reconstruction of the crime. He told Curtis that he wished to speak to the Judge himself, and to shout his defiance at the witnesses as they told their stories. He was brought to Guildford every day by train, and was allowed to converse with the newspapermen; his jailers were most pleasant to him, though they could speak not a word of his language; he was met with politeness wherever he went; he was never roughly handled, and it seemed that all the court officials were anxious only to see that he was comfortable. Gradually, Jean Vaquier came to a certain conviction about this trial; such exemplary conduct on the part of police officials could mean only one thing; they believed him innocent, and the trial was only a formality.

But in the mind of his counsel, who had made him sign papers stating that it was left to him how the case was to be conducted, there was no such confidence.

Once or twice Vaquier aired his wit to his interpreter. A witness was referred to as a builder and mortician.

"Ah, I understand!" said Jean. "He accommodates you above and below ground—is it not so?"

He passed innumerable notes to Sir Henry, making this and that suggestion, demanding to be given the opportunity of himself conducting the cross-examination of adverse witnesses. Sir Henry, worried already by the way the case was going, curtly requested him to leave matters alone.

The crux of the case was the evidence of Mrs. Jones, widow of the dead man. Sir Edward Marshall Hall, tall, dignified, handsome, conducted the examination. She was in the witness box almost all the first day, and most of the second, when Sir Henry plied her with questions regarding her relationship with Vaquier, about the management of the hotel, about the circumstances of her husband's taking the poisoned salts. When Mr. Justice Avory, that most stern of English judges, asked whether certain questions were relevant, Sir Henry replied, "I am attacking this lady's credit absolutely, in every way."

Part of Sir Henry's plan for the defence was already revealed. He was establishing that there had been discussion between Vaquier and Mr. Jones concerning a project of his own; he wanted Mr. Jones to finance a café in the South of France. He established further that Mrs. Jones had lent him money, on the strength of his expected sale of his sausage machine patent. Therefore, Sir Henry was going to suggest, because of the café project and the hope of obtaining a further loan from the Jones family, it was not in the interests of Jean Vaquier that Mr. Jones should die.

But when Sir Henry put his own witnesses into the box, and made an attempt to explain away the purchase of strychnine poisoning, it was obvious—to all except Vaquier—that here was the weak link in the case for the defence. Vaquier had not even mentioned these purchases in his first statements to the police. He had not thought them worthy of explanation; and now, the only reason he was able to give for requiring the deadly poison, was that it might come in useful for his wireless experiments!

But Curtis, in his final address to the jury, cleverly turned round these points, that seemed so adverse to his client, and made them appear favourable. Was it not natural, he said, that a Frenchman, not knowing the laws of this country, must think that he should have a reason—any reason—for buying poison? Was it not also natural that while he knew he was to be accused of the crime of murder, he should consider every other person in close contact with the Jones family, and accuse each one in turn? "It was far more advantageous to Vaquier that Mr. Jones should live than that he should die," said Sir Henry. "Vaquier had possessed this woman in Biarritz, Bordeaux, Paris, and London; but the infatuation was ended, and there had recently been no guilty relations between these two; the passion had burnt out. Why then should Vaquier desire the death of the woman's husband?"

He scouted the suggestion that Vaquier had admitted the murder to Mrs. Jones with the words, "Yes, Mabs, for you." He did not understand English, and could not speak it. "I am not going to impress matters of that sort upon you," said Curtis, "because Mrs. Jones is a witness whose evidence you cannot rely upon."

He concluded: "Vaquier is a stranger in a strange land; if there is a reasonable doubt in your minds that the Crown has not proved its case, then I ask you to say, by your verdict, that Vaquier is not guilty, and so allow this ill-starred visit to come to an end, and enable him to return to his native country...."

The Judge, in his long summing-up, would not give the jury a lead on whether the credibility of Mrs. Jones had been destroyed. "It does not follow that, because a wife has been unfaithful, she is never to be believed," he said. "But, because her evidence has been attacked, I suggest that you confine your attention to the evidence of other witnesses when you consider the accused's movements on the day of Mr. Jones' death. A suggestion has undoubtedly been made by counsel that she may have been a party to the destruction of her husband, but you must remember that the accused himself has asserted that she is entirely innocent."

The Judge went on to the question of the motive for the murder. The prosecution suggested that he was urging Mrs. Jones to leave her husband so that he might possess her completely; she had refused to leave him, and therefore, said the Judge, it was suggested that, for a man of Latin race, there existed a most powerful motive for removing him. Vaquier had himself admitted that he had pleaded with her to leave her husband; yet she had some affection for him, even though she had been unfaithful to him, and she had refused. "You are entitled to take into consideration the possibility of such a motive," said the Judge with meaning.

It was fairly evident to everyone in that court that there could be but one verdict. Except one man. Jean Pierre Vaquier stroked his beard, swept his wide, luminous, hypnotic eyes round the court seeking admiration, and smiled confidently. He was the hero of a great trial; his vanity was fed with glances of awe and, perhaps, admiration for him as a great lover. And soon it would be over.

"I will ask you now to retire and discharge the duty which you have undertaken by your oaths," said the serene, parchment-faced Judge. "That is, to find a true verdict according to the evidence, regardless of the consequences and regardless of everything except your desire to do justice between the Crown and the accused. Will you now consider your verdict?"

Sir Henry bent over his papers for a moment, then left the court. His heart was heavy. Whatever he thought of that excitable, pomaded Frenchman, he feared that in a few hours he would be stricken down by the blow of the jury's verdict. Jean Pierre Vaquier had not understood; he *would* not understand that he was very near to the gallows. He had mistaken the attitude of that court, misinterpreted the calm unprejudiced kindliness of the officials, thinking that if he had been in danger of being convicted, they would have subjected him to roughness and humiliating treatment. It was cruel kindness: he stroked his scented beard and smiled at his counsel, awaiting his vindication.

He had not long to wait. In an hour and a half the jury were back.

"Gentlemen of the jury, are you agreed upon your verdict?" intoned the Clerk of Assize.

A WHITELAW CARTOON

"Improbable!"
Mr. Norman Birkett, K.C., is cross-examined by Sir Henry Curtis-Bennett, K.C.

"We are," said the foreman.

"Do you find the prisoner at the bar, Jean Pierre Vaquier, guilty or not guilty?"

"Guilty."

His interpreter translated the dread word. Vaquier stood transfixed, fear and amazement darting from those eyes which portrayed the human emotions so clearly, that had looked on Mrs. Jones with passion, on Mr. Jones with hate and cruelty. He was speechless while the Clerk of the Assize continued with the old formula: "Jean Pierre Vaquier, you stand convicted of wilful murder. Have you anything to say why judgment of death should not be pronounced upon you according to law?"

Then the storm broke. From foaming lips, there came a torrent of shouted protest. From his eyes, there came tears, the look of a whipped dog.

"Monsieur le Président—" he began.

That calm, deadly voice of the Judge cut him short.

"I can only listen to any reason in law why I should not pronounce sentence upon you," he said.

"I can only say I am innocent!" shouted Vaquier, while with his carefully tended hands he beat a tattoo of despair upon the rickety ledge of the temporary dock. "I swear on my mother's and my father's graves, still fresh, that I am quite innocent of the crime of which I have been accused!"

Once more, the voice of the Judge, the voice of Destiny.

"Jean Pierre Vaquier, you have been convicted by the jury of the most serious crime known to the law of any civilized country. I can see no reason whatever to doubt the righteousness of the verdict. You have been tried according to the law and procedure of this country, which are more favourable to the accused than the laws of other countries, and you have had further the advantage of one of the most able and experienced counsel at the English Bar. Having been so convicted, it is my duty to pronounce upon you the sentence which is prescribed by law for this wicked and detestable crime. The sentence is that you be taken from this place to a lawful prison and thence to a place of execution, that you be there hanged by the neck until you are dead, and that your body be afterwards buried within the precincts of the prison wherein you shall last have been confined before your execution. And may the Lord have mercy upon your soul!"

The black cap had been placed ready to his hand. Mr. Justice Avory now placed it on his head—for perhaps the fiftieth time in his career.

"Amen!" said the chaplain.

But now the tattoo of Vaquier's fists and arms on the frail ledge of the dock had quickened to frenzy. He was savage, demented, his beard flecked with saliva.

"Je demande la justice!" he screamed. "Monsieur le Président, you have given an iniquitous verdict!"

Warders tore at him, trying to release his hands clenched on the brass rail of the dock. His voice rose, and he changed to wild vituperation.

"I can listen to nothing more," came the voice of the Judge. "Let him be removed . . ."

From Wandsworth prison, he wrote impassioned letters to Sir Henry and to friends. He became calmer, and once more his confidence returned, for he could not bring himself to realize that justice would overtake him in a foreign land. "Cher maître," he addressed Sir Henry, and implored him to visit him in jail. To a friend he wrote saying that he left the future confidently in the hands of that "wise and good counsellor," and said he thought there could be no doubt that he would "see again the fair land of France." "I have bled for France," he wrote, "and I would gladly have given my life for my country." He gave the address of the prison, impishly, as "Wandsworth Palace."

On July 28th, Sir Henry made his appeal for his life, submitting that there was new evidence. His client's ignorance of the law in England, he said, had caused him to suppress certain facts, which he had since been able to prove. He had been waiting throughout the trial to be "confronted" with one of his accusers, when he would have produced this evidence. But he had waited in vain; he had not told Sir Henry of this evidence, and it was important to his case.

"If this sort of thing is to be allowed," said the Lord Chief Justice, "the oath to be taken by prisoners will have to be altered to 'I swear to tell the truth, five-eighths of the truth, and nothing but the truth; I will keep the remaining three-eighths for the Court of Criminal Appeal.'"

The Appeal Judges did not even call upon counsel for the prosecution to reply to Sir Henry. The appeal was dismissed, and once more Jean Pierre Vaquier, gripping the rail of the dock, screamed his indignation, foamed at the mouth, rolled his eyes in angry despair.

He went to the scaffold a fortnight later; a small, pathetically pompous, vain creature who for a time had imagined himself the great lover; who succeeded in being only a blundering sausage-machine vendor who stumbled blindly into the greatest of crimes.

Chapter Fourteen

GREAT MURDER TRIALS

SHORTLY after the War a young and handsome man who took an inordinate interest in his clothes and personal appearance, assaulted a servant girl at Chertsey and received five years penal servitude. His name was Patrick Herbert Mahon, and he used his good looks and his considerable expenditure on clothes to make an impression upon almost every woman he met. He was married, but he had not learnt his lesson, and had no intention of settling down to a domestic life. The fault was not on one side only, for women pursued him, and he frequently had difficulty in ending his romances once he tired of them. In 1924 he was still under police observation as an ex-convict: But neither the interest of the police nor his marriage vows prevented him from pursuing his romantic instincts. And when he met a woman who lived in a Soho flat, he took her to dinner and she became a victim to his masculine charm at their first meeting; her name was Emily Kaye, and she did not intend that this should be merely a casual romance. She had a considerable sum of money in her possession and she wished to spend the rest of her life with Patrick Mahon. This proposal was not at all well taken; but Emily suggested that they try a "love experiment" by living together in a bungalow on the Crumbles at Eastbourne.

Emily had another reason for desiring a more or less official partnership with Mahon. She had become pregnant, and although Mahon denied later that he knew of her condition, it is very probable that she had mentioned this as a further reason for making him responsible for her future. Mahon was persuaded to give in. He had not yet completely tired of his passion for her, and at the end of a few days, he thought, he could drive her to leave him and he could then entertain the lady of his subsequent passion—when she had departed—using the bungalow as his home. He therefore rented the bungalow, which Emily had seen advertised, and she came down to stay with him. She had every confidence that eventually she could persuade him to live with her more or less indefinitely, and to this end she parted with a large sum of money which was the proceeds of the sale of securities. Emily was to take up residence on April 12th. On April 10th Mahon met another woman, "Ethel," and immediately decided that she should be the next recipient of his favours. On April 12th he made some curious purchases in London. He bought a knife and a saw which he said were for use in the bungalow. On April 15th Emily Kaye and Mahon had a quarrel. No doubt Emily was telling him again that she could not be happy away from him, and pleading that their "love experiment" had been successful. Mahon, with the thought of Ethel in his mind, resisted the suggestion. There was a fight. Mahon's version was that the woman threw an axe at him which bruised him in passing and broke into two pieces when it struck the wall. Then they engaged in a violent struggle—again according to Mahon. The strong and well-built girl, he said, forced him to the ground and knocked him unconscious, while she herself had fallen and split her head open against the coal scuttle.

Recovering consciousness, Mahon had found that she was dead. He had rushed out of the bungalow and, becoming calmer, had realized that he was in a terrible predicament. He had already invited the other woman down to live with him three days later. He might stand accused of murdering Emily at any moment. In a frenzy he dragged the body into a bedroom and locked the door. Nothing must interfere with his plans. Next day he went to London and met Ethel and accompanied her back to the bungalow. She noticed that there were a number of women's clothes about the room, but Mahon explained this by saying his wife had recently visited him there. He saw the danger of the secrets in that room for which he now bought a new Yale lock. Therefore, he sent a telegram to himself and told Ethel that they must return to London as soon as possible. Weighing on his mind was the thought of that body in the bedroom and he went to the bungalow with a new plan.

Looking round, he saw near by the instruments which would serve him well. With the carving knife and saw he cut the body of Emily Kaye in pieces, limb by limb, and thrust the limbs some into the stove and some into a cauldron of boiling water. There was the head with its long flowing blond hair. He thrust it into the stove, and as the hair caught alight he watched the features of the face contract into an almost living expression of agony: and at that moment, as he covered his eyes in horror, the heavens opened and over the Crumbles swept a terrifying storm that was preceded by one detonating clap of thunder. Mahon packed the various members of the body into a trunk, into a biscuit tin, and into a hat box, and stowed them in the bedroom.

On April 28th, he packed the knife and several pieces of Emily's blood-stained clothing into a bag, sprinkled them with Sanitas, and left it at Waterloo Station. There was no plan in his mind save to keep away from that house where he would ever be reminded of that last grim scene where the features of his mistress contracted before him. He knew, however, that it would be unsafe to leave the bag in the check room. On May 2nd he returned to Waterloo and produced the cloak-room ticket. As he turned, there was a hand on his shoulder. The police had been too quick for him. The bag was opened in his presence and he was arrested for murder.

They asked him at Scotland Yard how he could account for the grim contents of the bag. "I am fond of dogs," he said. "I suppose I have carried some meat for the dogs in it." But late that night he made a long statement, which left little to be discovered. He told his story of those sordid days and nights in the Crumbles bungalow and left nothing to the imagination. He gave every detail in picturesque language—how he had cut up the body—and devoted great attention to the storm which had shaken his courage when he had watched the eyes of Emily Kaye opening as the flames devoured her hair.

His solicitors briefed Mr. J. D. Cassels, K.C., for his defence. Yet it almost happened that Curtis-Bennett was briefed. A young magazine writer had offered to pay for the whole of Mahon's defence and expressed a desire that it should be in Sir Henry's hands. This proposition, however, came to nothing.

Curtis was briefed for the Crown, and seldom encountered a prisoner for whom he had greater dislike. He could hardly restrain the instinct to show his disgust of this calm, good-looking man who appeared so eager to inspect every gruesome exhibit in the case.

It was noticed, when the trial began on July 15th at the Lewes Assizes, that Mahon was looking considerably more healthy than at the police court proceedings shortly before. He seemed sunburnt and fat, although there was a striking contrast in the colour of his hands, which were pale and delicate. As a fact, Mahon had expressed a wish to obtain some chemical tan while in jail and had actually attempted to give his face an artificial tan with tobacco juice. He had bought a new nine-guinea suit especially for the trial, and his clear-cut handsome features radiated confidence. The trial excited national interest, although few legal niceties were to be debated and the attention of the public—and of an American judge who sat beside Mr. Justice Avory—was concentrated upon the shocking details of this most callous killing.

Before him Sir Henry Curtis-Bennett had the knife and saw together with keys of the bedroom and the little coal scuttle which, according to the prisoner, had caused the death of

Emily Kaye. He had also a perfect model of the bungalow, built to scale, the bedroom furnished and the wall paper identical with that in the house of death. Sir Henry's opening speech was no more than a catechism of the known facts with the conclusion: "If these facts are proved it will be my duty to ask you for a verdict that Patrick Mahon is 'Guilty' of the murder of Miss Kaye." As in the Field and Gray trial at the same court, before the same judge, and with Curtis and Cassels opposed to each other, the illness of a juryman meant five hours' delay, while Curtis restated his case; but by the end of the second day the prosecution had concluded, and Mr. Cassels put Mahon into the box. He was anxious to "make a good impression" in court. He was overeager and obsequious, smiling round at the jury, nervously trying to please. But he succeeded in being merely irritating. He had a habit of replying "Quite," to his counsel's questions. He was glib and unashamed as he told the story of the "love experiment." Describing Emily Kaye's behaviour just before, according to him, she threw the axe at him, he said: "I realized from her manner that a crisis was coming; she seemed so hysterical and overwrought." But Mr. Justice Avory did not like this manner.

"This is all description," he said, "a sort of narrative. We want to know what happened, not what you thought and what you imagined, but what happened."

Patrick Mahon broke down when he came to the scene when Emily threw the axe and rushed at him in a savage attack. "I was astounded by the suddenness of the attack," he said. "In a second Miss Kaye followed up the throw. She leaped across the room, clutching at my face, and—"

The calm voice of the Judge urged him to continue. "We have got as far as she was clutching at your face," he said to the weeping figure in the dock.

"I became absolutely uneasy with fear and fright," said Mahon.

"You did?" queried the Judge.

"I did, my Lord. And with almost a last despairing throw I pushed her off and we both fell over the easy-chair to the left of the fireplace. Miss Kaye's head hit the cauldron, and I fell with her." (Later, this version of the struggle was to elicit the open disbelief of the Judge.)

Mahon said that Emily, usually good-tempered and placid, had suddenly become as angry "as an infuriated tiger." The incident that had led up to this sudden change was the writing of a letter by Miss Kaye. That night, she had pleaded with her lover to go abroad with her—to Paris and thence to South Africa. Mahon was breaking coal with the newly purchased axe, and, finishing his task, he put the axe on the table where the girl was writing. "Pat," said the girl, "I am determined to settle this matter one way or another tonight." She tossed over two letters that she had written, and asked Mahon to sign them. They were to friends, saying that he was leaving England.

"I cannot do it," Mahon told her, according to his own statement. "Why cannot we be pals?"

The woman flared up. "What is the use of palship to me, to one of my nature?" she cried.

But another version of that incident was suggested by the Judge. Mahon had said that he intended to tell his wife of his association with Miss Kaye—after he had ended his friendship with her. "Rather than sign the letter, or do what she wanted, I would tell my wife the whole thing," he said. "Do you think it is perhaps possible that what really took place was that *she* said: 'If you do not do this which you promised to do, I shall tell your wife the whole thing'?"

But, whatever the facts of the incident which led up to the quarrel, Mahon gave details of his feelings of horror when he realized the girl was dead.

He described how he went out of the bungalow just before dawn, and returned to find the girl dead. "It suddenly struck me what a fool I had been not to call for assistance, and it suddenly dawned on me what a horrible thing it was, she was there and dead. I think the realization of the fact that she was dead flooded my mind—"

Once more the stern Judge disapproved of these sentiments. "You were asked what you did," he said, "not all this imagination. You were asked what you did."

"I am trying to remember what I did, my Lord. It is not easy to remember . . ."

He came to his actions on that fateful Good Friday. "I had been wondering how to conceal what had happened," he said. "I determined to cut the legs off the body and put it in a trunk. I eventually did cut the legs off and then found I could not get the body in itself, the rest of the body into the trunk without taking the head off, to fasten the trunk up. . . ."

But he came to another decision about the disposal of the body of his sweetheart. The trunk would not close. Terrified, fighting down his nausea, Mahon took the body out of the trunk again, and began to burn it. Some portions he boiled; others he flung upon the fire in the stove of the little bungalow. With many a wild glance towards the door, he had steeled himself to complete his awful task. Then Mr. Cassels—perhaps remembering the story of Patrick Mahon, of how when he had burnt the head the skin had contracted and the eyes had looked at him, and of how at that moment a storm had swept over the lonely Crumbles—came to his questions about the burning of the head.

"On the Tuesday you burned the head?"

It seemed that Mahon was about to reply with a full description of that ghastly moment. In another moment he might have shocked the court with that graphic picture of the hair catching fire, the skin lifting, the eyes opening, as the storm cracked and rolled away.

But just at that moment, as he had begun, "That is so," there broke over the courtroom at Lewes a shattering cannonade of thunder and lightning. The heavens opened, and for a moment there was no word spoken in that court, men and women shuddering before the sudden onslaught that had come out of a blue sky that pleasant summer's day.

But only to two men in court was the full significance of that storm apparent: Patrick Mahon and his counsel. Alone in court, these two knew that the coincidence of that first clap of thunder had seemed remarkably like a sign from the heavens, an omen of terrible meaning. Mahon shuddered and cowered in the corner of the dock. He was shaking, harried by a terrible fear. The calm voice of his counsel continued with a few more questions. But when Sir Henry rose to cross-examine, he was faced with a man who had the fear of God in his heart, a beaten and trembling creature who had detected the hand of the Almighty in a summer storm.

Sir Henry took him through, detail by detail, the grim hours in which he had tried to dispose of that body. He riddled him with keen questions regarding the purchase of the knife and the saw. In a statement to the police, Mahon had said: "I put the body in the spare room and covered her up with her fur coat. I came up to London, and on return, took with me a knife which I had bought at a shop in town. I also bought from the same shop a small saw. When I got back I was so excited and worried that I could not then carry out my intention to decapitate the body . . ."

Mahon now said that he did not intend this to read that he had bought the knife for the purpose of performing the grim deed; he had bought them for an innocent purpose.

"The knife was the one with the name of the shop on it?" said Sir Henry.

"Yes, it was."

"Did the knife with the name on it *happen* to be in the bag which you left at Waterloo Station?"

"Yes."

Another example of Sir Henry's skill in confounding a witness into exposing an obviously farfetched theory was the following:

"Is your case that you were really being seduced by this lady from your wife? Is that your case?"

"It might be so put."

"Did the other woman—Ethel—seduce you away from your wife?"

"Of course not."

"Now I understand your case. The seduction by Miss Kaye of you from your wife was becoming repugnant to you, was it, and you wanted to stop it?"

Mahon's confidence ebbed, drained away. Curtis came to examine his story of how he had broken some of the dead woman's bones with his fingers; how he had put the boiled flesh in the trunk, and thrown the broken bones from the window of the train. Mahon recovered something of his composure. And when he came to the final speech for the Crown, Curtis asked the jury whether, in view of his previous callous behaviour, they thought that his emotions were sincere.

"After cutting up the body of Miss Kaye, Mahon met another woman, stayed with her in the room that had been used by Miss Kaye and himself, took her out to dinner, and went to Plumpton Races. Nobody noticed anything untoward about him at all, and you may have your opinion as to whether the feeling he showed in the witness box was real or not. . . ."

Mr. Cassels spoke very briefly. It might be said that Mahon was immoral, he said, but immorality was not visited with capital punishment. Did men murder after they had received money? Did the delay in disposing of the body point to the conduct which might be expected of a murderer? Was it not possible that his refusal to leave home and live with Miss Kaye for always, roused her to anger? The jury would remember the lines:

Heaven has no rage like love to hatred turned,
Nor hell a fury like a woman scorned.

"It has been suggested that the breaking down of the prisoner was not genuine," he concluded. "Remember all that this man has been through, all the things that, guilty or not guilty, he has done: can you conceive that possibly on the threshold of eternity you would get play-acting from a man in such a grave position? Have you before you such an inhuman monster?"

Avory's summing-up was dead against Mahon. Was it conceivable that considering the relations between them, having taken precautions to avoid such a result, Mahon did not know that the woman was pregnant? Was it possible that a woman under these circumstances, knowing what her condition was, would try to strangle the man whom she loved with this absorbing love which the prisoner had described, and the man to whom alone she looked at that time to save her from this situation in which she found herself?

"In asking yourselves whether his subsequent conduct is consistent with any view that this was a death happening without his intention and desire, you have to look at the evidence of his taking this other woman to the bungalow on Good Friday, sleeping with her in the very room which he had occupied with the deceased woman for the three nights, and actually taking the precaution, before she arrives there, to go there himself and cut the head off, in order that he may pack it in the trunk out of sight. Is that conduct which you would expect of a man who feels any kind of remorse at a death which he neither desired nor intended? He took the trouble to burn the head and collect the bones. Why this trouble? Why take this meticulous care to destroy every fraction of the skull unless it were for the purpose of concealing the injuries on the bone of this head which might afford conclusive testimony to what had really happened on that night, instead of the mere fall on that rickety old coal cauldron?"

The cold voice of England's famed "hanging judge," as he was often called, swept on with the string of damning questions. Until he concluded by asking whether there was anything in his story, even if they believed it whole-heartedly, which would justify a verdict of manslaughter or self-defence? Emily Kaye was said to be strong and athletic. But was there any ground for saying that without a deadly weapon at hand Mahon's life was in such danger that he was justified in killing her in order to save himself?

From Patrick Mahon's lips there came a bitter and defiant protest as the death sentence was about to be pronounced. "I am too conscious of the bitterness and unfairness of the summing up," he said, and as he was led away it was seen that the artificial sun tan with which he had hoped to impress the Court, was not proof against the deathly pallor that had spread over his hands and features. He had a colour perhaps, appropriate to the awful history of his acquaintanceship with poor Emily Kaye who was starved of romance: he was yellow.

"Man of Prey," the Press called him while giving attention to the fact that his previous record was not revealed in court until after the death sentence, to the astonishment of the Judicial Observer from America. They called him the most remarkable criminal who had ever stood in an English dock: But when Curtis-Bennett, after the failure of the appeal at which he was not called upon to argue, and the execution in September, looked back upon his own part in the trial of Patrick Mahon, he thought of him only with loathing as the most callous and brutal murderer he had ever known.

One last macabre detail marked the final moment of Mahon's existence. He was "doubly hanged." It seemed that he had a certain amount of knowledge of the procedure of the executioner. He knew that his feet must stand within two chalk marks as the rope was adjusted round his neck. He knew that immediately after the fixing of the hood, the executioner would move swiftly to a lever and cause the platform on which he stood to swing away from under him. As he sensed that Pierrepoint moved to the lever, Mahon jerked his bound feet forward in a wild attempt to place them on the stationary part of the platform. At that moment the lever was pulled and his body swung back, the base of the spine striking with terrific force against the sharp edge of the platform. That blow killed him, and half a second later the spine was again broken at the neck by the jerk of the rope.

Now Sir Henry's evenings were occupied with a new brief which had come into his chambers. The brief was for the Crown against John Norman Holmes Thorne, a young poultry farmer who was charged with the murder of a typist. It was said that Marshall Hall had been approached to defend him, but he returned the brief since he was still occupied in the famous Dennistoun case. As well as being again at the Lewes Assizes, several features of the case were very similar to those of the Mahon trial. Mr. Cassels, K.C., was once again defending the prisoner; there were the same grim exhibits and the same gruesome evidence concerning the cutting up of a body; once more three thousand members of the public applied for admittance to a court which accommodated only fifty. But on the bench was a judge who was experiencing his first murder trial—Mr. Justice Finlay.

The trial began on March 11th, and Curtis outlined the grim and dramatic narrative of a young man who was being driven into marriage. Norman Thorne was a religiously minded man, a Sunday school teacher and Band of Hope preacher, and also belonged to the "Alliance of Honour." In 1921 he was "walking out" with a girl named Elsie Cameron. In 1922 he started a poultry farm at Crowborough. That Christmas the couple became engaged. The next year it appears that they anticipated the wedding ceremony and became on the most intimate terms, Miss Cameron staying at the little hut which was Norman's home on the poultry farm. The girl, according to the young man who now stood in the dock, was the more passionate of the two: "I persuaded her to join the 'Alliance of Honour' because she was growing very passionate," Thorne said. The young man's life was further complicated by a fascination exerted over him by another young woman who lived actually in Crowborough, one Elizabeth ———, and as his passion for Elizabeth grew, the fascination of Elsie died. Elsie appreciated the position immediately and wrote to her fiancé: "Please arrange about getting married as soon as possible. Things will soon be noticeable to everybody."

Elsie, it will be seen, was employing a ruse to force her young man into marriage. Although she was now a member of the "Alliance of Honour," that did not prevent her from attempting the most cowardly and most ancient of all deceits: she was telling Norman that she was about to become a mother. In the most tragic circumstances, this was proved to be false.

She knew all about Elizabeth and wrote: "You say you did not know last week what you know now, so am I to take it that you have got this other girl into the same condition as you have me? Oh! Norman, you have broken my heart. I expect you to marry me and finish with the other girl and as soon as possible. My baby must have a name and another thing, I love you in spite of all. Oh! you have deceived me; my heart is really broken."

Elsie Cameron was highly strung and nervous, liable to hysteria, and frequently ill from mental strain. And it was to calm her that Norman Thorne eventually told her he would agree to marry her. On December 5th, however, she was not satisfied that he was making any preparations to carry out his promise. She announced that she was coming to his hut, to stay there until she was made "an honest woman." Now there is perhaps little doubt that when Elsie wrote that letter to Thorne, she was convinced that she was pregnant. It was not the first time that she had had the same fears. Moreover, the periods of doubt made her ultranervous and hysterical, and it is worth while noting that the majority of women who commit suicide do so during their menstrual periods. But the medical evidence—by no means emphasized during the trial—was to the effect that during that evening, Elsie Cameron must have realized that her fears were once again incorrect. She was not going to have a baby, and she knew it. The threat with which she had tried to bludgeon Norman Thorne into marrying her (probably in honest apprehension) was gone; there was now no reason why he should marry her and cut loose from his association with her rival.

It has been said that perhaps Elsie knew this before she ever arrived at the chicken farm. Almost certainly she must have known when Thorne told her that he had already made an appointment to meet Elizabeth that night. And there naturally occurred a scene in the confined quarters of the hut, possibly a violent scene, with Elsie standing with her back to the door, pleading with her lover not to desert her for a rival in this her hour of need.

But the truth of that encounter will never be known. Norman kept his appointment, leaving behind him the hysterical, tragically minded, and jealous young woman who had just discovered that she had lost her power of threatening the man she wished to call husband.

On December 7th, Thorne wrote a letter addressed to Elsie Cameron: "My own darling Elsie—Where did you get to yesterday? I went to Groombridge but you didn't turn up. I suppose you were detained unexpectedly. . . ."

But the letter was not delivered to Elsie, for she had not been seen again at home; and she was never again seen alive. The search for her began, for Thorne was saying that, as his letter showed, he had not seen her at all. He appeared to be perfectly frank with the police and anxious to help them, and on December 18th he went to Crowborough police station and asked if there were any further developments. The police told him that people had seen Elsie walking towards his hut, and asked for permission to search the place. He readily gave it, but they could find no trace whatever of Miss Cameron. But on January 15th, the police were more suspicious and began to dig in the chicken run. A few feet under the ground they found parts of her body, dismembered with a saw. Norman Thorne then told the police that Elsie had indeed come to his hut and had committed suicide by hanging herself on a beam while he had gone out to keep an appointment with Elizabeth. He was arrested, and the police asked him to demonstrate exactly what he had found when he returned to the hut. He pointed to a crossbeam and said he had walked in to find her suspended by a piece of string knotted tightly round her neck. He had cut her down hastily and carried her to a mattress. She was not dead when he found her; but as he staggered across the room and collapsed with her on the mattress, she died. The realization that had come to Mahon now struck Norman Thorne with equal strength. He was dazed and nearly out of his mind. He rushed out of the hut with the intention of getting a doctor's help. But the night air brought with it the chill dread that he would be immediately accused of murder. He stayed throughout the night in an agony of despair, and at dawn his mind was made up. He cut the body to pieces and dug a shallow grave.

The body was buried again at Willesden. On February 4th, however, another post-mortem examination was made by Sir Bernard Spilsbury and Dr. Bronté. Sir Bernard was to be called by the Crown: Dr. Bronté by the defence. These two experts had formed different opinions, and were to give in court precisely opposite views of the circumstances in which Elsie Cameron had died.

Curtis outlined the case for the Crown as being that Elsie had become a nuisance to Thorne because of his affection for the other girl. "That evening of December 5th, Thorne murdered Elsie Cameron, and having murdered her he cut up her body and disposed of it. From that time he told lies continually until finally when the body was found, he made a statement."

Mr. Cassels had prepared a magnificent defence. He was fortunate in having an opinion from Dr. Bronté, the great pathologist, that was favourable to his case. He proceeded to prove by cross-examination that Elsie Cameron was a girl of highly nervous temperament and had previously threatened to commit suicide. He put it that, though she was wrong, she sincerely believed she was pregnant, and he was able to produce witnesses who spoke of quite serious illnesses she had suffered as a result of her nerves. The police were not satisfied with Thorne's explanation of the hanging of Elsie. There were no marks on the beams such as would have been made by a string. And Sir Bernard Spilsbury said in reply to Curtis that there were no marks on Elsie's neck that signified she had been hanged. Mr. Cassels was suggesting that there was an attempt at hanging, and that the body was cut down before death, Elsie dying from shock immediately after being cut down. "Were there creases on Elsie's neck?" asked Mr. Cassels. Sir Bernard replied that there were normal creases in the skin. This was the vital point of the defence, and Mr. Cassels promised to bring Dr. Bronté and several other medical witnesses to say that those creases were not natural and were consistent with the pressure of a rope upon the neck. Microscopical slides had been made showing the pressing of minute blood vessels. "The challenge of the defence," said Mr. Cassels, "is that those slides from that part of the neck prove the case of Norman Thorne. If you think that there was some crushing of the neck, my submission is that that must mean a verdict of acquittal. . . ."

In the witness box Thorne conducted himself well and told his story without emotion. He had to tell how he had divided the body, and what he had thought in those terrible hours while he determined on the attempt to conceal a tragedy. "I flung myself on the bed and I cried like a baby," he said. "I realized the awful end that neurasthenia had brought her to. I realized the terrible position in which I was placed, and thought of suicide myself. I made a big effort to pull myself together. I succeeded."

What was there to support this story? It has been suggested that in her nervous state, Elsie Cameron staged a "sham suicide" as a last resort to terrify and perhaps convince her lover of her devotion. Her plan was that when he came into the hut, he should find her hanging, and, shocked at the consequences of his callousness, would revive her and protest his love again for this poor, frightened creature who had tried to kill herself rather than live without him. With this end in view, Elsie, according to this theory, prepared the grim masquerade. She tied the loop in the rope, set the chair ready to be kicked away when she heard Thorne's footsteps, and steeled herself to carry out the dangerous experiment. And then—then the sham suicide had ended as many such adventures end. She had reckoned without her own clumsiness and dangerous state of nerves; perhaps she kicked the chair away too early; perhaps the tension had acted on her nervous system so as to impair her accuracy. And when Thorne came in, she was dead or near to death.

Thorne himself, in a letter to his parents, put forward this theory. "What prompted her to come to Crowborough for some very sudden reason? Was it not that she was experiencing the first indications that something was on the way. . . . What was her state of mind when I left her—she might have done any mad thing if she suddenly realised she would not be married. . . ."

Certainly, Elsie's ambitions were exclusively devoted to being a wife. She was an ineffective, frail, inconsequential girl, with a record of lost jobs behind her, with very little opportunity of obtaining security. She was content even to share the hopeless squalor of Thorne's hut, the uninspiring life of a chicken farmer whose debts were accumulating.

Thorne's ordeal really began when, after lunch on the third day of the trial, Curtis stood up to cross-examine.

"On the morning of December 5th," began Curtis, "which of these two girls you were in love with did you desire to marry?"

The question was one of terrible difficulty. It was a typical opening query of Sir Henry's. Apparently unimportant, it was surprising enough to shake the equanimity of any man facing Curtis across the court. If Thorne had said he wanted to marry Elizabeth, then he had admitted a reason for wishing Elsie out of the way. If he had said Elsie, then he would also have admitted a further series of lies in his letters to Elizabeth. Thorne made perhaps the only answer: "Well, I don't know I was particularly desirous of marrying either just at that time."

Another question of Sir Henry's caused Thorne to pause in contemplation of his own predicament. Thorne had said Elsie knew he would marry her if she were pregnant, and when he went out that night she believed he would keep his promise.

"Then why did she commit suicide?" asked Curtis quietly.

Thorne: "Why? She left no message behind and I don't think it is safe for me to say."

But the real battle was between the expert pathologists. One of those called by Mr. Cassels said he thought Sir Bernard Spilsbury was very skilled: "But if I may say so—a trifle dogmatic."

Dr. Bronté differed completely from Sir Bernard Spilsbury in his opinion of the injuries. Sir Bernard was certain that Elsie had died from bruises. Dr. Bronté said Sir Bernard had not examined the marks microscopically as he had done: "The cause of death was partial hanging with ensuing shock."

Sir Henry was not happy about the trial. Dr. Bronté and the other medical experts had made a most impressive showing for the defence, and he could see that Mr. Cassels had, with his customary skill, pieced together a very credible narrative which was supported by the evidence obtained during the cross-examination. Sir Henry had done something towards shaking the testimony of these experts, but he was not satisfied. There appeared to be a complete stalemate, and everything depended upon which of the experts was believed by the jury. Before adjourning on the Saturday afternoon, the Judge suggested that three of the medical experts should meet on the Sunday with the object of comparing the microscopic slides which each had prepared. And over the week-end Curtis was engaged in long deliberations with his associates, and on the Monday, after obtaining leave to recall Sir Bernard Spilsbury, he introduced a new point that greatly strengthened his case.

In a statement to the police, Thorne had said that when he returned to the hut to see the body of Miss Cameron the eyes were "puckered up." "Assuming unconsciousness had intervened at that time, if not death, I just want to find out from you what would have been the condition of the eyes," said Curtis.

"There would be no puckering," said Sir Bernard. "The eyes would not be completely closed or completely open."

And once again Sir Bernard Spilsbury was emphatic that the string said to have been used by a suicidal Elsie Cameron would not have caused the creases in her neck. Mr. Cassels put one of his experts into the box, and the position was one of stalemate once again.

Now there was a further point, of value to the defence, in this theory of the creases in the dead girl's neck. Thorne had taken some pains to enclose the severed head in a tin can before burial. Why did he do this, knowing that through this move it was likely that the head—the part that would most clearly identify Elsie Cameron—would be preserved better through the years? One theory has it that Thorne was anxious that if the worst came to the worst, and his crime were discovered, he could point to the creases in the neck, in the well-preserved head, and declare that Elsie had committed suicide by hanging. Moreover, it seems that he took similar pains in the decapitation of the body to preserve the neck. He did not slice off the head in the usual manner; he cut down towards the collar bone, making a V-shape of the head. The task took him considerable time—and it cannot be supposed that he would delay his grim business unless he had a very good reason. He always insisted that those marks proved his case, and it may have been that the marks were indeed made on Elsie's neck by a rope—but after she was dead, Thorne trying to manufacture evidence that would substantiate his story.

It should not be forgotten that the medical experts who testified that the marks on poor Elsie's neck were from the pressure of a rope, were men of renown. They were convinced of the circumstance that a rope had been in contact with the dead girl, and that it might have caused death. Dr. Robert Bronté, for instance, the great pathologist, said that while the naked-eye appearance of the marks would give no evidence of hanging, his microscopic slides led him to the opinion that "they were consistent with pressure of a rope around the neck between two grooves." "I should not have expected to make these discoveries if these had been natural creases or grooves," he said. "A rope would certainly produce that effect. . . . In my opinion the cause of death was shock following an unsuccessful or interrupted effort of self-strangulation. . . . My experience is, of people jumping over bridges and intending to drown themselves, and not dying from drowning but dying from shock—immediate shock. I have had experience of cases of attempted hanging producing death from shock. One case was of a man who had the rope tied round his neck and was dead before he had time to tie the second knot on the rope. . . . All my experience teaches me that death may be sought in one way and actually acquired in another."

Curtis-Bennett cross-examined Dr. Bronté on that point. Handing him the piece of string with which, according to Thorne, Elsie had tried to hang herself, he asked whether it was possible that, after suspending from that thin piece of cord, the marks could disappear after death within a quarter of an hour. Dr. Bronté said it was possible.

"If your hypothetical case is correct, Thorne must have come in just before death?" asked Sir Henry. "And otherwise the whole of your case falls to the ground?" Dr. Bronté agreed that this was so.

It seemed that the verdict must be upon the medical evidence alone, and Mr. Cassels, in his address to the jury, recalled that he had warned them that the issue might depend on a microscopical slide. "Was I far wrong?" he asked. "What a tragedy of human justice it would be if the life of a man is to depend on the accuracy or fallibility of one individual! We can all admire attainment, take our hats off to ability, acknowledge the high position that a man has won in his sphere, but it is a long way to go if you have to say that because that man says one thing, there can be no room for error."

The layman, reading the case, might be excused for expressing wonderment at the situation. The prosecution stated that Elsie died from bruises inflicted on the head with an Indian club. The defence asserted that she died from the shock after partial asphyxiation by hanging, and accounted for the bruises by saying that Thorne stumbled with her and accidentally bruised her in falling. The doctors could not agree whether or not she had indeed suffered at all from a rope or string being drawn round her neck.

Naturally, therefore, Curtis was worried. In his address for the Crown he commented on the evidence which had tended to show that Elsie had suicidal tendencies. "If one went back into the lives of most people, I wonder whether one would not be able to find some such incidents as have been pointed out to you in this case. What motive had she that night to commit suicide? Thorne had a strong motive, and you must remember that the man who said his nerves were so affected by the sight of the hanging girl, was shortly afterwards to dismember the body. . . . I submit that on the evidence you have listened to in the last four days, no reasonable man could doubt that Elsie Cameron did *not* die as a result of suicide but died as a result of murder."

The Judge said there was no doubt that Norman Thorne was between two fires. Could they say that Elsie actually had suicidal tendencies? Were Thorne's actions consistent with innocence? "Your verdict should be based on a fair dispassionate consideration of the evidence. If, after considering it alike for prosecution and defence, your minds remain in doubt, then the prisoner is entitled to be acquitted."

None could say that Mr. Justice Finlay had favoured either the prosecution or the defence by this summing-up, but the jury were absent only half an hour before pronouncing a virdict of "Guilty." And when Mr. Cassels, who had now been joined by Mr. Jowitt, K.C., appealed for the life of Thorne on April 7th, their Lordships did not call upon Counsel for the Crown to argue. An appeal was also made for the appointment of a special medical commissioner to consider the question of the bruises on Elsie Cameron's body. Mr. Jowitt said that there had never been a stronger case for using the Act of 1907 which provided that a judge might be guided in scientific matters by a skilled medical assessor. But the Lord Chief Justice remarked that the unanimity of twelve jurymen was convincing, and when, on the second day, their Lordships gave their decision, it was a refusal of the application. There was no ground whatever for the suggestion in the present case that the jury failed to appreciate the conflicting views put before them in the medical and surgical aspects of the case.

The *Law Journal* reported that in the legal profession there was regret and profound disquiet at the result of the appeal. "The verdict of the Jury on a question of pathology is valueless," it said: "Thorne is entitled to feel that he has been condemned by a tribunal which was not capable of forming first hand judgment, but followed the man with the biggest name."

Thorne was hanged. Curtis, while he was convinced that justice had been done, knew that but for his earnest hours of thought during that vital week-end, his friend "Jimmy" Cassels might have brought off one of the greatest victories of the decade.

But in the little hut where Thorne lived, the police, on searching, found something of no little interest—many newspaper cuttings of the Mahon trial. . . .

Chapter Fifteen

WHEN CURTIS TALKED

WHEN Curtis talked about "the finest profession in the world," it was to give a review of the work of a barrister which would serve as a valuable and complete survey of the profession. He spoke well, enthusiastically, and at length on the subject with a fund of human understanding and a wit that made it possible to listen to him with intense pleasure. One of the questions asked of him by his nonlegal friends was the inevitable one that is put to all barristers. It runs: "How on earth can you possibly put heart into the defence of a man whom you know to be guilty?"

The answer, said Curtis, was extremely simple. He never did. If a client came to him saying he was guilty he would reply: "I cannot put before a court a defence which I know to be untrue. But it is my duty to relate any mitigating features there may be in your case in an endeavour to induce the Judge to pass upon you a more lenient sentence than he would otherwise do."

Sometimes the client was thunder-struck and said: "I thought lawyers were there for me to tell them the truth, and for them to get me out of my troubles." But if, in spite of saying he was guilty, the client insisted on a plea of "Not guilty," then Curtis told him he must seek another counsel. "And if you wish to be defended on a plea of 'Not guilty,'" he advised, "don't tell him you are guilty."

A complementary question equally inevitable was: "But surely you, as a man of the world and not as a barrister, don't swallow all the stories you are told." Curtis would reply: "It's not our duty to judge the man. It is our duty to see that he is not convicted unless there is proper evidence against him. It is for the Court to say whether or not he is guilty. To quote the best simile, we are like taxis on a rank. We are merely hired *to put a client's case before the Court,* but of course, we must not knowingly allow the Court to be misled, we being ourselves officers of the Court. It is not our duty to invent a defence: we deal with facts as we are told them—but there are cases where a client is charged with an offence which is complicated in law and there might well be a doubt as to whether he has committed an offence or not. Therefore, even if a client says he is guilty we *are* entitled to make the prosecution prove the case. In order to effect this, we must plead 'Not guilty' and listen to the evidence. At the end we may submit that there is no evidence to go to the jury that our client has committed the offence, and if the Judge is with us there will be an acquittal. But if he is not with us, and decides that the case must go to the jury, then we cannot be a party to putting up a defence which we know to be untrue. I should say, 'I call no evidence, m'Lord,' and let the Judge sum up and the jury decide as to whether the evidence has been sufficient."

To some this sounded like a strange exposition of a barrister's duties; but Curtis claimed it was perfectly logical. "Suppose," he said, "a man comes to me with a story of innocence and I say to him, 'well, I don't think I believe your story, and I am not prepared to put it before a Court.' That man would be deprived of the services of a barrister he wanted to defend him solely because of my personal opinion. I should indeed be taking to myself the functions of a jury."

This, then, was the simple test he applied, in order to show the logic of the barrister's position. He developed that theme many times in his career for the benefit of members of the lay-public who confessed that they had always been confused by this point. Other matters of which he used to talk were of greater interest to the legal profession itself, and on these matters he had a common-sense attitude that was of benefit to dozens of young men who looked up to him as a kindly adviser. When he called it the finest profession in the world, he did so with a personal knowledge of the risks and disadvantages which cannot be excluded. "You are absolute master of yourself," he said. "You have no regular office hours, and theoretically you can take your holidays when you want them. But only theoretically. You must be prepared to sacrifice or postpone a holiday at a moment's notice, and you are at the beck and call of a telephone. Further, you are absolutely dependent upon your health, for few people realize the physical strain of a day in court, consultations when you return to chambers in the late afternoon, and long hours into the night when you are reading up the next day's work: One day of illness and you are losing not only the work but the money. Other people have to do your work, and a reputation for being a doubtful starter is very hard to live down. But there are days when a case falls through or a defendant is ill, and you find yourself with an afternoon free. Those days are as pleasant as afternoons stolen by a truant schoolboy—far more exciting than holidays prearranged and long thought over."

Curtis himself had been very fortunate. He appreciated that he had received a number of complimentary briefs from firms such as Freke Palmer as a result of his father already being a magistrate. Many other young men have waited years for such briefs; there are a thousand pathetically briefless barristers in practice—many of them with brilliant scholastic careers behind them, who obtained their degrees at Oxford or Cambridge with high honours. But these complimentary briefs have their disadvantage, for many people are apt to say that they have been secured only because of the family name, and in addition they come at a time when perhaps the young barrister is less able to do the work than at any other time in his career. The solicitor may have a great admiration for the family name; but, first and foremost, he must consider his clients, and if they suffer materially, the solicitor will find himself abandoned in favour of another. "Of course it's all a leap in the dark when you come to the Bar," said Curtis. "But the Bar confers the greatest prizes in the world. There is nothing that is not within the reach of those who scale the heights of the legal profession—a judgeship, the Lord Chief Justiceship of England, the Lord Chancellorship, a Cabinet position, premiership, the Viceroyalty of India. For the not-so-successful, county court judgeships, Metropolitan police-court magistracies, and judgeships abroad and in the colonies. Great prizes indeed, but only to be acquired after years of hard work of the most exacting kind."

Early in his career Curtis was given to understand that for the asking he could have been made one of the Treasury Counsel at the Old Bailey, that is to say, one of the counsel whom the Director of Public Prosecutions instructs to present his cases. An income of nearly a thousand a year is assured to a junior Treasury Counsel. That certainly would have meant a great deal to Curtis in his younger days. But with much trepidation he declined to enter for the post, since it would mean losing the greater part of his defending practice. It was a most important decision and, as it proved, a wise one. The leaders of the Bar whose names are familiar to the public today may have appeared in some of the more sensational criminal cases, but they were not like Curtis, appearing every day of their lives in criminal cases. Edward Marjoribanks makes it quite plain, in the admirable biography of Marshall Hall, that his earnings at the Criminal Bar were a fraction of his total income. He made the rest of his money in the big cases in the Law Courts in the Strand.

In 1914, a year after his father's death, Curtis had refused another tempting offer—that of the position of a Metropolitan Magistrate. The post carried with it an income of £1,500 a year, and with his wife's income, Curtis could have been comfortably established for the rest of his life. He would never have lived to enjoy the increase in salary up to £2,000 a year as it is now, but it is curious to look back on the possibility of his sitting as a Magistrate to the end of his life.

At one stage in his career at the Bar, but at a time when his name was becoming well known, he thought of the position of Chief Commissioner of the Metropolitan Police. Sir Edward Henry was likely to retire, and to some of his friends Curtis mentioned that he would like the post. Cassels said to him: "Can you ride a horse?" Curtis had not thought of that. The idea did not get any further.

Members of the Old Bailey Bar, before rebuilding took place in 1907, were slightly looked down upon by their brethren in the High Courts in the Strand. Their methods of advocacy were not always in accordance with the highest traditions of the Bar, but with the modernization of the actual building, there came also an improvement in the standard of advocacy and etiquette. Men like Horace Avory, Charles Gill, Richard Muir, Travers Humphreys, and Curtis were leaders of that change, and today the Old Bailey Bar and its members enjoy an equal distinction with others of their craft. But still there persisted for many years an air of superiority among young men who knew no better, and who affected to despise the Criminal Bar. This drove Curtis to anger. "How is it possible for anybody to be interested in the least," he said, "as to whether one company pays another company a sum of money? That is the bulk of the litigation in the High Courts. But at the Criminal Bar we see life: We are defending or prosecuting people who might go to prison and who might be hanged. The liberty of the subject, life and death, these are everyday matters to us. We deal with real human stuff, the drama of life itself: there is no satisfaction like that of winning a case in which there are concerned men and women of flesh and blood."

Indeed, one of his greatest treasures was a bundle of some

four or five hundred letters from clients whom he had defended: All expressed their thanks and their appreciation.

But Curtis came across advocates who said in a superior way: "I don't care for coming to the Old Bailey, and I shan't come again."

"Well, I hope you keep your promise," Curtis would reply. Sure enough, at the next Session, provided the opportunity and the fee were there, these "superior" advocates would make an appearance.

Curtis took a pride and a real delight in every detail of the old-fashioned ceremonial and custom of the Law. Just as he enjoyed the cosmopolitan life of a great restaurant, the activity and the efficiency of a railway station, and the camaraderie of the House of Commons smoking room, so he enjoyed the formal invitations of the Sheriffs of the City of London when the Central Criminal Court was in session and the hospitality of the Bar Mess when he was on a circuit. He was an ardent supporter of every survival of that etiquette which dated from another age when transport through England was more of a problem. The circuit system survived from the days when the judges and counsel set out from London on horseback to various circuit towns to dispense justice.

Those members of the Bar who had influence in any particular county would join the circuit of which that county was a part. Hence it came about that lawyers banded themselves together into circuits to deal with the various areas of the country. Owing to the difficulties of transport they were rarely interchangeable. It is for that reason that, even today, a defendant who is due to appear at an Assize town, cannot brief a barrister outside the circuit without paying a special fee of 100 guineas, for a leader, or 50 for a junior, in addition to the brief fee, which is rarely less than a similar amount. Curtis was frequently briefed "off his circuit"—one of the greatest compliments that can be paid to a barrister. He became guest of the Mess of the circuit and, far from the strain of

London, free from the worry of arranging the next day's plans, he was able to spend restful periods at his hotel and enjoy the experience of making new friends. He afterwards repaid the hospitality shown him by sending a case of champagne to the Bar Mess as is the custom. He travelled many thousands of miles throughout England in the course of these special briefs; they were some of the most enjoyable experiences of his legal career.

In his first chambers, Curtis had for his clerk Sam Humphreys, a great character at the Bar, at one time a judge at the Dunmow Flitch Trial, and well known as a mimic who used to imitate Curtis behind his back almost to perfection. He was followed by John Winckworth, who had been clerk to Sir Richard Muir. Winckworth died shortly after entering his service, and he was followed by Hollis, former chief clerk to Sir Travers Humphreys, who had been elevated to the Bench. When Curtis left Plowden Buildings, where he had been for over twenty years, to go over the road to No. 1, Temple Gardens, he and Hollis remained as close personal friends to the end of Curtis's life.

Hollis had been well known as one of the best clerks in the Temple. Curtis was fortunate to have secured his services, for a clerk can go a long way towards forging the success of his principal, just as a bad clerk can contribute to his ruination. The clerk is the tactful, intelligent and confidential adviser and friend. There is no known training for such a job, although the duties demanded of him are such that require all the virtues. He must be an expert organizer, and a courteous and methodically-minded guardian of his principal's interests. It is perhaps not surprising, therefore, that many barristers' clerks make more money than some barristers, and in the Temple today there are several members of that efficient profession who have large houses of their own and luxurious motor cars. By usage, no solicitor can approach a barrister except through his clerk. Theoretically, the barrister is only "rewarded by an honorarium" and no discussion takes place about the fee between barrister and solicitor. It is only when the clerk has dispensed with these mundane matters that a conference is arranged between the barrister, the solicitor and the client.

But this is only a part of the clerk's work. Often enough he has several barristers in his chambers whose work he must arrange: he must communicate with the clerks of various Courts to ensure that his principal's programme for the day's work shall not clash; he must ask many favours of Court officials, and must be certain that while asking for fees which reflect glory on his master, he does not drive away solicitors with their clients' purses as their first consideration. Small wonder then, that a good clerk is a prize beyond purchase: and that from all the junior clerks who begin work in chambers by answering the telephone, there arises only now and again a genius who can claim all the virtues, and call himself the most valuable adviser of a famous Counsel.

The most characteristic picture of Curtis that remains is the memory of him standing in the Mess Room of the Old Bailey surrounded by young barristers. Curtis was always invited to lunch with the sheriffs and the judges, but before the end of the luncheon adjournment he would join his more humble brethren and stand against a coffee trolley, smoking one of his long cigars. The best stories would be heard round Curtis; he joked with everyone, knew by name everyone he had ever met before. It seemed that he had not a care in the world, though perhaps throughout the morning he had been engaged in a long and bitter battle in court. There would be but a few moments of conversation round the trolley. Then at the last possible moment he would walk towards the court, pause a moment at the door, take a last regretful puff before throwing away his cigar, and stride impressively into court to do battle again.

He timed these entrances perfectly. At the beginning of a

case his clerk would enter carrying his brief, a number of coloured pencils, and a little box containing Sir Henry's favourite lozenges and place them on the desk nearest to the dock: A moment after he entered there would be a stir in court and men and women would nudge one another and whisper his name.

These young men who listened to stories, most of them against himself, learnt also a great deal from his methods. In the old days, some prosecuting counsel at the Old Bailey were a bullying and loud-voiced lot. But Curtis was a member of that company which changed the methods of the cross-examination and established a new reputation for the Old Bailey. He did not believe in shock tactics; he believed in putting a witness at his ease, sometimes too much at his ease. The witness would see rise in front of him the figure of a man whose reputation he already knew. But in a few moments he would lose his fear and his guardedness under the influence of a few gently spoken questions. Curtis wanted him to think: "Here is a nice, kind gentleman, much kinder than the other man who has been asking questions on the other side; he only wants me to tell what I know of the case." The answers would come quite freely; but after a little time that suave enquiring voice would harden, and the witness would realize that an all-important question was coming to which there could be—as a natural consequence—only one reply—the reply he least wished to give.

"The art of cross-examination," said Curtis, "is not necessarily to know what to ask, but to know what *not* to ask. It is quite easy to ask a long series of questions in an angry tone and to think it is getting you somewhere. The real art is never to ask a question unless you know the answer beforehand. Sometimes you have to take a chance, but even then it is often possible by careful approach to get an idea of the answer before the question is asked. And it may even happen that you decide after all to move to another line of enquiry. If you can't catch a witness out in half an hour or so, you never will. You can cross-examine a truthful witness all day, and the only result will be that he is telling the truth more obviously at the end of your efforts than when you began. There is also the common mistake of putting one question too many in order to emphasize a good point: You should be satisfied with nearly establishing your point: If you try to obtain a more emphatic answer, you may find the witness has had time to think, and you will get an answer that will destroy all the good you have achieved."

In Sir Henry's entire career, the nearest he ever came to an open disagreement with a prominent judge was during the hearing of the Hayley Morriss trial. Curtis was briefed for Mrs. Morriss, the pretty young wife of the owner of Pippingford Park; having formerly been his housekeeper, she had married her employer shortly before the case. They were to be tried together. But on the 12th of December, 1925, Curtis, having received certain instructions, stood up to ask Mr. Justice Avory for a postponement until the next sessions. Last August, he said, his client became in a certain condition, and her medical advisers were sent for, since there were symptoms of a miscarriage. "She is in a serious condition of health, and her doctor will tell the Court that it would be impossible for her to stand her trial for three weeks at least."

But when the doctor gave evidence, he was closely questioned by Sir Edward Marshall Hall, who appeared for the Crown. Did the doctor know that he was only called in after the committal to the Assizes? Did he know the legal advisors? And the Judge asked if he knew that Mrs. Morriss had recently been seen in the town? Sir Edward wanted an independent examination of Mrs. Morriss, and the Judge agreed. "I will then consider whether the trial ought to proceed . . ."

Hayley Morriss, who was anxious that the trial should not be postponed if it could be helped, was defended by Curtis-Bennett's old friends Roland Oliver and St. John Hutchinson.

On the following Monday, when the names of both the defendants were called, Mrs. Morriss was present. She had walked over from the local hotel, pale and weakly.

"Do you wish to hear the report of the medical expert appointed to examine her?" asked Marshall Hall.

The Judge: "The fact that she has surrendered is the best answer to any question on that subject. She is here."

Sir Henry was on his feet. "Before the trial I wish you to hear the medical evidence of two of her doctors," he said. "I submit it is not a question whether or not this woman could be brought to the court, but whether or not she is in a fit condition to undergo a long trial and a considerable period in the witness box. On those two questions, which I submit the Court will have to determine, I certainly require to call the medical men."

This was a strong way of putting his point. The Judge was very stern and emphatic as he replied: "I decline to hear the evidence. In my opinion there has been a deliberate attempt already to deceive the Court in this case, and I am not sure that there may not have been something worse—conspiracy to defeat the ends of justice. The defendant is here, and the case must now proceed. If she requires medical attention she will receive it quite as well here as if she were not in this Court."

Curtis had difficulty in concealing his indignation.

"In view of the circumstances, I submit that evidence should go before the Judge as to the condition of the girl. A medical man of repute has stated on oath that in his view it would be dangerous to the health of this girl to attend and stand her trial."

The Judge: "Sir Henry, I have decided this matter. I must decline to hear you further."

Sir Henry: "Your Lordship will at any rate allow me, on her behalf, to protest against that being done without the evidence which I have in my possession being produced."

The Judge: "I have heard your protest. I must assume that you were deceived by the instructions you received. I have not been equally deceived. There is an end to the question."

Sir Henry: "May I say that neither Sir Travers Humphreys [his junior] nor myself consider that we were deceived by the evidence which was put before us."

This, then, was the dramatic opening to a case which attracted large crowds of would-be spectators to struggle for admission. Curtis was never able to call that evidence, and the young wife stood her trial, a wan and slim figure in the dock.

And again the castigating tongue of Mr. Justice Avory was heard when he summed up. Of Mrs. Morriss he said: "I am still satisfied that she was, if she desired, fit to give evidence on oath."

Curtis bitterly resented the way he had been treated by the Judge. He believed that someone had falsely told Mr. Justice Avory that Mrs. Morriss or her advisor was anxious to find a reason for taking the case away from that Judge, and that Mrs. Morriss had been seen in the town recently. It must be clear that something of the sort happened, for it is astonishing that Mr. Justice Avory, who knew the work and was fond of both Sir Henry and Sir Travers Humphreys, should insinuate, if not actually say, that such distinguished members of the Bar had been party to a false application. It was not a false application, and Counsel had come down specially to make it the week before the trial started so as to give the Court fair warning. Had it been a false application, it would have been much easier to appear on the day of the trial without Mrs. Morriss.

One of Sir Henry's most remarkable murder cases was one in which the accused, while in jail awaiting trial, wrote a letter to his sweetheart describing how he had committed the crime. This was told during the trial of two soldiers, Ian Maxwell Stewart and John Lincoln, for the murder of

Edward Richards, a commercial traveller, at Trowbridge on Christmas Eve. Both had pleaded not guilty at the police court proceedings. But while in prison, Lincoln asked if he might write a letter. He did not trouble to read the prison regulations, which were to the effect that unsealed letters were read by the officials. He gave his letter to a warder with the envelope open. The authorities read a full description of how he had committed the crime.

Curtis was appearing for Stewart, and at the close of the case for the prosecution, applied successfully for the discharge of his client. Both men had been engaged in the burglary during which the unfortunate Richards was shot dead, and counsel for the Crown maintained that if Stewart knew that his friend was armed, then Stewart too was guilty of murder. The Judge, however, agreed with Curtis that there was now no proof against Stewart, and directed the jury to discharge him, though he was rearrested on the charge of robbery with violence; the next day the Crown offered no evidence on that count, and he was again released, to be rearrested on another charge.

The murder was callous and futile, for one of the most trivial reasons in the history of violence in this country. For these two young soldiers, after drinking a considerable amount of liquor on that ill-starred night, had entered the house of Richards, where they thought there was likely to be a large sum of money. Lincoln had a gun and some ammunition. When they entered the house, they could find no money, but drank half a bottle of brandy and left; as soon as they were outside, they returned to fetch two bottles of beer. And according to Lincoln's letter, those two bottles of beer caused the murder of Richards, who returned and surprised them at that moment. Richards was armed. It is possible that he fired first at the dim shape of the intruder who was passing through a door; and as he fired, he was killed by a blaze of rapid fire from his unseen assailant. "You have only to keep the trigger pressed and the bullets fire automatically," wrote Lincoln.

His counsel, while protesting at the conduct of the prison authorities in omitting to warn Lincoln that his unsealed letters would be read, could do little for him save to draw from him the admission that he was drunk at the time of the murder.

"Drunkenness, or the effect of liquor, is no defence whatever in a case of this kind," said the Judge, and the jury took only fifteen minutes in which to come to a decision of "Guilty."

A curious incident occurred before the case. Stewart's father was said to be well-known in the theatrical profession, and attempts were made to collect money for a defence fund with which to brief Curtis. When, however, a famous actress was giving a donation to an equally well-known man in a restaurant in the Strand, the hotel detective stopped him receiving the money. But the money was collected without any other obstruction, and Curtis received a special fee since this case, heard at the Wiltshire Assizes, was off his circuit.

Chapter Sixteen

"HYDE PARK CASES"

BY THIS time Curtis had found that he had overestimated his strength when he endeavoured to combine his duties in the House of Commons with his legal work. There was also an added duty to be performed as deputy chairman of the Essex Quarter Sessions. The chairman at that time was Mr. Collingwood Hope, K.C., and apart from him there was no other with outstanding legal training.

From the first time he had taken his seat at the Quarter Sessions, it was obvious that this was but a step towards his cherished ambition of the Recordership of London. Every barrister practising at Chelmsford wished his cases to come before Curtis, to the possible annoyance of the chairman in the other court. Therefore, since he had a large licensing practice as well as criminal work in the county, his acceptance of the post involved considerable personal sacrifice.

But when he next saw his medical adviser it was to receive an ultimatum on the ground of health: Either he must give up politics, or he must give up the Bar. His answer was obvious. Politics would go by the board.

He had determined, however, to stay on in the House of Commons during the lifetime of the present Government. But while he was still deliberating, a bombshell fell into the domestic circle of his life and made it imperative for him to come to a decision. His wife intimated that she was going to divorce him.

They had been married for twenty-three years, and their children were aged twenty-two and sixteen. Curtis, however, had put himself in a position where divorce proceedings could be brought against him, as many other men have done before him. One day he received an urgent telephone message from a well-known firm of solicitors, who requested him to see them at once on a matter of the highest importance. Curtis had no idea what this could be: it was unusual for a solicitor to ask a barrister to go to his office. For a moment he imagined that another fat brief was on the way, but on a moment's reflection he realized that if this were so the solicitor would be visiting him.

He emerged from that office shaken and ill, and weighed down with worry. For perhaps the first time in his life he was powerless and helpless, for he knew that he could not answer the evidence which had been collected against him. He saw complete ruin ahead, socially and financially; but when he could think logically his paramount feeling was one of bitter regret that he should lose a wife who had worked with him and helped him through the early days, had built for him a home which ran upon oiled wheels, and had eased him in moments of anxiety with loyalty, love, and affection.

Several efforts were made by friends of the family to smooth the matter over, but without avail. And when he came to consider the more material aspects of his future, he saw only the blackest outlook. His wife had money, and Curtis had never thought it necessary to save much himself. He had not contemplated retiring for some years, and by that time, with perhaps the coveted Recordership, he could retire from the rough and tumble of the Criminal Bar and enjoy years of comparative leisure. But there was a further evil which he feared would even prevent him from maintaining the high level of his earnings. Before him there had been barristers who had passed through the divorce court; but there was none who had done so at the height of his career. Curtis feared that his practice was so personal, and solicitors perhaps were so old-fashioned, that his practice would at least be halved. He feared that he must say farewell to that hope of a judgeship: he knew that people would say he would not receive that honour because he had been through the divorce court. Fears that he would not be able to leave his family in a comfortable position assailed him, and for a time he was a man harried by doubts, in an agony of mind.

This at any rate had decided his political career. Quite legitimately he applied for the "Chiltern Hundreds" on the ground of ill-health. The coming divorce had increased tenfold the nervous strain under which he was suffering, and it was with complete frankness that he told the Conservative Central Office the immediate reason why he had decided to resign.

It is perhaps not surprising that his first reaction was a desire to forget the coming disaster. He went abroad for a long motor tour, but now even this familiar and infallible panacea failed him, and he came back still convinced that magistrates and juries and judges would think the less of him because he had been the "guilty party" in a divorce action. He sold his favourite Bentley in a fit of panic, and flung himself into his work. None of his clients knew that their brilliant defender was himself in an agony of mind, a man who felt himself destined for complete ruin.

But the crisis he feared was less serious than he had imagined. Curtis felt that everyone he met was talking about him; but in actual fact his friends were most sympathetic, and the Press was most generous in making only brief mention of the proceedings in court. His misery was further lightened by his receiving the high honour of being made a Bencher of his Inn. He was called to the Bench on November 17, 1926, the same night that his son was called to the Bar, and Mr. Justice Astbury, Treasurer of the Inn, made particular reference to this curious coincidence. His wife was in the gallery watching the proceedings, and but for the tragedy which overshadowed them the occasion would have been one of immense pleasure.

The following year his practice did indeed fall to £7,000—a considerable drop from over £10,000 and a matter of some importance to Curtis since he had always hitherto known that his budget would be increased by his wife's money.

In September, 1927, Curtis was in yet another "street offence case." A schoolmaster and a former Oxford Blue was convicted of being a rogue and vagabond and of "persistently importuning," and was sentenced to three months by Sir Chartres Biron at Bow Street. Curtis appeared with Mr. J. D. Cassels and Mr. Eustace Fulton at the London Sessions and secured a magnificent reversal of the conviction. The police evidence had been uncorroborated, and Curtis soon had a police witness contradicting himself on the time factor. "There would appear to be nothing more dangerous than for an unsuspecting person to go for a walk by himself in London," said Curtis in his address to the Court.

The Court quashed the conviction, and on Sir Henry's application gave costs to the appellant. The case received additional prominence in the Press because that very week a conviction on an almost similar charge had been reversed. Again this was the uncorroborated word of a single policeman, and the case had been heard by Mr. Mead. "How many men can spend £300 and more in defending their good name? There are scores of cases of which the general public never hear," said the Press.

In October of that year Curtis again successfully appealed against the conviction of a clerk. The sentence had been three months' hard labour but at the appeal the police evidence as to identification was torn to pieces.

The public agitation, however, come to a head during the next year, after Sir Henry had successfully represented Sir Leo Chiozza Money, former M.P. and Government servant, against a charge of indecency in Hyde Park. Sir Leo had been arrested with a young friend named Irene Savage, who was not, however, required to go into the witness box. The magistrate, Mr. Cancellor, said he had heard enough and discharged both defendants. "In cases of this sort, the police ought to take every opportunity of getting corroborative evidence," said the magistrate. "In my opinion, in this case, that opportunity was not grasped. . . . I cannot help thinking that the police officers should send their reports forthwith to headquarters. If that had been done, I think this case would never have been brought and a great deal of pain would have been spared the defendants."

Curtis obtained costs against the police, and it was apparent that public agitation would only be satisfied by a strict inquiry. Shortly afterwards the Home Secretary called for a full report and the question was asked in Parliament "whether in view of the results of recent prosecutions in such cases, the Home Secretary is satisfied that sufficient care is taken to establish the trustworthiness of the evidence before the charge is made."

Part of the statement by the strait-laced and unhumorous Sir William Joynson Hicks, the Home Secretary, made people howl with laughter. "It is not illegal for any young member of the community to take any equally young lady to Hyde Park, to sit in the park, and it is not illegal to salute her with a chaste embrace," he said. Cartoons show the chaste embrace taking place with Sir William as Cupid making a careful inspection with the aid of two constables with flashlights. But the Savage case as such paled into insignificance beside a new sensation that arose from Sir Henry's much publicized fight for the honour of the politician and the girl. On May 15th, two weeks after the dismissal of the case, she was invited to visit Scotland Yard. She was there questioned by Chief Inspector Collins as to what had occurred with Sir Leo Money in the Park. As a consequence of what she said happened to her at Scotland Yard, a parliamentary tribunal was set up to inquire into her allegations. The Home Secretary undertook that the State would bear the whole cost and expenses of her appearance before the tribunal. Miss Savidge briefed Patrick Hastings, Curtis-Bennett, and Walter Frampton, while Norman Birkett led for the police.

Many people have since been confused by the fact that whereas it was a Miss Irene "Savage" who was charged with Sir Leo Money, the hearings before the tribunal were always known as the "Savidge" Inquiry. Her real name was Irene Savidge, but when the police had first charged her she found her name was spelt in the more usual way: She, therefore, felt there could be no criticism if she kept to that version of the name. During the first day of the Inquiry, Sir Patrick Hastings outlined his case for the girl. He said that, following a number of questions in the House of Commons, the Director of Public Prosecutions had instructed the police to take a further statement of the circumstances of Miss Savidge's acquaintance with Sir Leo Money: "At Scotland Yard," said Sir Patrick, "her examination seemed to have been directed not so much to finding out whether there was any case against the police, as to have been deliberately designed to get something from Miss Savidge so that there would be no prosecution of the police. I shudder to think what might have happened if Miss Savidge had been the daughter of someone in a different social sphere."

According to the girl, continued Sir Patrick, Inspector Collins had been by turns threatening and affectionate, and had suggested that she was muddled with wine, and that Sir Leo had done something without her knowledge. That could only be designed to quash the chance of a prosecution of the two policemen, although Sir Henry at the police court had stated that it was not his case to make any charge of perjury against the police.

Miss Savidge gave evidence for a day and a half. She was

a perky and courageous witness, and when Mr. Birkett pressed her during a long cross-examination she always had her reply:

"I say that you asked for a cigarette," suggested Mr. Birkett. "And I say that you are wrong," replied the pretty twenty-two-year-old girl.

"If you have been done a grievous wrong and Parliament wants to put it right, why should you not go and tell the truth?" "It wasn't Parliament that asked me—but Scotland Yard."

In her evidence in chief, she said Inspector Collins at first threatened her with the words: "Look here, Miss Savidge, we have you here to tell us the truth, and if you don't tell the truth you and Sir Leo Money will suffer severely. Do you realize that these two police officers have the best of characters and also have their wives to think of?"

Inspector Collins gave the tribunal some interesting details of the methods of Scotland Yard when witnesses were being questioned, but he denied emphatically that they ever practised anything in the nature of "third degree."

In their final speeches Mr. Birkett and Sir Patrick both emphasized the gravity of the issues involved, and Sir Patrick even went so far as to say that the police would never get another young girl into Scotland Yard. He commented on the "horrors of cross-examination" and the outrageous methods by which she had been induced to accompany the police officers. Not the least interesting side light was contained in a statement by Sir Archibald Bodkin, the Director of Public Prosecutions, who spoke of Sir Leo and Miss Savidge "having very foolishly been in Hyde Park." "Why, very foolishly?" asked the public. Was it foolish to sit on a bench because of the risk of being pounced upon by policemen and falsely charged with improper conduct?

The Report of the Savidge Tribunal was published on July 13th. Briefly, the majority report was of the opinion that the police officers concerned with taking Miss Savidge to Scotland Yard were not to blame: "Because, and only because, they were following what is apparently the established practice at Scotland Yard." But that was not to say that they approved of that practice in this particular case. They further stated that they were satisfied that Miss Savidge was not intimidated; that the alleged demonstration did not take place, and that the remark complained of had not been made. No lack of propriety had been shown. Finally, the report stated that the Tribunal was unable to accept Miss Savidge's statements on matters in which there was a conflict of evidence between her and Inspector Collins, "and we acquit him of any improper conduct during the taking of the statements."

This was the majority report signed by Sir John Eldon Bankes and Mr. J. J. Withers, M.P., but Mr. H. B. Lees-Smith, M.P., presented a minority report in which he censured the police officers, and gave it as his opinion that Miss Savidge was misled as to the nature of the Inquiry she would undergo. "In the witness box she gave the impression of a frank, simple and somewhat childlike witness whose evidence remained unshaken under cross examination. The police officers did not give the impression that they were equally frank in their evidence, but denied both the probable and the improbable with equal force."

His report went on to say that a number of questions should not have been asked her, and that her replies were misrepresented: He considered Inspector Collins responsible. "Great perils to private citizens and to civil liberty have been revealed by Miss Savidge's experience and there is need for an investigation into still wider fields of police administration and control."

The ultimate result of the whole matter was that the questioning of private individuals who might later be witnesses or even defendants, was put under much stricter control.

Curtis made another great fight in September, 1928, when he made an appearance in defence of two London constables

A WHITELAW CARTOON
"The Indian Elephant, or Curtis-Bennett"

who were charged with conspiring to proffer a false charge against "Helen Adele," and to pervert the course of justice. The case was extremely involved. Helen Adele, who admitted in court that she had not given her correct surname, and whose real name was not asked for by either side, was an unfortunate woman who had been charged at a Clerkenwell police court with using abusive language outside a garage. She had been arrested by Police Constables C—— and Charles Victor S——. Their evidence was that she was making a disturbance and refused to go away. It was four o'clock in the morning, and as a consequence of her behaviour the officers had arrested her. Both the policemen gave evidence, but when she came into the witness box she told an extraordinary story. She denied the allegations, and said the officers had faked the charge against her because earlier that night she had refused the improper suggestions made to her by C——. Often enough Helen Adele did not possess two shillings to pay for a bed; when this happened she was in the habit of going to a certain taxicab garage and sleeping the night in one of the cabs which had been left there to be washed.

This was done with the connivance of the garage staff, and when she had kicked off her shoes and made herself comfortable Helen frequently sent one of the staff out for a cup of tea. Long after midnight on the night in question she had made her weary way to the garage. She said she had opened the door of a new cab which had frequently served as her bedroom and inside had seen C——, his tunic off and his helmet on the floor, preparing to go to sleep. C—— had invited her into the cab, and she had wearily consented. But, when the policeman began to make improper suggestions to her, she resisted. Tea had been brought to them, and while the door was open she discovered that C——'s friend S—— was in another cab. Both of them were supposed to be on duty, and after a heated argument C—— had said to her: "You are not getting out of this —— cab, putting in a squeak over us." He also said that he would charge her for shouting in the road.

Mr. Dummett, the Magistrate, discharged Adele and ordered that a full inquiry should be made into her accusations. The result was that on September 13th, Sir Henry, Mr. St. John Hutchinson, and Mr. Derek Curtis-Bennett stood in the Old Bailey to defend the policemen and Mr. Percival Clarke, Mr. G. D. Roberts, and Mr. Anthony Hawke appeared for the Director of Public Prosecutions.

The policemen had sworn that the girl's story was untrue, and although Curtis was quiet in his cross-examination Helen Adele, during a three and a half hours' ordeal of answering his probing questions, had to admit many strange secrets of her pathetic career. At the end she said: "I do not know what I am talking about." Curtis had confronted her with written statements which she now had to admit were untruths. And for the defence he promised a row of witnesses who would speak for the good character of the prisoners.

The most prominent witness was the sergeant on the beat, who said that at the time when, according to Helen Adele, they were in the garage, he had actually seen them together. And Curtis cleverly turned round to his advantage a point that seemed to be against Constable S——. Helen Adele had said that she had had relations with S—— on many occasions: "I suggest that is very important in favour of the constables," said Sir Henry. "Is it conceivable, if that were true, that S—— would have made a false charge against a woman who could so easily ruin him in the police force and destroy his domestic happiness?" He ridiculed the testimony of the prosecution witnesses. One of these was a car-washer who had confessed to having perjured himself in the police court. Another was the boy who brought the tea—and who admitted that he was frightened of the police. "You are asked to convict two members of the police force on the word of Helen Adele, plus that of a self-confessed perjurer," he said. He put the constables in the witness box, but Mr. Clarke's cross-examination made very strong points against them when he established that the noise for which they had arrested Adele was heard by nobody else in the neighbourhood. The sergeant was asked how it was that he marked the time on that particular night when he saw the constables on the beat. He replied that it was shortly before he himself went to the station for his refreshment. The prosecution pounced on that and suggested that, in point of fact, he had not been to the station for his refreshment that night. He had no proof; and the allegation was put forward that, since he was a representative of the men on the Disciplinary Board, he had perjured himself to save the policemen.

Curtis made one of the best speeches of his career in defence of the prisoners. "It is an amazing story in many ways. I doubt whether any jury has heard of a more amazing story —because of the nature of the charge—because of the character of the witness—and because of the suggestions Mr. Clarke has thought right to make against police officers in general.... Helen Adele told a story which was untrue in many ways.... It is said sometimes that the public are at the mercy of the police, but do not forget the police are also very much at the mercy of the public. I doubt whether even in the army there is any supervision so constant and strict as in the Metropolitan Police. If the conditions of the force are such as have been suggested in this case, it is far worse than any anti-police fanatic has ever suggested, for it has been said that constables are perjurers and leave their beats at any time and for any time that their sergeants are prepared to perjure for them and that sergeants do not even go round their beats in the rain.... There is a limit to the number of coincidences that take place every twenty-four hours. If this story is true, these men ought to suffer; but if it is untrue, how much at the mercy of the underworld will the police force of London become!"

Certainly there has seldom been a case in which such diametrically opposing versions of incidents on the same date have been put forward. The prosecution now suggested that the sergeant, whose evidence was all-important, had not made a mistake in saying he had seen them on the beat, but had agreed to help a comrade rather than help this poor girl. "You have to do your duty," said Mr. Clarke, "taking care not to discredit a great force."

But when Mr. Justice Humphreys summed up, he would have none of these suggestions that the reputation of the police force was at stake. A condemnation of "Guilty" would be no condemnation of the force as a whole: If anything, it would show that members of the force had succeeded in bringing to justice two men unworthy to be members of it. . . . "Perjury and foul perjury has been committed in this court. . . . I think you will agree that if this case depended on the evidence of Helen Adele alone, one would say it was not safe to convict. I am not referring to the fact that the wretched girl is either a prostitute or something near it: it is not a question of morality, and I hope most of us feel more pity than blame."

The summing-up had lasted two and one-half hours, and Curtis had lost his case. A verdict of Guilty was returned, and the policemen were sent to the second division for eighteen months' imprisonment.

Here was yet another in the long list of police scandals, or allegations of police scandals, in which Curtis had appeared. He himself had very decided views about the conduct and honesty of the police. But he sensed with a degree of concern that the public attitude to the force was changing. Confidence was waning, and regrettably there was a large section of the public prepared to go to any extremes, even paying to strike a blow against individuals in the force as well as the system.

Chapter Seventeen

STRANGE CASES

IN NOVEMBER, 1928, Curtis was briefed to appear for San Dwe, a young Burmese elephant-keeper at the London Zoo, who was charged with the murder of another native elephant attendant, in a fit of jealousy over the care of a sacred white elephant from Burma.

There was something of Eastern mysticism and mythology in this bizarre jealousy of one humble resident of London against another. San Dwe and Said Ali slept in the same room at the Tapir House at the Zoo. Like many of his race, Said Ali hoarded his money, and from the tips earned from parents for taking their children for a ride on the sacred elephant he had amassed a considerable fortune of over a hundred pounds. The elephant had come from Burma. There was some talk of an ancient myth that presaged disaster to all concerned with the animal when it had left its native land. That prophecy was tragically fulfilled; "for one night San Dwe rose from his bed and struck his friend eight times on the head with a sledge hammer with a ferocity that was beyond belief," said Counsel for the Crown. He did not touch the money that was concealed under Said Ali's mattress; but he left the house by the window, and in an hysterical condition he told the police that four men had entered their room and killed his friend.

Curtis called no evidence in San Dwe's defence, but simply stated that the case had not been proved, and in a short speech said that the condition in which his client was found, "terror-stricken, foaming at the mouth like a demented mad man . . ." was not consistent with his having been the coldly calculating murderer. Mr. Justice Swift invited him to produce evidence of insanity, but he only drew attention to the state of his client's mind. San Dwe was found guilty and sentenced to death, but during King George's illness the first document signed by Queen Mary as a member of the Council of State was the reprieve of San Dwe. Curtis had helped to draw up the petition for reprieve; he had thus helped to modify that strangely verified prediction of Buddhist monks who said that evil results would follow the journey of a sacred white elephant from Rangoon to Regent's Park.

Over Christmas there was a great weight on his mind. Early in the new year he would have to appear in the most serious of the cases connected with the morale of the police. He had been briefed by Sergeant Goddard to defend him against a charge of conspiracy with Mrs. Kate Meyrick and Luigi Ribuffi.

Goddard, who had been twenty-six years in the police force, had been appointed a special plain-clothes officer to examine into complaints against night clubs in the West End of London. He had personally superintended over a hundred raids on clubs, and had been commended many times for his industry. The work was difficult, for the police had to make sure that no hint of their intentions came to the ears of the proprietors of undesirable clubs, and often enough, when they made their sudden swoops upon cellars and garrets and front floors with barred windows, they found that the "intelligence service" of the clubs had made their visit fruitless. They knew that the Law was being defied; but it was becoming increasingly difficult to obtain evidence. Clubs, houses of assignation, and disreputable cafés, all seemed to be able to obtain advance information of the movements of the police. Young men were being fleeced and led into evil ways; enormous profits were being made by men and women—many of them foreigners—who sold whisky at thirty shillings a bottle and more, and who employed the worst type of women to lead visitors into spending small fortunes in the mistaken belief that they were seeing the "Bohemian life" of London.

In the autumn of 1928, anonymous letters were received by Scotland Yard, suggesting that the reason why the police could not put a stop to these practices was that there were traitors in their own ranks. The letters mentioned one man in particular—the man who was in chief control of the force detailed to investigate complaints. "Goddard has a beautiful car and a large house at Streatham," read one letter. "Goddard has financed his brother-in-law's business. Goddard not only accepts bribes, but has a financial interest in the most notorious houses and clubs in London."

Scotland Yard gave Goddard the letter and asked him to give an explanation. But, first, independent investigations had been made. In his reply, Goddard said that he had been very thrifty for seventeen years, and had managed to save a few hundred pounds. His wife had money of her own, and in addition he had made a lot of money by backing horses and by speculation in foreign exchanges.

"Then no doubt," said Chief Constable Wensley, "you will bring to Scotland Yard the private safes that you have at Selfridge's and at the Pall Mall Safe Deposit, and will let us see what is inside them."

Before him, they turned £470 worth of bank notes out of one safe, and £12,000 out of another. "I am ruined," said Goddard. The notes were traced back. It was found that many of them had been in the possession of Mrs. Kate Meyrick, the notorious proprietress of the "43 Club" in Gerrard Street, and others in the possession of Luigi Ribuffi, the director of Victor's Club in Leicester Square. It was recalled that, whenever complaints had come regarding the management of the "43 Club," Goddard had reported that they were unfounded; the police, having suspicions about his honesty, had made an independent raid and had found drinking going on after hours.

Curtis had a difficult case. Mr. Percival Clarke took three days in which to outline the case for the prosecution and produce his witnesses, among whom was the junior detective who had formerly worked with Goddard. Sir Henry Maddocks, K.C., for Mrs. Meyrick, suggested that one of the most outspoken of the anonymous letters, in which it was said that Goddard had a financial interest in a notorious resort of known crooks, and persons of ill repute, might well have been written by the police. Curtis, however, did not contest the genuineness of the letters so strongly as he presented the "complete explanation" of Goddard for all the money found in his possession. He put up a splendid defence, detailing an amazing run of luck that Goddard had enjoyed both in gambling ventures and in business. In the witness box, Goddard said that he had made over £7,000 on betting in the last fifteen years; he had made £6,000 in seven years from a share in a music publishing office, and part of the money found in the safe deposit was on trust, and the property of his partner; another source of riches had been a share of Wembley Rock kiosks at the British Empire Exhibition, from which he had made £6,000.

"How much of the stuff would have to be sold to make that profit?" he was asked.

"It cost me £68 a ton," said Goddard, "and we sometimes worked for one penny in the shilling profit."

"Visitors to the Wembley Exhibition must have gone about in a very sticky condition," was the comment of Mr. Justice Avory.

There was also a big source of profit in the foreign exchange speculation; but in all these affairs Goddard was unable to show accounts, either on his own behalf or from the partners who duly came to court to support his evidence under the examination of his counsel.

The other prisoners also lent weight to his denials. Mrs. Meyrick, for instance, said that she was always exactly the reverse from friendly towards Goddard. He had reported against her club on occasions, and since her imprisonment, there had been no occasion for her to bribe a police officer, for there had been no infringements of the law. And when Curtis, on the sixth day of the trial, stood up to address the jury for his client, he was most emphatic that there was a wide gulf between what the Crown had sought to prove, and what they had proved. "The prosecution has made suggestions without evidence," he said. "A man like Goddard might easily have been the victim of an anonymous letter-writer. Goddard has explained how he came by the money; was it likely that he would store bank notes that could be proved to have been at some time in the possession of night-club proprietors? He has been stupid in dealing with matters that he had no right to deal with, but I ask you to say you are not satisfied that he accepted money for an improper purpose. . . ."

But the Judge was very stern when he told Goddard that he had wrecked what might have been an honourable career in the police force for the sake of filthy lucre. The jury returned the verdict of Guilty against all the three prisoners, and Mr. Justice Avory said: "It would have been well if you had written inside your notebook the words:

"'Turn from glittering gold thy scornful eye
Nor sell for gold what gold can never buy.'

"You hoped to live in luxury by this money, which you had amassed by these unlawful means; none of that money could have given you a moment's peace if you had any conscience, which is doubtful."

Goddard's sentence was intended to make the punishment fit the crime. Imprisonment for eighteen months, with hard labour; but of the £20,000 which the prosecution said he had amassed through taking bribes from the very people he was detailed to watch, he had to pay a fine of £2,000, and to pay the costs of the prosecution, which amounted to some £3,000. For the defence, he paid Curtis 280 guineas. The day after the trial, every night club in London had a notice on its doors announcing that it was closed. "Illegal drinking in London is finished," said the Press. "Night life of a disreputable character is dead." But the phrase seemed familiar; and in a very few years it was announced once more that the police were making a "new drive" against the type of establishment which sells false glamour and shoddy vice and unblushingly presents an exorbitant bill as the dawn creeps over Mayfair and Soho.

In 1928 Curtis at last received convincing proof that his divorce had been forgiven and forgotten. On the recommendation of Sir William Joynson Hicks, the Home Secretary, he was made Recorder of Colchester following the elevation of Sir Malcolm Macnaghten to the Bench. The appointment was dated December 21, 1928, and, as King George was ill, bore the signatures of Queen Mary, Edward, Prince of Wales, and Stanley Baldwin, who were "well satisfied of the ability and integrity of the said Sir Henry Honywood Curtis-Bennett." He discharged his duties with great distinction—not only when presiding over the quarter sessions, but when attending each year the Colchester Oyster Feast. At the annual visits his speeches were on a more serious note than his usual witty addresses at London banquets. He looked forward to the feasts and was invariably called upon to make one of the most important speeches.

One of the strangest clients ever to enter Sir Henry's chambers was Lillias Irma Valerie Arkell-Smith, who briefed him in April of 1929 to present one of the most remarkable defences ever heard in a court of law. The name may not be familiar; the figure who stood in the dock of the Old Bailey in a mackintosh with the collar turned up, and with the face of a handsome man, was better known as "Colonel Barker."

Mrs. Arkell-Smith was thirty-three. She had married an

Australian Army officer in 1918, and after parting with him, had lived with another Australian, by whom she had two children. In the War she was a "land girl," dressed in breeches and shirt. The local chemist, a Mr. Howard, believed this masculine woman when she said that she was Sir Victor Barker, a captain in the Army and the holder of the D.S.O. "Sir Victor" asked the chemist's daughter to marry her. They went through a form of marriage and lived together as man and wife for three years, the elder woman saying that "he" had suffered an abdominal injury during the War.

But this story, told in a calm voice by Mr. Percival Clarke for the Prosecution, was eclipsed when he proceeded to tell how he himself had prosecuted a certain "Captain Barker" in 1927, for being in possession of firearms without a licence. The "captain" was then in the National Fascist movement. "On that occasion," said Mr. Clarke, "she came into Court with her eyes bandaged, and was led into the dock by a friend. It was explained that the defendant suffered from blindness owing to War wounds, and not a soul in Court knew that there was other than a man standing in the dock. She was acquitted."

In 1929 she was dressed as a man, acting as reception clerk in a Strand hotel. A receiving order in bankruptcy had been made against "Sir Victor Barker," and the reception clerk was arrested. Not until she was taken to prison was it found that she was a normal woman. "I submit that these facts show that this person has a total disregard for the truth or for the sanctity of the oath," continued Mr. Clarke. "If she had wanted to marry another woman, she could have gone to a register office; there was no justification for her abusing the Church."

Curtis was now defending her against a charge of swearing in court that she was a man, and making a false entry in a marriage register that she was a bachelor.

"The defendant's legal advisors considered for a long time

before advising a plea of guilty," said Curtis, "for such a thing as had happened in the present case had never been contemplated. The defendant did not obtain any money through her 'marriage' to Miss Howard, and in fact supported her. There have been many distinguished figures in history who have lived as men, and in a much smaller sphere she has lived a respectable life, earning her living; she is more sinned against than sinning; it is astonishing that the misery of this woman can be made into a sort of entertainment by people who increase her wretchedness by coming here to stare at her. Has she not been punished enough?"

The Recorder, Sir Ernest Wild, thought not.

"Colonel Barker" broke down and wept. But it was with a squaring of her manly shoulders, and a military turn of her heel, that she went out of the dock to serve her sentence of nine months' imprisonment.

In August, 1929, Curtis married again. His bride was Miss Lillian Mary Jeffries, and after the honeymoon, he appeared at the Old Bailey again to receive the congratulations of judges and colleagues. He settled down more quietly at Boreham, still keeping his flat in Piccadilly. One morning in September, when once more he was touring France in his car with his wife and his son and daughter-in-law, he was reading the *Continental Daily Mail* at a café. The newspaper heading was, "Hatry Arrested."

When he returned on September 29th, he learnt that Edmund Daniels, charged with Hatry, had made an approach to obtain his services. From that moment, until the great trial opened on January 19, he was immersed in the complicated history of that case, which shook the city of London, destroyed public confidence, and was ever afterwards said to mark the beginning of the great depression.

Hatry was defended by Mr. Norman Birkett and Mr. St.

John Hutchinson; Mr. Cecil Whiteley and Mr. Walter Frampton appeared for John Dixon.

The public had heard little of the true facts of the case except that Hatry had failed for a huge sum of money; but on October 14th there was some inkling of the gravity of the issues involved when the applications made by counsel for bail for the accused were refused. Although it was proved that the defendants had placed themselves in the hands of Sir Archibald Bodkin, the Director of Public Prosecutions, and had been helping Sir Gilbert Garnsey, the accountant, prepare a statement of the position of the companies concerned, they were refused bail, the High Court giving an opinion that, although they had confessed, they did not then know the gravity of the charge. Curtis said that the airports were being watched as well as the ordinary ports. "If you have means, you need not go through an airport," was the reply. "We are not satisfied that, if granted bail, the defendants will appear to take their trial."

The charge against Hatry was one of conspiracy, forgery, and fraudulent conversion; in January there appeared with him in the dock, as well as Daniels and Dixon, Albert Tabor. For weeks before the hearing, Curtis had visited the Old Bailey, where his client came from prison to go through the mass of papers relevant to the charges. Daniels, who was only thirty-two, had been a prominent man in the City for eight years, largely because of Hatry's influence. On September 19th, after a week of alarm in business circles, during which the Hatry stock was tumbling relentlessly, Daniels had come with his chief and his associate to Sir Gilbert Garnsey. Their faces were drawn and haggard. They spoke of irregularities; they said that the liabilities would be nearly £20,000,000.

Sir Gilbert Garnsey had warned them, asking if they knew the seriousness of their statements. Hatry had replied that they knew exactly what it meant and what the punishment would be. They offered to go to the police, but Sir

Gilbert, staggered by the enormity of the fraud to which they had confessed, asked for time to consider the position. That night, Hatry returned to him; Sir Gilbert said that he would go to the Director of Public Prosecutions.

Their decision to juggle with their stocks, they revealed, had been made at a meeting one Sunday afternoon when their affairs were already in a complicated and dangerous position. Five of Hatry's associates had met in a private house near London. They talked of ruin, not in thousands of pounds, but in millions. There was one course—a dishonest one—which might stave off the evil day. "Unless you take that course," said one of them, "I will blow my brains out!" That was the beginning of the fraud of the twentieth century, which rocked the confidence of the City of London.

Hatry, Daniels, and Dixon pleaded "Not guilty" to the indictment charging them with conspiracy, and "Guilty" to other indictments. For three days the Court heard the story of the collapse that had followed on the heels of those rumours in the financial columns which had been so disturbing. Mr. Norman Birkett's final passage in his speech for Hatry was long remembered: "No punishment inflicted on Hatry can fill the cup of suffering from which he has most bitterly to drink, more full than it is now. He has been four months in prison with time to think, to brood, to reflect, to see what might have been and what is. . . . The appeal I make to you is that you should impose such a sentence as will vindicate the law, but which will not crush or break or destroy, but will permit Mr. Hatry to maintain the hope—which is the last earthly thing he has—that one day he may live to redeem that career which has been so finally and tragically shattered. . . ."

Hatry accepted the responsibility for the entire affair. Curtis revealed that fact in the first sentence of his address for his client. Daniels was working on a salary the whole time, said Curtis. The defendants did not wish to enter into an agreement to defraud, but even when they went to Sir Gilbert Garnsey, they had in mind the thought that a great number of people could still be saved from the crash. His client, in point of fact, had not made a penny piece out of the frauds.

But Mr. Justice Avory's words—words which rang with intense meaning, and which read as well as they were spoken—left little doubt in the mind of Clarence Hatry that he would be made to pay heavily for his influence on these men who together had caused the solid foundations of the commercial world to rock. "You stand convicted of one of the most appalling frauds that have ever disfigured the commercial reputation of this country," he said, "—more serious than any of the great frauds upon the public within the last fifty years." He did not think there was merit in Hatry's confession, and he poured scorn on the pleas for mercy that had been made. "You were merely succumbing to the inevitable," he said. "What does your plea amount to when stripped of its rhetorical language? It is nothing more than the threadbare plea of every clerk or servant who robs his master and says that he hoped to repay the money before his crime was discovered by backing a winner. Except that your crime was on a large scale, there is no difference between that excuse and the excuse which is made daily by the dishonest clerk or servant. . . ."

Fourteen years was the sentence on Hatry. He turned to go. "Stay!" said the Judge. And Hatry was brought back to hear further sentences which were to run concurrently.

To Daniels, the Judge said: "There is no question that you have taken a leading part in the perpetration of these forgeries and frauds, but I give effect to the statement that has been made by Hatry that he was primarily responsible." Curtis's client received a sentence of seven years. The fraud of the century had taken only a few days to retail in court.

The case for the Crown totalled some quarter of a million words—nearly three times the length of this volume, while the speeches in defence by various counsel were of approximately similar length.

Chapter Eighteen

"LAUGH AND GROW FAT"

DURING that year, 1929, Curtis had been taking things easier. He could afford to refuse briefs that did not bring in their hundred guineas in fees. He could put into practice a rule that he had often commended but seldom followed: that a leading barrister should only appear in court for a fifty-guinea fee. Licensing cases provided the big sums still, but he had not been in the public eye in big cases as in the great years 1922 or 1924.

His practice had not receded since those great days, save for a short time after his divorce, but the remark was often heard, "You don't see Curtis-Bennett's name in the papers now as you used to do." Yet the fact of the name being in the papers was by no means a fair representation of the work he was doing. Curtis used to comment on it himself. Often a friend would say to him: "You've been busy this week; I'm seeing your name in the papers every day." But after he had gone Curtis would say: "That's funny, for this week I seem to have done less work than I've done for the last six months. People seem to think that when my name is not in print, I'm not working."

But while the approaches made to him to conduct a case were as frequent as ever, he now learnt the wisdom of giving his brain a rest as often as he could. His idea of leisure was found peculiar by many people, for it consisted either in sitting at the wheel of his car for hours at a time, or of lunching with his legal friends and talking on the subject that was his work. One of his pleasures was to take lunch at the Savoy

Grill with his old friend, who stepped into his shoes on his appointment at the London Sessions as one of the most distinguished leaders of the Criminal Bar, Mr. St. John Hutchinson. He called him "Hutch," and many were the days when Manetta could be seen showing these two portly and genial men to their favourite table just off the aisle in the middle of that famous meeting place. Comment in the Grill would invariably turn on what chance had allowed these two legal luminaries to spend two hours on a leisurely luncheon. Newspapermen would come over to their table to talk with Curtis, and would find him genial as always.

He was always a favourite with newspapermen, and although he held strong views about the "interference" of the Press in the lives of private individuals, he raged more strongly against that senseless and morbid crew, the crowd of fashionably dressed men and women who flock to a great murder trial or a peculiar sex case. "It is disgusting!" said Curtis. "They are treating this as a spectacle; they do not know that they are watching a poor wretch undergoing the greatest agony of his life!"

By the year 1930 Curtis weighed some eighteen stone. His doctors put him on diets, but he confessed that he could not keep to them. They warned him against City dinners, which tired him out though they formed one of his great pleasures. But, though he had made attempts to spare his constitution the great strains he put upon it, he could not keep to the diets. "I'd rather die than live the miserable sort of life I'll have to if I keep to this," he would say, and another good resolution would go. Sometimes he starved for a week or more, but he believed in the old adage "Laugh and grow fat," and certainly his figure suited his geniality and his good humour. And though he was ever conscious of the weakening of his heart through the strain of his weight, he kept amazingly good health, having a constitution that was proof against most of the common ills. His only recurrent malady was a sudden "petit mal"—a dizziness that sometimes overcame him at the most critical moments. None knew that he had been visited by this malady, but sometimes he would sit down after a brilliant cross-examination and say afterwards: "I've had another of those attacks." For a few moments he would have a blurred vision and complete dizziness, and for the rest of the day he suffered from a headache that could not be shaken off. Even his closest friends knew nothing of these attacks; his happy philosophy was such that he was regarded rather as a happy-go-lucky, extravagant and careless buccaneer of the Bar; the account books and worry, the hours of painstaking inquiry, were secrets from many of his most intimate friends; and when he died, there were few people who knew that he was one of the most methodical men, a stickler for efficiency in his private life. They did not know that many of his cases tore the heart out of him and left him exhausted; that faculty for shouldering the burdens of others, that from his clients' point of view was invaluable, was from his own point of view a terrible weight to carry. He would never leave to another a part of the work that he could do himself; he believed that his clients should know and appreciate that they "were getting their money's worth." And indeed there was no barrister who was so conscientious in making a personal appearance in court when he had made a promise to do so; too often, however, Curtis had to admit that a client judges the conduct of the counsel only by the result, and when the verdict has gone against him, can find only criticism of his counsel, never imagining that a great fight has been made over a hopeless case. . . .

In the Goddard case, to quote an instance of how Curtis would not allow his health to interfere with his work, he had a high temperature, and almost completely lost his voice. It was obvious that he was in for influenza, and the doctor ordered him to bed. But Curtis consulted a famous specialist who treated opera stars when they lost their voices, and, muffled to the eyes, went to court, knowing that he could talk for so long and no longer. He made his presence felt very forcibly that day; and there was nobody who knew that, by rights, he should have been in bed.

An attempt to recoup, and to rest himself fully, he made in 1930, when he varied his usual physically exhausting holiday by making a trip to South America. But he was restless on the boat; he did not particularly care for the company to be found on cruises; and he never tried the experiment again.

In March, 1930, Sir Henry found himself once more in familiar company at the Sussex Assizes at Lewes. Once again, the Court listened breathlessly to the story of a shocking murder. But now there was heard a tale of such cold-blooded brutality by a young man on his sick and aging mother, that Curtis was at times during the case personally affected. The accused was Sidney Harry Fox, a twenty-eight-year-old youth who had no job and no money. Curtis was appearing for the Crown with the Attorney-General (Sir William Jowitt, K.C.) as his senior and Mr. St. John Hutchinson as his junior, while Mr. J. D. Cassels, K.C., and Mr. T. T. James appeared for the defence.

The woman Fox was alleged to have murdered was sixty-three years of age. Sidney appears to have been the favourite son, and although the old lady had no worldly possessions of any value she had made out a will in favour of Sidney and with pointed partiality against the eldest of her family. But it was a pathetic document, for in truth Mrs. Fox possessed only a pension of ten shillings a week and except for a few rings had nothing of value in the world. Mother and son had a joint income of eighteen shillings a week from their two pensions. The old lady did not even possess night attire or toilet materials and travelled with a small paper parcel.

But during October Sidney and his mother, having given up all hope of increasing their income, seem to have let caution go to the winds. They stayed at a good hotel in Canterbury for a week, spending considerably more per day than their pensions for the week. They left with half the bill unpaid, and from there went to the Hotel Metropole, Margate, where Sidney Fox glibly told the reception clerk that their luggage had been sent on from France. They took two rooms in the hotel, and Sidney managed to cash a worthless cheque with which he paid a small proportion of their bill at the end of a few days. But the young man had a plan: all he needed for its success was the ability to conjure up in himself sufficient courage for a terrible deed. There were some insurance policies about to lapse on his mother's life. They were for short terms only, but if a fatal accident happened to his mother within the next forty-eight hours, then Sidney would be paid a sum of over three thousand pounds. He took some trouble to find out from the insurance companies what type of accident Mrs. Fox must suffer in order to make the policy in order. He asked clerks in local offices whether food-poisoning in a restaurant could be classified as "death from external accidental means"; he asked if the money would be paid if she were accidentally drowned in her bath. But, receiving the reply that these accidents might be subject to questioning, he decided that within forty-eight hours his mother must be burned to death.

But Sidney doubted whether the "accident" would occur within the time limit stipulated by one of the policies. This insurance became invalid at noon on October 23rd: he therefore extended the policy until midnight, paying a few shillings for the extra premium.

It is worth noting that during the previous six months the total income of this strange pair was £22. 10s. Of this, £10 had been paid as premiums against the woman's accidental death.

Fox had in mind the possibility of doctors examining the body of his mother after death. There might be, he thought, some bruises on her limbs: casually, therefore, he mentioned to an acquaintance in the hotel that his mother was so much improved in health that they had engaged in a playful "sham fight" the previous day. And that afternoon of October 23rd he went and bought a bottle of port: Dutch courage for a man about to commit matricide.

He went to his room at half past ten that evening. "If by any chance," said the Attorney-General at the trial, "Mrs. Fox died by violent external means in the course of the next hour and a half, Sidney Fox was entitled to receive the sum of £3,000."

At twenty minutes to twelve, a commercial traveller sitting in the hall saw Fox race downstairs scantily clad in his undergarments and shouting: "Where is the boots? There is a fire!"

The traveller rushed upstairs with Fox, and after being driven back from Mrs. Fox's room by clouds of smoke, crawled in again on hands and knees and dragged out her body.

"Has the money been found?" shouted Fox. "There was twenty-five pounds in her bag. Have they got it?"

The case for the prosecution was that Fox went upstairs that night with murder in his heart. "If murderer he was, you can have no doubt of his cunning and skill: his bed had been lain on and he came down those stairs partially undressed. But in all these cases, Sir Bernard Spilsbury will show you what the true facts are."

Now although there were several witnesses who could tell of significant facts that would, in the mass, lead to the inevitable conclusion that Fox was guilty of the crime of matricide, there can be no doubt that his worst witness was himself. Fox was a sexual pervert—and his kind do not make good witnesses. He was vain and a poseur, and it was remarked that such was his effort to present a pleasant appearance to the jury, that he could not devote the whole of his mind to what he was saying. Otherwise, how could he have fallen into the appalling mistake that sent a gasp of amazement round the court? It was while Sir William Jowitt was taking him through that period when, in bed according to his own story, he smelt smoke, and went to see if the smoke was coming from his mother's room. He opened the door, saw the smoke clouds, and realized that his mother was in great danger.

"You must have been greatly apprehensive for your mother?" he was asked. "I was," he replied.

"Fox, you closed the door!"

"It is quite possible that I did."

"Can you explain," demanded Sir William, "why it was that you closed the door instead of flinging it wide open?"

Fox must have been day-dreaming, for in a second his subconscious mind spoke the truth.

"My explanation of that now is that the smoke should not spread into the hotel," he said calmly.

But apart from that fatal revelation, Fox had already laid a trail of guilt that could easily be followed up. He had always been careless in his life of crime. When he had forged cheques, he must have known that sooner or later the police would track him down. When he had represented himself as a member of a famous London club, and affixed a military title and the prefix "Honourable" to his name, it was with no possible hope that he would be believed for long. His had always been a mean and detestable character. When he was arrested for impersonation and fraud, and had picked up a letter addressed to him at the Royal Automobile Club, he had readily given away the name of the man who had written to him. The writer was an English Army officer who had signed his initials to a most compromising letter from another famous club. The letter led to his exposure and the sentence of being cashiered from the Army. Fox could probably have saved him; instead, he gave away the name.

Again, when he had made himself charming to an elderly Australian woman, and had actually made love to her for the sake of her fortune, Fox had bungled an attempt to murder her by gas poisoning, for the sake of the money she had left him in her will. As he stood in the dock, his name appeared as the co-respondent in a divorce action brought by the husband. He still carried with him the woman's will, leaving him her property, though after the attempt at murder, she had immediately come to her senses and written another.

His old mother, there is no doubt, knew and connived at his deceptions on hotels and trusting tradesmen. She had unbounded admiration for the son who could give her ease and comfort in good hotels, and she never knew that that same son came to look upon his old mother as his last asset, the means whereby he might bring off his greatest coup. . . .

It might be surmised that the strange couple found people very trusting. When Fox had represented himself to titled people as a distant relation, they had gladly cashed his cheques on banks the other side of the country. When he had come to hotels, he had played the old trick of depositing parcels "of valuable documents" with the hotel management. He had always explained away their lack of luggage by saying that it "was being sent on." He cashed a cheque for £2 written on a piece of the hotel note paper, with stamps affixed, at the local chemist's shop. And daily, he inquired about the extent of his bill, giving the impression that he was being careful to live within his means.

The manager of the hotel was a man who had his suspicions. He sent up the bill daily to Fox, though he did not press him. Then, when the manager's wife was comforting him after the death of his mother, she had said: "It is a strange thing, but his hair smelt of smoke, and he did not go into the room; and he said he had not been in the room before. . . ." The manager and his wife looked at each other; they read suspicion in each other's faces.

But, as often happens, it was an insurance company that finally led to his exposure. Mrs. Fox was buried, and the poor belongings of the dead woman had been given away. Fox had even made a present of his mother's false teeth to a chambermaid. He had not paid the bill at the hotel, but it was thought callous to intrude with such a matter upon a young man obviously grieving for his mother's sad death. He had asked for the address of a local solicitor, and it was thought at the hotel that that fact in itself showed that he had funds. Actually, the introduction worked the other way, for Fox, on the strength of his forthcoming withdrawal of £3,000 insurance money, had borrowed some £40 from the solicitor. . . .

But insurance companies are always wary when called upon to pay large sums of money as a result of an "accidental death" that occurs within a few minutes of the expiring of the policy. Fox, it is true, could point to the fact that for years past, the couple had paid a substantial sum of their small income for insurance policies. Nevertheless, an investigation seemed in order, merely to check on the background of the young man who was soon to be paid that large sum of money. It was easily found that many of his statements were untrue. He had said that, the day of the tragedy, he had cashed a cheque for £25 on a London bank, and that notes amounting to that sum must have been burned in the fire. It was readily found that the statement was untrue.

He was asked for his address, and he gave the name of a house that did not exist. When a detective who knew his previous record saluted him with a "Good morning, Fox!" he replied, "I do not know you." The manager of an hotel he had bilked a few weeks before wired to the Hotel Metropole. And the Metropole manager began to remember his own and his wife's suspicions.

The chambermaid, the manageress, and others in the hotel were completely deceived by his show of grief. And indeed, it may have been that Fox always had an affection for the old lady, whose life he had undoubtedly tried to make easier, and whom he had rescued from a home for the improvident and from other circumstances less comfortable.

Perhaps Fox had never envisaged the possibility of Sir Bernard's examining the body and proving that he had strangled his mother. He did not know that death from burning would leave soot in the windpipe: or that the pathetically slight pressure that he had to put upon his mother's throat with his bare hands would leave a mark on the tongue that Sir Bernard said indicated plainly that she was dead before ever the flames crept to her chair. They produced in court the clerks with whom he had arranged extension of insurance coverage until he had gathered courage. They produced the pieces of paper with which he had set fire to the carpet and a cane chair. They set up in court the gas stove, and the furniture, and Sir Henry unrolled the carpet and arranged the fender so that the jury could see exactly how he had gone about his grim business.

For his defence there was produced an eminent pathologist who gave directly contradicting evidence to that of Sir Bernard Spilsbury. He had never known a case of manual strangulation with so few signs of violence, said this expert. But the jury were absent only a short time after Sir Henry had delivered a final speech for the prosecution. The verdict was "Guilty."

Another clumsy murderer had been trapped by the expert evidence of that calm, good-looking official who is known as "the perfect witness." The memory of one of the most callous and mercenary killers was wiped out by a notice posted on the wall at Maidstone Gaol.

It was a relief to Curtis when he appeared in a case in which a little laughter was permissible. One of the most light-hearted prosecutions was one which concerned the penny-in-the-slot machines which tempted the coins from mill hands on holiday at Blackpool. Curtis was taken north to defend the management of an amusement arcade on Blackpool Parade. The police had been watching the summer crowds flocking to a machine called "the little stockbroker" which offered a gamble on a miniature stock exchange to anybody who would like to risk a penny. The owners gave further instructions as to how to win back 90 per cent of the money "invested," and some complicated directions were exhibited above each machine. But the case for the police was that the holiday public in Blackpool were so anxious to put their pennies into the machine that no man could spend enough time to read the instructions. They were said to be complicated in the extreme, and Curtis had expended a small fortune in pennies on the model of the machine in court without being able to persuade the Bench that these instructions were perfectly simple to follow. Prosecuting counsel also used the ratepayers' money in showing the working of "the little stockbroker." Mr. J. C. Jackson, K.C., had considerable luck with his first venture; for to the general amusement he drew four pennies. "Put it in the till," said Curtis. Mr. Jackson: "It is not out of the till. I have played so long and it has cost the ratepayers threepence."

Curtis suggested that the Bench should dismiss the summons, saying that it was perfectly plain that the Lancashire lads and lassies who came to Blackpool could not lose money if they followed the directions provided with the machines. But a police inspector had said that at the amusement arcade there were no kind gentlemen giving a kindergarten lesson as Sir Henry had done to those who wanted to play. The case was sent to the Quarter Sessions, and once again the machine was produced in court and Mr. Jackson placed the ratepayers' money into "the little stockbroker" and demonstrated that on each occasion he lost money. Curtis again submitted that there was no case and said he hoped the Postmaster-General would never have to meet a charge of keeping gaming houses as a result of building telephone boxes in which the rules of play were as complicated as those for manipulating "the little stockbroker." "Unless you read these instructions in telephone boxes it is a game anyone can play," said Curtis.

"There is a certainty that you will never get more out than you put in," said Mr. Jackson.

But Curtis lost his case and the defendants were bound over; Mr. Justice Avory confirming the decision some weeks later at the Court of Criminal Appeal. "Anyone wishing to make a certainty of winning would have occupied the machine for the best part of a day," said the Judge in dismissing the appeal.

A remarkable feature of 1931 was Sir Henry's success in motoring cases. These were on the increase and although the police were taking more trouble in ensuring that their evidence was technically correct, he was able time after time to shake their evidence sufficiently to obtain an acquittal. In two years he appeared in eight outstanding motoring cases in which he secured the acquittal of the defendant. The courts listened to his expert submissions, and there were few men, witnesses, juries, or judges, who appeared to contest his statements and his arguments.

One of the most outstanding defences was when he contested the evidence of the police in regard to the skid marks alleged to have been made by his client's car. The evidence seemed convincing when it was first given: Curtis, however, took the trouble to make a minute examination of the photographs. He discovered that the marks referred to were shown as beginning with a clear-cut line made by the tires; they ended with a gradual tapering off of the impression made upon the macadam road. With a few questions Curtis was able to convince the police witness that the application of brakes resulted in the gradual checking of the wheel and that on releasing the brake pedal, the skid marks would end abruptly. "Is it not more probable, therefore, that these skid marks were made by a car travelling in precisely the opposite direction?" submitted Curtis. The Judge agreed with him, and his client was acquitted.

In another case there was revealed a very human side of the Law. A notable public personage was accused of driving to public danger, and the most valuable witness for the defence was a man who said he had been driving behind the defendant and could testify that he was proceeding at a very moderate speed. The offence was alleged to have been committed in the West End of London. Sir Henry's witness duly testified as to the speed of the car in front of him, but when he was cross-examined he seemed unwilling to answer a question as to why he himself was proceeding at a mere fifteen miles an hour. For some time it seemed as though the testimony of this witness would lose its value, for he persistently refused to say why it was that he was proceeding at less than his normal speed. Sir Henry was greatly troubled. The case was obviously in the balance in the mind of the magistrate; but during the short and rather puzzling silence in the court the witness suddenly came to a decision to tell the whole truth: "Well, if you must know," he said, "I was trying to pick up a girl."

"It's our case," said Curtis; and he was right.

He secured the acquittal of a young army officer charged with manslaughter, wanton driving, and being drunk in charge of a motor car by a superb defence that evolved almost into an attack on the police. His client had passed with flying colours a test which Mr. Justice Charles said would have beaten almost any man. The police had asked the officer to pronounce the words "British constitution," "Royal Field Artillery," "Aberystwyth," "Buenos Aires," "Pernambuco," and "Ecclefechan." They had asked his client who had won the last bye-election, where it was, and why General Smith-Dorrien was sent home from the War! In another case a racing trainer had been charged with drunkenness when driving because he had been sarcastic with a policeman. "Have a joke with a judge if you like," said Curtis, "but never joke with a policeman when he is on duty." He secured the acquittal of a Cheltenham colonel accused of being drunk in charge and said of a naval officer accused of driving to the danger of the public: "His car is a noisy little one, and it is an extremely stupid thing to drive a car which makes a noise. Rich people can drive Rolls Royces quite quickly without any attention because they drive quietly. But it attracts attention if you make a noise."

In the case of a young Oxford undergraduate who was acquitted of manslaughter, Curtis said: "There is no speed limit in these days. When they hear of thirty-five miles an hour, people hold up their hands and say 'thirty-five miles an hour,' but if any of you have driven a car during the week-end and have touched thirty-five miles an hour or forty, did you think that if you had the misfortune of seeing someone step out in front of you, you could be charged with manslaughter?"

As Recorder of Colchester, he decided that a man charged with being drunk while driving was equally liable even if he were driving in a private road leading to his own house. His point was that the public—the butcher, the grocer, and the baker—had access to that road. Sir Henry said he would give a certificate for an appeal on the point of law to the Court of Criminal Appeal.

He even defended a man who was subjected to three medical tests in one night and after being arrested in one county was rearrested fifteen minutes later in another. But one of his greatest triumphs in that period was dismissal of the charge against Lord Howard of Effingham, who was accused of manslaughter, a coroner's jury having returned a verdict of criminal negligence on his part after the death of a labourer on the Henley Road. Lord Howard drove up to a constable at Maidenhead and said he had run into something: His windscreen was smashed and the window was dented: The body of the labourer was found on the footpath the next morning. The prosecution could not prove whether the labourer had been on the path or the road and there was said to be a thick fog. Curtis vigorously criticized the conduct of the coroner's court. "As an example of the atmosphere at these proceedings," he said, "Lord Howard, who was a stranger in the district, was asked why he went as far as Maidenhead to report. If we found ourselves in a strange part I doubt if we should know where the nearest policeman lived. Yet even that was put down against him."

Five minutes later the Bench returned with a decision that there was not sufficient evidence to send Sir Henry's client for trial.

Again in January of 1933 he had the Recorder of Oxford stopping the case against another man, accused of driving under the influence of drink. The police surgeon described his tests on the defendant and referred to "the peak hour" of drunkenness after taking alcohol. "This is a new one to me," said the Recorder. Sir Henry: "I have never heard of the peak before." The doctor said he tested defendant's susceptibility to pain. "What did you use for that?" "A pin."

Sir Henry: "I see. You stick a pin into him, and if he jumps he is normal." The doctor agreed. Almost simultaneously the Recorder asked the jury if they had heard enough.

Two good successes on appeal to Sir Henry's credit were when he represented Brenda Dean Paul, who had been sentenced to six months' imprisonment, and when he appealed for the "thousand a year woman golfer" who was convicted of stealing a ten-shilling note from a handbag. His appeal for Brenda Paul was most moving. "I propose that she be taken into the country and looked after," he said. "Do try this proposal. She having tasted a little of what imprisonment is like would never do anything again to put herself within prison walls.

Curtis had himself defended a woman at the police court

for the alleged theft of a ten-shilling note at her golf club. A detective had marked a note and left it in some bag in the dressing room, and said he had watched while she took possession of it. After her conviction she cabled her husband—an important official in Ceylon—to return to England, and expressed her determination to take the matter to the Home Office. "Some people think the police cannot make a mistake," said Curtis. "It is clear that they can."

Apparently the Court thought so too, for the appeal was allowed.

Chapter Nineteen

GREAT ACQUITTALS

SIR HENRY's first case of importance in 1933 was his defence of Compton Mackenzie, the author, when charged with an offence under the Official Secrets Act in connection with his book "Greek Memories." Mr. Mackenzie had pleaded "Guilty," and the public were not to know very much about the confidential secrets which he was alleged to have referred to in his book. The famous author, Curtis revealed, usually received over £2,000 for a novel, but for each of a series of books of "memories" he received only £500. He did not have money in his mind, but had written the book to tell the truth about M. Venizelos. This was the first case heard *in camera* since the War, and the fine was £100, the Judge telling Mr. Mackenzie: "I do not say the Attorney-General has succeeded in persuading me that the document you published is of so much importance as some of His Majesty's Servants attach to it. The Prosecution are satisfied you had no intention to do anything hostile to the interests of your country. I hope this case may do something to warn those whose urge to write is greater than their discretion."

One of Sir Henry's biggest criminal cases which concerned the financial world was his defence of Harry Geen, who was charged with receiving large sums of money from the Broad Street Press knowing them to have been obtained by fraud. The prosecution said that Geen had been extradited from America on these charges, and that the method of a number of conspirators was to start a financial paper, *The City News*, giving advice about stocks and shares. At first the advice was sound and trustworthy, but after gaining the confidence of the public they employed share-pushers and touts to purchase worthless paper. One of the moving spirits, it was said, was Jacob Factor, who was still in America, and who had always appeared as a substantial man of business to Harry Geen. The trial lasted for ten days, and Curtis' brief was marked 1,000 guineas. In his address for the defence he emphasized his point that Geen had been duped by "that extraordinary figure" Jacob Factor, through whose account there had passed £800,000 in 1928, and nearly twice that sum in 1929, when there was no suggestion of fraud. "Let the right people suffer," said Curtis, "not the underlings who were misled into the positions they held and merely carried out the instructions of a much greater personality."

Curtis also appeared in the "Great Fire Trial." For thirty-three days Leopold Harris and his associates were sitting in the dock which had been fitted to accommodate them in the Old Bailey. Curtis was appearing for Jarvis, and in an impassioned appeal, after announcing that his client had withdrawn his plea of "Not guilty" to certain counts in the indictment, said that Jarvis had had a life which could be described as "hell upon earth." It had been admitted by the prosecution that he had not been active for some years, and not only had admitted his fault but had refrained from making any suggestions of perjury against witnesses for the prosecution. Jarvis received three years' penal servitude. It was in many ways the most remarkable trial that Curtis had ever listened to. The prisoners had increased in number from day to day as the police roped in their suspects. The chief witness for the Crown was the spy in the enemies' camp: Camillo Capsoni, who had been in the pay of the prosecution for more than a year while enjoying the complete confidence of the fire gang. "We use him and seek to use him merely as an instrument of justice," Mr. Oliver had said for the prosecution, and indeed, during those days of waiting, in Capsoni's story of how he had worked with Mr. William Charles Crocker, the solicitor whose name suddenly became famous, and with Leopold Harris and his gang of fire raisers, there was drama in every sentence, which added to the infamy of this unscrupulous gang which had pillaged the insurance world in London.

There were many innovations in the court that had never been known at the Old Bailey. Apparatus for the deaf was installed. There was a complete telephone service from Mr. Oliver's table to a library of papers and exhibits in a room below. A hundred thousand documents were filed by a staff of clerks for immediate reference; 121 witnesses had given evidence during preliminary proceedings, and their statements had totalled half a million words. The cost to the public for the satisfaction of knowing that a national scandal had been exposed was £100,000.

It was in September of 1933 that Curtis found himself briefed to appear for Sir Leo Chiozza Money, who had been summoned for assault by a young girl who alleged that he had forcibly kissed her in a railway carriage. The defence was a denial that he had forced his kisses upon her. Sir Leo said in the witness box that he had kissed her hands, and that as an author and journalist he liked to talk to all and sundry on general matters. Curtis spoke of the girl as being unusually sensitive. "I think this will be a lesson to many of us not to speak to people to whom we have not been introduced. I have no doubt this sensitive girl got frightened and thought that something might be going to happen."

Sir Leo was fined, the Bench saying that his conduct had brought him within the charges preferred against him.

During this year and the next Sir Henry's success in defence was really remarkable. He seemed to be in a winning streak, and his notebooks record an unceasing series of cases in which he defended the accused and obtained an acquittal either on the first hearing or on appeal. He successfully defended one of the newly elected sheriffs of the City of London in October,

1933, against a charge of insulting a woman servant: in November he succeeded in extracting from a judge a statement that the conviction of a doctor convicted of manslaughter in a motoring accident ought not to result in his being struck off the Register; he secured a verdict of "Not guilty" for a Kent man accused of the manslaughter of a boy while driving; he successfully represented a Mr. Jones, who was accused by his wife of attempting to poison her with arsenic; he was unsuccessful in defending Eric Hatry, the barrister, against a charge of cruelty to a cat; but when a young schoolboy rugby footballer was charged with the manslaughter of his best friend after a birthday party, Curtis successfully defended him and established that the blow was struck by accident.

In an important case in which he appeared for the Crown, a verdict of "Guilty" was returned against Albert Probert and Frederick Parker, accused of the Portslade Shop murder. In August, 1934, he was one of three famous K.C.'s who were briefed by Dorothy Sibley, a rich young girl in a case which the magistrates described as something very near "Alice in Wonderland." The charge of obtaining goods from Harrods by false pretences was before the court six times. Miss Sibley had first briefed Mr. J. D. Cassels, then Sir Henry, and finally Mr. Norman Birkett.

In 1935 he gave some typically audacious advice to motorists when he appeared for the defence in the case of a man charged with manslaughter. "If you are ever stopped by the police," he said, "don't for goodness' sake touch the car in any way, or you will be said to be leaning on it for support. Don't sway at all when you are walking, or you will be said to be staggering under the influence of drink. Spring smartly to attention, stand upright outside the car, and say: 'I am not guilty of whatever you are about to charge me with doing.'"

In another motoring case he secured the acquittal of Captain William George Mells charged with manslaughter after a prolonged trial at Northampton Assizes. Once again he cited that most valuable judgment in Rex *v*. Bateman in which the Lord Chief Justice had stated that, "in order to establish criminal liability, the facts must be such that the negligence of the accused went beyond the mere matter of compensation between subjects and showed such a disregard for the life and safety of others as to amount to a crime against the state."

Sir Henry had made a great effort at the first hearing to induce the magistrates to say that there was no case to go to the jury. He had then urged that it should go for trial at the Old Bailey, but again he failed and secured the acquittal after a magnificent address in which he said: ". . . forty miles an hour sounds a good deal more in a court of justice than it does when you are upon the road. Not so many years ago ten miles an hour was considered fast; then twenty miles an hour was the speed limit; now thirty miles an hour in built-up areas is the speed limit; forty miles sounds a good deal more than it really is with modern cars and modern brakes."

Another fine defence was made on behalf of a former chief of police in Tanganyika, who was charged with manslaughter. The coroner had received many communications, and Sir Henry rightly emphasized that the prosecution depended entirely upon circumstantial evidence. "Circumstantial evidence is sometimes stronger than direct evidence," he said. "But I suggest that in this case you have seen a terrible example of what may go wrong."

All these were important and remunerative cases; but from the point of view of legal interest, of paramount importance was the "Golf Links Murder Trial" in which Curtis prosecuted Percy Anderson, who was accused of murdering his sweetheart and leaving her body in a water tank on the East Brighton golf links. A suggestion of insanity was put forward by Mr. Eric Neve for the defence, and Anderson in the box told of a "blank moment" that he experienced while he was having a quarrel with the girl. Anderson admitted that his sweetheart seemed to have been strangled by his own scarf;

"Are you telling the Jury that after the girl was shot at and murdered by the scarf being tied tightly round her neck, for the first time in your life you had a blank moment?" Curtis asked. The answer was in the affirmative.

The Lord Chief Justice paid an outstanding compliment to Curtis for his prosecution. "In all my experience of listening to criminal cases—I am sorry to say for well over thirty years —I have never heard of a charge of murder more clearly, more concisely, or more fairly opened to a jury than this case was opened by Sir Henry Curtis-Bennett."

This was the last time Sir Henry was to appear before the Lord Chief Justice, and the tribute pleased him greatly.

Lord Hewart went on to an interesting and authoritative thesis on the meaning of a "defence of insanity." "It is a question about which more than one profession is cultivating loose, lax and sloppy views," he said. "Every man is presumed to be sane and responsible for his crime until the contrary is proved. . . . To establish a defence on the grounds of insanity, it must be clearly proved that at the time of the committing of the Act, the party accused was labouring under such a defect of reason from disease of the mind as not to know the nature and quality of the act he was doing; or, if he did know it, that he did not know that he was doing what was wrong."

Mr. Neve in his final speech had concluded by asking the jury to let the accused man go out and see the sunshine and hear the larks singing. The Judge's comment was: "It seemed to be suggested to you that unless you came to a conclusion in the prisoner's favour, you are interfering with the solar system and breaking off the singing of birds. I am sure you will not have any consideration of that kind present in your mind. The solar system is much more likely to be interfered with, and the song of birds much more likely to cease, if juries upon a sentimental exhortation fail to do their duty. . . ."

Anderson was sentenced to death.

In June, 1935, Curtis had another excellent success in the Court of Criminal Appeal on behalf of the Duke of Manchester, who had been convicted and sentenced to nine months' imprisonment on two charges of obtaining money by false pretences. Curtis had defended at the Old Bailey before the Recorder of London, and the Recorder's summing up on that occasion received a severe criticism from the Lord Chief Justice in the Court of Criminal Appeal.

Curtis had pleaded that His Honour Judge Gregory had left great confusion in the minds of the jury as a result of his summing up, and Lord Hewart agreed, saying that it was insufficient and unsatisfactory. He continued: "Nor does it appear that, if the summing up had been what it ought to have been, the jury would certainly have arrived at the same conclusion or would inevitably have convicted." The Court allowed the appeal and the conviction was granted.

On July 4, 1935, Curtis was appointed chairman of the Essex Quarter Sessions in succession to Mr. Collingwood Hope, K.C. "My father was always very anxious to become chairman of the Essex Quarter Sessions, but he never achieved that ambition," said Curtis, "and I am honoured because I am an Essex man."

More than once Curtis was opposed by his son Derek in licensing cases. He usually had a word to say for the opposition that he knew was coming from "my young and learned friend whose name I seem to recognize." And in reply to his occasional sarcasm his son would say: "My learned friend ought to have known what I was going to say, for I learnt at his knees all that there was to learn for and against licensing. Do not be lured by the art and attractiveness by which out of his sage experience he can present such applications. The way he submits his argument puts you in a sort of anaesthesia for a time. When you come out of it—and I hope you are emerging now—you realize that there is absolutely nothing in it at all."

In those years Curtis added to the reputation he had already gained as a master in representing the brewery companies before magistrates. His name, indeed, deserves to go down through the history of the strange laws of England for having been responsible for the ending of that curious situation, a source of ridicule to every visitor, which made drinking on one side of Oxford Street legal and on the other side illegal. Time and again Curtis had crossed swords in friendly fashion with representatives of the Church who appeared to contest his applications. In one case it was asked: "How would Sir Henry Curtis-Bennett like to have a public house placed near his house at Chelmsford?"

"There is one," said Curtis.

He urged upon Justices the argument that convictions of drunkenness were diminishing all over the country. "You can hardly see a drunken man nowadays," he said. "You can trust your public, and who knows better what the public desire than the license holders?" And in reply to the Bishop of Willesden concerning the Marylebone licensing hours, he said: "It is typical of the history of our country that minorities shout loudest. Today, no doubt, opposition will be led by my Lord Bishop, who will have canons to the right of him and canons to the left of him. Respectable workingmen are being driven to certain types of clubs because the public houses are closed too early."

But it was not till 1935 that the Oxford Street drinking anomaly was ended. As early as 1925 Curtis was applying for a reform: "It is unfair to restaurant proprietors on the north side of the street," he had said, "and there is little doubt that the increase in night clubs has had some relation to the restrictions."

The Licensing Act had been passed in 1921, but it had taken thirteen years for the licensing justices to be convinced that it was an absurd situation for men in the inns on one side

CHAIRMAN OF THE COUNTY OF LONDON SESSIONS
Photograph by Keystone

of the street to be ejected at closing time, only to walk through the traffic to drink for another half-hour within the law.

On December 12, 1935, Sir Henry appeared in what may prove to be the last "Trial by Peers" held in England. From time immemorial it has been laid down by statute that a Peer must stand his trial for an alleged felony at the Bar of the House of Lords before his "Peers." He must not be asked to appear before a judge and a jury of "twelve good men and true." His judges must be the ermine-robed members of the House of Lords. Such is the statute, jealously guarded by English tradition. And although it was felt by many of the public, and perhaps by the Peers themselves, that the custom was out of date and out of keeping with the times, and efforts were subsequently made to abolish the necessity by Act of Parliament, nothing has so far been done, and the position remains that when a member of the Upper House stands charged with a serious offence, he must submit to the judgment of his Peers, and appear in that hallowed chamber amid all the panoply and pomp of a more leisurely and decorative England.

The Peer who was now required to stand his trial before Their Lordships was young and lanky Edward Southwell, Lord de Clifford: member of an ancient family; man-about-town; popular sportsman whose first interest was in motoring. He was a brilliant motorist, and had competed in many of the Continental endurance "rallies," in which it is required to drive cars through all conditions of roads and climate, day and night, sometimes for thousands of miles. Quite recently, Lord de Clifford had broken every record in an astonishing drive from Calais to Athens, averaging a very high speed. He was well known in the industry for his skill, and could be counted as one of the most experienced motorists in Europe.

At three o'clock in the morning on the 15th of August, 1935, Lord de Clifford was driving a small Lancia car along the Kingston Bypass away from London.

The Kingston Bypass had become known as one of the most dangerous roads in the country, and time and again coroners have had occasion to comment on its evil reputation. Lord de Clifford saw the lights of another car approaching him. To his astonishment they appeared to be on the wrong side of the road, that is, on the same side as his car was travelling. As they came nearer and as it became obvious to Lord de Clifford that there was likely to be an accident, he drove over to the off-side of the road in an effort to prevent a calamity. His speed was about forty miles an hour, but he gained the impression that the other car was travelling much faster and was "out of control." As he reached the offside of the road Lord de Clifford realized that the oncoming car was, in fact, now on its correct side of the road. He made an effort to drive back to the left-hand side, but at a point in about the middle of the road, the two cars collided. It seemed that the driver of the other car had also altered his direction on seeing the Lancia. Both the cars were badly damaged: But there was a far more serious result. Douglas George Hopkins, the driver of the Fraser-Nash car, was killed: His passengers—Miss Sheila Hopkins, his sister, who was sitting on the near side of the car, and Miss Rosemary Reynolds, who was seated in the middle—were injured. Lord de Clifford was also injured.

After the inquest, Lord de Clifford was arrested and charged with manslaughter. After a hearing at the police court he was committed for trial at the Old Bailey. The defendant being a Peer of the Realm and the crime alleged against him being felony, there was no alternative to removal of the case by writ of certiorari to the House of Lords to be tried "by his Peers" as a court of first instance. It was erroneously thought by many people that the decision to be tried by the House of Lords rested with Lord de Clifford, although his solicitors frequently reminded the public that this was not the case. Lord de Clifford's advisors retained Sir Henry Curtis-Bennett as counsel for the defence. In contradiction to the mistaken popular feeling, it can be said that Lord de Clifford's advisors would certainly have preferred the case to be heard before a jury to which Curtis was accustomed rather than before the unknown quantity—in both senses of the word—of the members of the Upper House.

The last occasion on which a Peer had been called before the House on a charge of felony was in 1901, when Earl Russell pleaded guilty to bigamy.

As usual, Curtis took immense trouble in acquainting himself with every detail of the circumstances of the accident. He himself went out in his car one night to the Kingston Bypass with another car and a Press photographer. He did not know what results would be obtained by his experiments but he was certain there must be good foundation for Lord de Clifford's belief that the Fraser-Nash was on the wrong side of the road. Several photographs were taken from the driving seat of one car of the road ahead with the other car approaching round the slight bend. These photographs, when they were developed, showed clearly that De Clifford might well have been misled by a strange freak of the road. The lights of the approaching car, which was driven well to its correct side, gave an unmistakable impression that it was in fact on the wrong side of the road.

Curtis also discovered that a kink in the road tended to throw a car onto its off-side. He had hundreds of these photographs prepared, and contemplated having a scale model of the road built to use as evidence. He made a most careful examination of both cars and spent hours of study bringing his unrivalled technical knowledge to bear on the most minute facts connected with the case.

For some weeks before the trial, great interest was shown in the event. Not only by the legal profession; for the tailors of London, grasping the opportunity, were advertising to their titled customers the special robes they would be obliged to wear at the occasion: the ermine and the purple; the knee breeches and silk stockings. Nor did the indignation felt by some members of the public at this needless expense, escape Lord de Clifford himself: He was not a rich man, and the trial by his peers was likely to cost him considerably more than the trial he would have liked, before judge and jury—open to any member of the public not enjoying the privilege of an ancient title. Lord de Clifford's position, indeed, was unenviable; from every point of view he would have preferred an ordinary trial; Sir Henry had agreed with him that there might be many members of that august assembly who were not conversant with the niceties of a motoring case; some members of the House of Lords are experienced, and one or two of the younger peers are motoring correspondents of the national papers; but the average age of the House is advanced; the average income is large; and therefore, more than the members of any other assembly in the country, perhaps, the members of the Upper House leave motoring matters to their chauffeurs, regard the automobile as a convenient method of travel, and nurse a secret preference for the horse and carriage.

But tradition must be served. Lord de Clifford himself, the Lord Chancellor, the Lord Chief Justice—none could alter the position.

In the grey December morning, therefore, the wealth and privilege of traditional England, in ermine and knee breeches, in cocked hats and capes, drove to the sombre building to hear one of their number arraigned on a charge of manslaughter. Eighty-five of them, earls and viscounts and marquesses and the four dukes, Argyll, Rutland, and Richmond and Gordon. With the Lord Chancellor on the Woolsack, and four judges of the High Court to advise on any question of law which might arise, they heard the Sergeant at Arms declare: "Oyez, oyez, oyez: Our Sovereign Lord the King strictly charges and commands all manner of persons to keep silence under pain of imprisonment."

The Commission was read, the sonorous voice of the Clerk

of the Crown in Chancery intoning the phraseology of another age, far removed from the busy workaday world that surged round Parliament Square outside those grey walls. "George the Fifth by the Grace of God of Great Britain, Ireland, and the British Dominions beyond the Seas, King, Defender of the Faith, to our right trusty and well beloved cousin and Councillor Douglas McGarel Hogg, Viscount Hailsham, Our Chancellor of Great Britain, Greeting. Know ye that whereas Edward Southwell, Baron de Clifford, stands indicted for felony . . ."

And then: "Very much confiding in your Fidelity, Prudence, provident Circumspection and Industry, have for this cause ordained and constituted you High Steward of Our United Kingdom . . ." Ending with the words: "By the King Himself Signed with His Own Hand."

The names of the Noble Lords present were called, beginning with the Junior Baron, and each rose and answered to his title. Then the Garter and Gentleman Usher of the Black Rod, after three reverences, knelt before the Lord High Steward, and presented to him a slim, white wand—the White Staff of Office. All this panoply and carefully ordained procedure, this stilted, history-soaked formality, had come into being, the puppets had dressed themselves and moved about their business, because of circumstances from another age and time, as a result of two split seconds of doubt and indecision at three o'clock in the morning on a motor-road. The words that were framed into stilted phrases in the days when England travelled by stagecoach were now heard as preliminary to a case in which there figured mile-a-minute automobiles; a speed road made for a speed-mad world; a world undreamt-of when the Lords of England first handed White Rods of Office, made their reverences, and heard messages "From the King, Signed by His Own Hand."

"Oyez, oyez, oyez," called the Sergeant at Arms once more.

"Edward Southwell, Lord de Clifford, come forward and save you and your bail or else you forfeit your recognizance!"

The tall pale figure was brought to the Bar, bowed three times, and, being "advised to give attention," was arraigned upon the indictment.

"What say you, my Lord. Are you guilty of the felony with which you are charged or not guilty?"

"Not guilty," said Lord de Clifford, in a strong voice.

The Clerk of the Parliaments: "How will you be tried?"

Lord de Clifford: "By God and my peers."

The Clerk of the Parliaments: "God send Your Lordship a good deliverance!"

The ceremony had lasted a full hour. And now, it was as if the world moved forward three centuries, like the transformation scene in a stage spectacle, save that the setting remained the same. The words on the actors' lips were of the twentieth century; bewigged men spoke of acceleration and gradients and gear-shifts; the Lords listened, switching their minds to the present which this rich ceremony had so far ignored.

For the Crown there appeared the Attorney-General, the Right Honourable Sir Thomas Inskip, K.C., M.P., the Solicitor-General, Sir Donald Somervell, K.C., M.P., Mr. Eustace Fulton, and Mr. Christmas Humphreys. Sir Henry had with him for the defence Mr. Ryder Richardson, Mr. Neville Faulks, Mr. John C. Tait and was instructed by Mr. J. Thomson Halsall.

The Attorney-General's opening dealt mainly with the facts and the measurements. Curtis had few questions to ask the first witness, but he did elicit some important facts regarding the probable speed of the car driven by the deceased. He elicited from one of the passengers in the car that until the collision took place they had seen no car approaching and from the other passenger he confirmed that immediately before the collision the three occupants had been conversing. Immediately after the case for the Crown was closed Sir Henry submitted that there was no case made out by the prosecution against Lord de Clifford for manslaughter. He had his witnesses ready outside the court and he was prepared to distribute his photographs and embark upon a lengthy explanation of the exact circumstances which had given rise to the accident. Lord de Clifford himself was anxious to give his explanation, but in a few forceful words Sir Henry had reminded their Lordships exactly how the law stood in regard to criminal negligence. Once more he used with destructive effect his old friend Rex *v.* Bateman. "In a judgement of my Lord Hewart the Lord Chief Justice," he said, "in order to establish criminal liability the facts must be such that in the opinion of the jury, the negligence of the accused went beyond a mere matter of compensation between subjects and showed such disregard for the life and safety of others as to amount to a crime against the State."

The mere fact that a motorist was on the wrong side of the road was not necessarily evidence of negligence. . . . The fact that the occupant of the other car saw nothing confirmed Lord de Clifford's account of his own actions. "Is this not a position in which any of your Lordships either driving a car or being driven might find yourselves even tonight? . . . Over and over again when you are walking on the proper side of the footpath, how often do you find somebody coming to meet you? You go to the wrong side and he goes to his right side and you go back on your right side and so does he, and you collide. Because Lord de Clifford did in the agony of the moment, just before the collision took place, what he believed at that moment to be the only course, is that to be said to be criminal negligence?"

With the agreement of the peers the court adjourned until after lunch. Although these were unfamiliar surroundings, Sir Henry had soon found that he had the sympathy of their

Lordships. After lunch the Lord High Steward, addressing Sir Henry, announced: "The Judges have unanimously advised their Lordships that your submission is well founded and that there is no case to answer."

The Peers were then asked whether the prisoner was guilty or not guilty, and the Clerk of the Parliaments, reading from a list, called on each of their Lordships by name, to which each replied: "Not guilty, upon my honour."

"My Lords, I declare that Edward Southwell, Lord de Clifford, is acquitted of the felony . . ." intoned the Lord High Steward.

The proclamation was read dissolving the Commission of High Steward, and the Sergeant at Arms announced: "Our Sovereign Lord the King doth strictly charge and command all manner of persons here present to depart thence in the Peace of God." The Lord High Steward, holding the Staff in both hands, broke it in two, and declared the Commission to be dissolved.

The spectacle was over; tradition had been served.

Chapter Twenty

"A NEW LIFE"

IN THE summer of 1936, Curtis took a well-earned holiday in France. His wife was with him, and his son and daughter-in-law were to follow by road and join him at Royat. He had said that if he could manage to visit Royat again, he would be quite recovered, and able to carry through the rest of the year without distress. But for the first time in his life he had complained that he woke up in the morning without zest for the day's work; he was always tired and unwilling to face problems and struggles; he relied entirely on Royat to correct the malady.

The well-remembered road south was as great a delight as ever, and there was no hint of fatigue in his handling of the big car. Those who welcomed him en route found him as genial as ever, and within a few days of his arrival at the Majestic Palace Hotel, he seemed to have recovered even more rapidly than ever. His son was delighted to find him cheerful again and active, and confident that he would return to London fully competent to enter the fray.

But it was not to be. Lady Curtis-Bennett, herself never very strong, fell ill during the third week of their stay at Royat, and Sir Henry was always immediately affected when she was ill. She suffered a severe attack of colitis and was in considerable pain for several days. Within twenty-four hours, the worry and helplessness felt by Sir Henry, his insistence on taxing his own strength unduly, undid all the good work of the brief holiday. When his son returned to Royat, at Sir Henry's request, after a few days' tour, he found him worse than when he had left London.

Curtis acted as day-and-night nurse. As ever, he would leave little to others and was unwilling to save himself a severe strain that he knew was unwise from his own point of view. He could not rest, nor feel confident of the outcome, unless he himself ministered to the hourly needs of the invalid. He put all thought of his own health aside, and made two invalids where there had been one. The long-anticipated holiday was a tragedy, and when he drove back, arriving in London on the 31st of August, he was in no condition to do battle with the briefs that awaited him at his chambers.

He walked into his chambers and saw the desk littered with briefs and other papers. Suddenly he felt, for the first time in his life, unwilling to settle down to them. Nothing could compensate him for the loss of that feeling of willingness for battle. More attractive than at any time in his career, there loomed the possibility of a judgeship.

There were other considerations, one favourable to the acceptance of such a course, the other unfavourable. Sir Henry had known that for some time there had been rumours or impressions in the legal world that he would never be offered a judgeship because he had been respondent in a divorce suit. It would be sweet justification to counter those rumours. On the other hand, he knew he must face an immense drop in income, at a time of life when a man is least suited to altering the style of his living. He could count on an income of £10,000 a year or so from his practice; the most that he could expect if he achieved what was his life's ambition—the Recordership of London—was £4,000 a year.

Could he readjust his life to that extent? Could he reduce his charity subscriptions, deny himself the privilege of giving lavish hospitality on the night of a big fight, perhaps reduce living expenses at Boreham and Deanery Street, depend on one motor car and partially retire from a social world that depended on first nights and important public banquets?

Men said that he was careless about money, but he himself knew precisely where he stood, and—undreamt of by most of his colleagues—he had a matter of £20,000 invested, saved year by year. But he was a man who liked everything about him to be efficient and perfect—and that cost money. It would be a revolution in his life if he did give up his practice, and he would find it hard to adapt himself to a reduced standard of living.

But leisure was the most urgent need of all; he had worked too hard, and the strain had told on him.

In September, as if to repay himself for the unfortunate holiday at Royat, he went to Scotland. Here there was a too-eloquent indication of his lack of energy. For he said he was tired of the Great North Road, and actually had his long car put on the night train that took him and his wife. At the station he fussed over the arrangements in his old style, and there was no indication of *laissez-faire* at any rate in his concern for its welfare. He chivvied railway officials, expressed doubts as to whether it would be taken off the train at Perth, and asked a hundred questions. The whole business, he thought, was being conducted in much too casual a manner. But on his return he had to admit that his fears were groundless, and that the railway officials whose efficiency he so gravely suspected had superintended the transport of his precious vehicle with calm precision.

This was like the old Curtis, worrying over every detail that was not in his own charge, fearful lest there should be the slightest hitch to wreck his careful organization. His nervousness was a sign of normality, and it would have been a more dangerous symptom if he had adopted a fatalistic attitude.

He toured Scotland for ten days, but it could not be said that he was better. He was still tired, still uneasy at the prospect of tackling another spell of hard work. Once again he had the car put on the train, and soon after he had returned to London, at a time when everything had conspired to make him less eager for the rough and tumble of the Criminal Bar, he was offered the opportunity of escape. Sir Percival Clarke died on October 5th, and shortly after he had a letter from Sir John Simon's private secretary. Would he accept the position of Chairman of the London Sessions?

Sir John's letter added that he would quite understand if he refused, but could he give an answer in twenty-four hours?

Curtis was crowded out with work. He was briefed for the defendants in the Girl Pat Case, and was most worried about it. He wanted to take on the case, but he realized it was no easy task; also on his desk were two other big briefs, for a murder case and another important case at Exeter Assizes; a third was for the defence of a solicitor.

Altogether Curtis would have to return 1,700 guineas' worth of work. He would have to refuse this for a salary of £2,250 a year.

But he was immensely pleased at being offered the position without applying for it. He knew that the Recordership of London would probably become vacant within a year or two, and he was going to apply for it himself. The Chairmanship of London Sessions would be the obvious stepping-stone; as one of his friends put it, "If you are prepared to be Recorder of London and accept a salary of £4,000 a year, in exchange for your present income, the Chairmanship of the London Sessions will smooth out the path." Curtis did not even make a pretence of considering the matter. Although he was appalled at the thought of the income and supertax that he would have to pay from a meagre salary, he was almost like a child in his pleasure. He accepted by return of post, and as he walked down Piccadilly that day, ordering wine and cigars at Fortnum's, a suit or two from his tailor, spending a hundred pounds before he reached the Temple, he said jocularly that very soon all he would be able to do would be to put sixpence in a machine for a packet of cigarettes.

On October 16th the appointment was officially confirmed. Many of his friends were surprised at his acceptance. They knew that after receiving an income averaging £10,000 a year, he would not look forward to one of £2,250. Many thought he could not do it, for, as has been said, he was falsely credited with a lavish extravagance. Yet the apparent freedom from care about his finances was the result of his studied methods of accountancy. The little diaries that recorded his worldly success saved him from doubt, and there was no man who committed his life to paper more minutely. He was making a great sacrifice, but he was prepared for it; and he knew that he had no choice. He almost admitted as much to friends who asked him how he was looking forward to the future.

By every post, there came letters of congratulation, from old friends, and men he had met but once, who had been impressed by his personality and his kindliness; letters not of congratulation, but of welcome to the London Sessions; letters from men he had flattered by remembering their names and their faces; five hundred letters signed by some of the most illustrious names in the legal world. And in not one single instance did he look at the signature and say: "I wonder who that could be?"

In the next two weeks he answered every letter by hand, postponing many engagements in order to fulfil his social duty. He scrawled, in the familiar, almost illegible writing, a few words of special gratitude to each. He wrote: "It is nice to have had such a charming letter from you, and you must forgive me for not having answered it before, but over five hundred take some time to write. I shall now get some rest after years of overwork and perhaps it may lead somewhere, one never knows. Best wishes."

On October 20th, Sir Henry took his seat as Chairman of London Sessions, and was welcomed by the largest gathering of barristers that had ever assembled at the Sessions House. He was most moved at the warmth of the welcome, and by the fact that it was his old friend "Jimmy" Cassels who spoke on behalf of the Bar. ". . . Some of us have known him since he was a junior waiting for briefs to come," said Mr. Cassels; "we have seen him become the busiest Silk at the Criminal Bar, and far from waiting for briefs to come he has waited for them to go out."

Another old friend, Mr. St. John Hutchinson, K.C., referred to the sacrifices Sir Henry had made for the purpose of serving the State, and in reply to these speeches, and to other tributes paid by Mr. Beaufoi Moore and Mr. T. M. O'Callaghan on behalf of the junior Bar, Sir Henry recalled that he was relinquishing thirty-four years of strenuous fighting.

". . . I start what is to me a comparatively new life," he said. "I think that the position of Chairman of the London Sessions is of greater importance than many people realize. It is a position in which it is possible to do good. I find myself transferred from the fighting ranks of the finest profession in the world to occupy this seat where I shall certainly strive to emulate the examples which have been set by my great predecessors. I shall take great joy in watching you struggle as I have struggled, and I shall try to hold the scales of Justice between you and between all men, fairly. Today, as a fighting member of the Bar—I bid farewell."

It was a great wrench: he knew he was leaving the arena for the serenity of judicial office. Everyone knew that with more than twelve years' experience as Chairman of the Essex Quarter Sessions he would make an excellent chairman. Even when he tried rating appeals, about which he knew next to nothing, counsel who appeared before him were amazed at his quickness in picking up points and at his knowledge of when to keep his mouth shut. He admitted that he found it difficult not to intervene, and to restrain himself from making jokes which he felt would sound undignified coming from the

Bench. He was most impressed with the kindliness of Sir Herbert Wilberforce, the Deputy Chairman, of John Dix, the Clerk of the Peace, and every official from the highest to the lowest. He made up his mind that he would enjoy the change and the rest to the full, take all his holidays at Boreham, and go abroad in his car although he knew that his standard of living must be severely restricted in the future. "I am so happy here, I doubt whether I shall even put in for the Recordership," he said.

On October 22nd, he went as usual to Colchester for the Oyster Feast, with his wife. It was the last time he was to speak at that occasion. He had never been so gay or so successful with his witticisms. He said he had noticed an unusual number of police officers, and presumed that immediately after lunch he would be arrested for obtaining lunch under false pretences, since he was no longer Recorder of Colchester. He had another story about his weight—and this time it was a true one. He was proposing the toast of "A Better Humanity," and with a change to a serious note he said that those in a position of administering justice must not be too censorious; they must consider the circumstances that had brought the defendant into the dock. "I do believe," he said, "that one has the power—and I hope to be able to exercise it—of doing some good to better humanity in the humble sphere in which I work. . . ."

The week-end of October 31st, he spent at Boreham, and it was on Saturday and Sunday that he wrote some hundred or so of his letters. On Monday he must expect a busy day; he had arranged to clear up his private papers in his chambers —a sad task, for it meant the end of his associations with that well-beloved room. In the evening he was to speak at the dinner of the National Greyhound Racing Society at the Dorchester Hotel. On the Tuesday, London Sessions opened, and thereafter he had made appointments throughout the week; old friends were to lunch with him—among them Sir

Archibald Bodkin. There was a first night to go to, and perhaps he would have more time now for the Garrick Club, for a more leisurely enjoyment of the company of his friends, without the thought at the back of his mind that he ought to be at home reading a brief. . . .

The visit to Temple Gardens was an emotional experience. All day he stayed there, talking to Hollis, his clerk. "We had a happy day," said Hollis. "Sir Henry was as cheerful as ever, and we just talked. But at the end of the day I did notice that he was tired, and he told me that he was going to a public dinner, and said: 'I think I shall give up dinners when I have to speak; they are too much strain.'"

There were many who, reading his letters that he posted that day, believed that these expressions of his gratitude contained a hint that he knew he was not to live for long. Many read a "premonition of death" into the words: "I shall now get some rest after years of overwork, and perhaps it may lead somewhere, one never knows." The supposition was perhaps natural, but in point of fact Curtis was relieved once he had made his decision, and was a happy man. He had plans for the future, and was looking forward in particular to an engagement on November 17th, when he was to dine with Derek to celebrate the triple anniversary.

Yet there were other matters which made Curtis-Bennett's last acts appear more than significant. He seemed anxious to conduct a general stock-taking of his position as well as to bid farewell to the atmosphere of Middle Temple Lane that had been his whole life. Derek visited him in chambers, and with him checked the exact value of the shares that were in the safe, from the financial columns of the *Times*. He thought he had scrip to the value of £20,000. He found that their value to date was a matter of £1,000 more. He was moving the scrip to the safe in his room at London Sessions, and packed his bag with Derek helping. As he packed it he showed his son an envelope and said: "This is for you to read when

I'm dead." His will and securities he packed, too, and queried whether to take the bag to Deanery Street that night or to collect it next morning on the way to Sessions.

That day, he took a last look round the pleasant room to which he expected to return only as a visitor. Then he said that he wanted Derek to have his desk that had been his father's, and his furniture, and said: "It belonged to your grandfather, it's belonged to me for years. We haven't done so badly. I hope you'll have it in your room."

He was thinking of himself and his father before him, and all the great dramas that had begun in that room in Plowden Buildings, and in Pump Court. It was a sad moment, and he knew he would miss the exhilaration of battle.

He was tired when he left, and Hollis offered to carry his bag out to the car. But he refused, and carried it himself, and as he got into the car, confirmed an appointment for the next day with his clerk.

By half past seven he was changed and at the Dorchester, where he was to speak at the dinner of the Greyhound Racing Society. The speech was in response to the toast of "Our Guest," and he had told Lord Donegall and Mr. Arthur Elvin, who sat next to him, that he was as "nervous as a kitten." Mr. Elvin asked how it was possible that he, who was accustomed to addressing judges and juries on more vital matters almost every day of his life, felt nervous at the prospect of a speech at a public dinner.

"The person who is not nervous before such an ordeal," said Curtis, "is not able to make much of a speech."

He rose to speak at twenty minutes to eleven, and his first words were: "I feel this is the last time I shall speak in public." Little did he realize how prophetic those words were. He made a worthy speech, timed perfectly; a new joke about his size. The audience in laughter, a snapshot taken of him pausing while the audience around him were laughing, and the next moment the end had come.

A few feet away from his brother, Sir Noel Curtis-Bennett, he suddenly lurched to one side and fell on the ground. It was over instantaneously, a coronary thrombosis. He, who during his life was in so many sensational events, caused the greatest sensation of all in the manner of his passing. For one who had achieved so much, it was a magnificent end. At the height of his career he had taken judicial office, having long thought that such a post would be denied him. He had not had the time to feel the financial stringency which would fall upon him. He would only know that it was pleasant at his job, and that he liked it. He had had no stroke which would paralyze him so far as work was concerned and keep him alive in a life worse than death.

One moment his friends were laughing round him, and the next moment he was gone, in exactly the same way as on the 2nd of June, 1913, his father had gone at the Mansion House: in the same way that his greatest friend Freke Palmer had gone on the 20th of January, 1932.

In the Courts of Justice in London and the Provinces, references were made that showed the unanimous sense of loss that was felt. At London Sessions, where Sir Herbert Wilberforce said: "We were proud when Sir Henry consented to preside here. We confidently hoped that unless he was called to some higher office—which seemed probable—he would sit here for many years and increase the reputation of the London Sessions. He was a great advocate, and he might have become a great Judge; and we lament and deplore his loss."

His friend Mr. St. John Hutchinson, K.C., was heartbroken, saying he had lost the greatest friend he had ever had. At the Essex Assizes Mr. Justice Hawke said: "He was one of the greatest advocates of his time and will be remembered in more Courts of Assizes and quarter sessions than anyone else. It would not be too much to say that the members of the Bar and others hold him in an affection that amounted to love. . . ."

He was buried in the churchyard at Kelvedon in Essex in the next grave to his father, in the same churchyard as his grandparents. He had obtained the faculty for the grave from the Bishop of Chelmsford shortly after his father's death. And on November 7th his friends and his colleagues of the Temple, judges and counsel and solicitors and their clerks and officials of the courts paid tribute to him at a memorial service at Temple Church.

An astonishing variety of tributes greeted his biographers' request for memories of Sir Henry. Among the hundreds of letters paying tribute to his courage and his kindliness, there were many recollections of those stories with which his name will ever be associated. One correspondent, indeed, wrote saying how sad it was that Curtis had not lived those few weeks to December 22nd when he would have known that the name of Curtis-Bennett was to be carried on to another generation. On that date Margot, his daughter-in-law, gave birth to a son weighing ten pounds: "What a joke Curtis would have made of his weight—He could not have resisted it."

Into fifty-seven years of life he had crammed the experience of three-quarters of a century. He achieved great success and had lived his life to the full.

He had known both joy and misery to their fullest extent; he had shown courage and endurance; he had earned and deserved the gratitude of many. There are many who, going into the Old Bailey or the London Sessions, or perhaps some Assize Court in the country, will pause and think and miss that ringing voice, that cheery face, that happy smile, that friendly pat on the back, that cheerful anecdote, that wonderful cross-examination, that brilliant speech, and that great and kindly man.

THE END

Index

Abortion cases, 72
Adele, Helen, see "Helen Adele"
Amonderain, Raymonde, 49-50
Anderson, Percy, trial of, 253-4
Ansley, George, 164
Argyle, Duke of, 260
Arkell-Smith, Mrs., trial of, 226-8
Armstrong, Major Herbert Rouse, trial of, 102-13; appeal against verdict on, 121-3
Armstrong, Mrs., dog on grave of, 107
Asthury, Mr. Justice, 211
Austin, Tex, 160-2
Automobile Association, 20
Avory, Mr. Justice, 34, 88, 199, 244; and trial of Vaquier, 164, 166-70; and trial of Mahon, 175-82; and trial of Mrs. Hayley Morriss, 204-6; and trial of Goddard, 224-5; and Hatry Case, 231

Baldwin, Stanley, 226
Bankes, Sir John Eldon, 216
"Barker, Colonel," case of, 226-8
Barrie, Peter Christian, trial of, 74-6
"Bella Donna," 141
Bennett, Arnold, 136
Beresford, Tristram, 69
Bevan, Stuart, 66
Birkenhead, Lord, 26, 123
Birkett, Norman, 214-5, 252; defends Hatry, 228, 230
Biron, Sir Chartres, 212
Bishop, Stanley, 146
Blackpool, penny-in-slot-machine at, 242-4
Bodkin, Sir Archibald, 36, 51, 66, 215, 229, 271-2
"Boles," trial of, 67-69
Boreham, Essex, 52-3, 60
Bosanquet, S. R. C., 106
Bottomley, Horatio, 150

Bournonville, Eva de, trial of, 46-8
Breeckow, Georg T., trial of, 42-3
Brewster Sessions, 29-30
Broad Street Press, 249
Brockdorff-Rantzau, Count, 49
Brontë, Dr., evidence of, 186, 187, 189, 191-2
Buckmaster, Lord, 101
Buschman, Fernando, trial of, 41-2
Bywaters, Frederick, 125-7; trial of, 128-33, 142-6

Cameron, Elsie, murder of, 183-93
Cancellor, Mr., 213
"Canteen Case," 29
Capsoni, Camillo, 250-1
Casement, Roger, 62
Cassels, J. D., 22, 85, 87, 158, 212, 252, 270; defends Mahon, 175-82; defends Norman Thorne, 183, 187, 189-90, 192-4; defends Fox, 236
Charles, Mr. Justice, 245
Chelmsford, election at, 155-7
Circuit system, 200-1
City News, The, 249
Clanwaring, Thomas, trial of, 90-1
Clarke, Sir Percival, 218-20, 224, 227, 268
Clifford, Lord de, trial of, 257-64
Cochran, Charles B., and Rodeo Case, 160-1
Coercion, doctrine of, 100-2
Colchester, Recordership at, 226; Oyster Luncheon at, 226, 271
Colchester Telegraph, 18
Cole, Dr., 115
Coleman, Frederick, 17
Coleridge, Lord, 66
Collins, Chief Inspector, and Irene Savidge, 213-6
Continental Daily Mail, 228
Coventry, Sir Reginald, 75

Criminal Bar, 198-200
Criminal Justice Act (1925), 101
Crocker, William Charles, 251
Cross-examination, art of, 203-4
Crotch, Walter, trial of, 91-3
Crowborough, murder at, 183-94
Crumbles, Eastbourne, murder of Irene Munro at, 85-7; murder of Emily Kaye at, 172-82
"Cummings, Jack," 45
Curtis-Bennett, Ann, 29, 155
Curtis-Bennett, Derek, 13, 218, 272-3; called to Bar, 211-2; opposes father, 255; in France, 265
Curtis-Bennett, Lady (mother), 28
Curtiss-Bennett, Lady (*née* Dangar), 6-7, 9, 12-13; divorce of, 209-10
Curtis-Bennett, Lady (*née* Jeffries), 228, 265-6
Curtis-Bennett, Margot, 150, 275
Curtis-Bennett, Sir Henry (senior), 2-4; son appears before, 8, 28; death of, 28, 273
Curtis-Bennett, Sir Henry, increasing weight of, 1, 31, 148, 234; ill-health of, 1, 38, 209, 234-5, 265-6; at Cambridge, 1-3; as cycle racer, 2-3, 31; diary of, 3, 4, 6-7, 9-10; as amateur actor, 3, 5-6; and choice of career, 5, 12-3; called to Bar, 6, 7; courtship of, 6-7; early briefs of, 7-8, 10, 12, 13, 197; marriage of, 9; account books of, 9-10, 18, 20, 74, 235, 269; advises young barristers, 11-2; son born to, 12; as motorist, 13-4, 19-20, 21, 25, 78-9, 108; for defence in murder trials, 15-6, 20-1, 79-84, 97, 98, 102-20, 121-33, 140-7, 162-71, 206-8, 221-2; motoring cases of, 17-8, 23-5, 32-3, 87-8, 244-7, 252-3, 257-64; in chambers of his own, 21; charged with speeding, 23-4; licensing briefs of, 28, 29-30, 151, 233, 255-6; audacity of, 30-3, 36-7; his ability to make friends, 34; his attitude to jury, 35-6, 94-6; at outbreak of War, 38; spy cases of, 38-50; Secret Service work of, 51-64; as judge of character, 56; lost practice of, 60; examines suspected spies, 61-4; "takes silk," 65;
fees paid to, by Freke Palmer, 66; defends a dog, 67-9; appears in Lords, 69-71, 260-4; for prosecution in murder trials, 85-7, 90-1, 175-82, 183-94, 252, 253-4; "Hyde Park" cases of, 89-90, 124-5, 133-8, 212-4; and Marshall Hall, 93-4; as a speaker, 96, 157-8; maiden speech, 96, 159; in House of Commons, 96, 158-60, 209-11; receives knighthood, 98-9; great speech of, 108-9; jests about his size, 148-52; witticisms of, 152-3; his kindliness, 153-4; stands for Parliament, 155-8; and client pleading Guilty, 195-6; on "the finest profession," 195-8; posts offered to, 198-9; special briefs of, 200-1, 208; clerks of, 201-2; his methods of cross-examination, 203-4; in disagreement with Judge, 204-6; desires Recordership of London, 209, 266, 268; deputy Chairman of Essex Quarter Sessions, 209; divorce of, 209-12; made Bencher, 211; defends constables, 216-20; Recorder of Colchester, 226, 246; second marriage of, 228; pleasures of, 233-4; conscientiousness of, 235-6; his advice to motorists, 245-6, 252; Chairman of Essex Quarter Sessions, 255; opposed by his son, 255; goes to France, 265-6; and reduction of income, 266-7, 268-9; in Scotland, 267-8; accepts Chairmanship of London Sessions, 268-71; leaves his chambers, 271-3; death of, 274
Curtis-Bennett, Sir Noel, 5, 274
Curtis-Bennett, Susan, 150

Daily Express, 136
Daily Herald, 157
Daily Mail, 156, 157
Danckwerts, Mr., 149
Dangar, Elsie Eleanor, *see* Curtis-Bennett, Lady
Daniels, Edmund, trial of, 228-32
Darling, Lord, 71-72, 158; and coercion of wife, 100-1; and Armstrong trial, 106, 110-1, 121
Davies, A. C. Fox, 90
Davies, Mr., 110

INDEX

Deane, Bargrave, 66
Dennistoun Case, 183
Ditcham, Major, 82-3
Dix, John, 271
Dixon, John, trial of, 229-32
Donegall, Lord, 273
Douglas, James, 137, 138
Douglas-Pennant Inquiry, 69-71
"D. S. Windell Bank Fraud," 22-3
Dumb Friends League, 161
Dummett, Mr., 218
Dunmow Flitch Trial, 22, 201

East, Dr., 114
Edward, Prince of Wales, 226
Elliott, George, 20, 22
Elven, 273

Factor, Jacob, 250
Fahmy, Madame, 147
Fahmy Bey, Prince, shooting of, 146-7
Farrow, Thomas, trial of, 91-3
Farrow's Bank Case, 91-3
Faulks, Neville, 262
Field, Jack Alfred, trial of, 85-7
Finger-prints, as evidence, 14-16
Finlay, Mr. Justice, 183, 193
Fitzroy, Sir Almeric, case of, 94, 124-5, 133-8
Flowers, John, 85
Forente, Marguerite, *see* Fahmy, Madame
Fox, Mrs., murder of, 236-42
Fox, Sidney Harry, trial of, 236-42
Frampton, Walter, 75, 160, 214; and Thomson-Bywaters Case, 128, 131, 140; and Hatry Case, 229
Fulham Murder, 113-20
Fulton, Eustace, 26, 212, 262
Fulton, Forrest, 26, 66

Garnsey, Sir Gilbert, 229-31
Garrick Club, 96, 272
Gattie, Vernon, 75
Geen, Harry, trial of, 249-50
George V, King, 222, 226, 261
German Intelligence Department, British agents in, 56-60; testing of applicants for, 57-8

Gill, Sir Charles, 66, 199; method of, 12; and Painted Horse Case, 75, 78; and Crumbles Murder, 85-7; and Society Turf Case, 100
Girl Pat Case, 268
Goddard, Sergeant, trial of, 222-6, 235-6
Godson, E. A., 106
Golden Ballet prosecution, 73-4
"Golder's Green Murder," 79-82
Golf Links Murder Trial," 253-4
Goslett, Arthur, trial of, 79-82
Goslett, Mrs., 79, 80, 81
Grahame-White Aviation Company, 67
Gray, William Thomas, trial of, 85-7
"Great Fire Trial," 250-1
Greer, Mr. Justice, 93
Gregory, Sir Holman, 66, 255
"Grey Car Case," 24-5
Guerrerro, Adolfo, trial of, 49-50

Hahn, Peter, trial of, 39
Hailsham, Lord, 261
Hall, Sir Edward Marshall, 12, 66, 67, 85, 87, 137, 147, 164, 165; compared to Curtis-Bennett, 93-4; cases of, 98, 198; as politician, 156; and Rodeo prosecution, 160-1; and Hayley Morriss trial, 204-5
Hall, W. Clarke, 66
Halsall, J. Thomson, 262
Hanworth, Lord, *see* Pollock, Sir Ernest
Harris, Leopold, trial of, 250-1
Hart, Frederick, 91
Hastings, Sir Patrick, 65, 70; and trial of Vaquier, 164; and Savidge Inquiry, 214-5
Hatry, Clarence, trial of, 228-32
Hatry, Eric, 252
Hawke, Anthony, 218
Hawke, Mr. Justice, 274
"Hay Murder Case," 102-13
"Helen Adele," 217-20
Hemmerde, E. G., 66
Henry, Sir Edward, 199
Hewart, Lord, 70, 91-3, 254, 255; on negligence, 263
Hicks, Seymour, 96
Hicks, Sir William Joynson, 213, 226
Hogg, Sir Douglas, 261; and Painted Horse Case, 77-8

INDEX

Hollis, Mr., 201, 272, 273
Holt, Daisy, 79-82
Hope, Collingwood, 209, 255
Hopkins, Douglas George, 258
Hopkins, Sheila, 258
Hopkins, Walter, trial of, 74-6
"Houndsditch Murders," 25-6
Howard, Miss, 227-8
Howard, Mr., 227
Howard of Effingham, Lord, 246-7
Hume-Williams, Ellis, 66
Humphreys, Christmas, 262
Humphreys, Mr. Justice, 220
Humphreys, Sam, 22, 201
Humphreys, Sir Travers, 26, 89, 158, 199, 206
Hutchinson, St. John, 66, 204, 218, 236, 270, 274; defends Clarence Hatry, 228-9; at Savoy Grill, 233-4
Hutton, Arthur, 3, 6, 7, 12, 66
"Hyde Park cases," 89-90, 124-5, 133-8, 212-6

Inskip, Sir Thomas, 262
Isaacs, Rufus, 66

Jackson, J. C., 243-4
Jacoby, Henry, 123
James, T. T., 236
Jarvis, trial of, 250
Jeffries, Lilian Mary, 228
Jenkins, Huntley, 75
Johnson, Jack, 26-8
Jones, Mr., murder of, 162-4
Jones, Mrs. Mabel, 162, 165-7
Jowitt, Sir William, 193, 236, 239

Katz, Dr., 49
Kaye, Emily, murder of, 172-182
Kelvedon, 2, 3, 275
King, Francis, trial of, 22-3

Laleham, 19
Lassen, Johann Christian Zahle, trial of, 48-9
Laurie, Mr. Allen, 154
Law Journal, 193
Lawley, Cyril, trial of, 75-6
Lawn, Alice Maud, murder of, 90-91
Lees-Smith, H. B., 216

Lewes, murder trials at, 85-7, 175-82, 183-94, 236-42
Leyel, Mrs. Hilda, 73-4
Lincoln, John, trial of, 206-8
Lody, Hans, 41
Lords, House of, Douglas-Pennant Inquiry in, 69-71; Lord de Clifford tried in, 257-64
Lucy, A. B., 164

McCardie, Mr. Justice, 114, 120, 123
MacDonald, Ramsay, 156
Mackenzie, Compton, 249
McClure, George, 152
"McNaughton Rules," 115, 119, 123
Maddocks, Sir Henry, 224
Mahon, Patrick, 172-4; trial of, 175-82; execution of, 182-3
Manchester, Duke of, 255
Manetta, Signor, 234
Marjoribanks, Edward, 198
Martin, Mr., 104-105; attempted murder of, 103-4, 109, 121
Mary, Queen, 222, 226
"Mask Murderers," trial of, 14-17
Mata Hari, 62
Matthews, C. W., 66
Matthews, Thomas, 102, 105, 107, 110, 111, 112, 121, 123
Mead, Frederick, 94, 212; and trial of Sir Almeric Fitzroy, 133-8
Mells, Captain W. G., 252-3
Meyrick, Mrs. Kate, trial of, 222, 223-5
Micklethwait, St. John, 106
Milstein, Luba, 26
Moller, Major N. H., 156
Money, Sir Leo Chiozza, cases of, 212-5, 251
Moore, Beaufoi, 270
Morning Advertiser, 8
Morriss, Hayley, trial of, 204-6
Morriss, Mrs., 204-6
Motoring, early days of, 14, 19-20; exceeding the speed limit, 17; cases, 17-18, 23-5, 32-3, 87-8, 244-7, 252-3, 257-64; police and, 24-5
Muir, Sir Richard, 15, 20, 26, 66, 133, 135, 199; and motoring case, 88; and trial of Ronald True, 115, 118, 120
Muller, Carl, trial of, 39

INDEX

Mullins, Claude, 34
Munro, Irene, murder of, 85-7
Murphy, Mr., 149, 151
Muskett, Herbert, 133, 134

Nation, Carrie, 21
National Canine Defence League, 67
National Greyhound Racing Society, 271, 273
Neve, Eric, 253, 254
News of the World, 13, 158
Night Clubs, 222-4, 225-6

O'Callaghan, T. M., 270
Official Secrets Act, 249
Oliver, Roland, 147, 204, 250, 251
Oxford Street drinking anomaly, 256

"Painted Horse Case," 74-8
Pall Mall Safe Deposit, 223
Palmer, Freke, 7, 13, 147, 197; fees paid by, 66; death of, 274
Parker, Frederick, 252
Paul, Brenda Dean, 247
Peel, Captain and Mrs., trial of, 99-102
Persse, Henry, 76
Pink 'Un, 137
Plowden Buildings, Curtis-Bennett's, Chambers in, 21, 201, 273
Police, evidence of, 25, 212-7, 244-6; scandals concerning, 216-20, 222-6
Pollock, Sir Ernest, 105-6, 110, 122
"Poplar Scandals," 21
Portslade Shop Murder, 252
Pretyman, Rt. Hon. E. G., 155
Priestley, J. C., 66
Prize-fight, case to prevent, 26-8
Probert, Albert, 252

Radley College, 1, 2, 79
Rayner, Cecil, 21
Rayner, Horace George, trial of, 20-21
Referee, the, 17
Rex v. Bateman, 253, 263
Reynolds, Rosemary, 258
Ribuffi, Luigi, trial of, 222, 223
Richards, Edward, murder of, 206-8
Richardson, Ryder, 262
Richmond and Gordon, Duke of, 260
Ries, Irving Guy, trial of, 44

Robert, trial of, 22-23
Roberts, G. D., 218
Robinson, S. W., 156
Rodeo Prosecution, 160-2
Roome, H. D., 164
Rosenthal, Robert, trial of, 40-1
Routh, H. G., 15-16
"Rowland, Reginald," *see* Breeckow, Georg T.
R. S. P. C. A., 160
Royat, visit to, 265-6
Russell, Earl, 17
Russell, Sir Charles, 66
Russian Revolution, official foreknowledge of, 53-6
Rutland, Duke of, 260

Said Ali, murder of, 221
Sallows, John, trial of, 24-5
Salter, Clavell, 66
San Dwe, trial of, 221-2
Sasun, Doctor Devi, 72
Savage (Savidge), Irene, 213-6
"Savidge Inquiry," 214-6
Savoy Hotel, 146, 233-4
Scotland Yard, and Savidge Inquiry, 213-6
"Security Services," 39-40, 45, 48, 56, 58-60
Selfridge's, 223
Semmens, Edwin, 82; trial of, 83-4
Shearman, Sir Montague, 66, 132, 140, 142-3
Shortt, Mr. E., 123
Sibley, Dorothy, 252
Silvertown explosion, 58, 90
Simon, Sir John, 26-7, 268
Slesser, Sir Henry, 158
Smith, F. E., *see* Birkenhead, Lord
Smith-Dorrien, General, 245
"Society Turf Sensation," 99-102
Somervell, Sir Donald, 262
South-Eastern Circuit, 13
Spies, trials of, 38-50; examination of suspected, 60-4
Spilsbury, Sir Bernard, 102; evidence of, 186, 187, 189, 190, 238, 242
Stanhope, Lord, and Douglas-Pennant Inquiry, 69-71
Stern, F. A., 131

INDEX

Stewart, Ian Maxwell, trial of, 206-8
Stratton, Albert, trial of, 14-7
Stratton, Alfred, trial of, 14-7
"Street offence" case, 212
Sunday Express, 137
Swift, Mr. Justice, 222

Tabor, Albert, trial of, 229
Tait, Mr. John C., 262
Thompson, Mrs. Edith, 125-7; trial of, 128-33, 140-6; letters of, 125-32, 140-4
Thomson, Sir Basil, and suspected spies, 43-4, 45, 46-7, 48, 49, 60-3
Thorne, Norman, trial of, 183-94
Times, The, 8, 108, 272
Trowbridge, murder at, 206-8
True, Ronald, trial of, 113-20; appeal against verdict on, 123-4
Turf Conspiracy trial, 74-8
Turner, Mrs. Dorothy, 133-6, 137, 138

Upjohn, W. M., 66

Vachell, C. F., 106
Vaquier, Jean Pierre, trial of, 162-71
Victor's Club, 223

Wallace, Sir Robert, 137
Ward, Barrington, 66
Wells, Bombardier Billy, 26-7
Wembley Exhibition, Rodeo at, 160-2; sale of rock at, 224
Wensley, Chief Constable, 223
Wertheim, Lizzie, trial of, 42-3
Wetherby and Sons, Messrs., 74
White, James, 26, 27
Whiteley, Cecil, 92, 142; and Hatry case, 229
Whiteley, William, murder of, 21
Wiesz, Norman, trial of, 75-8
Wilberforce, Sir Herbert, 271, 274
Wild, Sir Ernest, 139, 228
Willesden, Bishop of, 256
Winckworth, John, 155, 201
Withers, J. J., 216
Woking, murder committed at, 162-71

Young, Dr., 114
Young, Filson, 130, 132
Young, Olive, murder of, 113-120

Zeffertt, C. S., 74
Zinovieff Letter, 156

www.ingramcontent.com/pod-product-compliance
Lightning Source LLC
Chambersburg PA
CBHW031943080426
42735CB00007B/245